Great Jobs for Biology Majors

Blythe Camenson

SERIES DEVELOPERS AND CONTRIBUTING AUTHORS
Stephen E. Lambert
Julie Ann DeGalan

VGM Career Horizons
NTC/Contemporary Publishing Group

Library of Congress Cataloging-in-Publication Data

Camenson, Blythe.
    Great jobs for biology majors / Blythe Camenson ; series
developers and contributing authors, Stephen E. Lambert, Julie Ann
DeGalan.
       p.   cm. — (Great jobs for—)
    Includes index.
    ISBN 0-8442-1917-7
    1. Biology—Vocational guidance.   I. Lambert, Stephen E.
II. DeGalan, Julie Ann. III. Title. IV. Series.
QH314.C35   1999
570'.23—dc21   98-45285
                                                     CIP

Published by VGM Career Horizons
A division of NTC/Contemporary Publishing Group, Inc.
4255 West Touhy Avenue, Lincolnwood (Chicago), Illinois 60712-1975 U.S.A.
Copyright © 1999 by NTC/Contemporary Publishing Group, Inc.
Printed in the United States of America
International Standard Book Number: 0-8442-1917-7
  01 02 03 04 05 MV 20 19 18 17 16 15 14 13 12 11 10 9 8 7 6 5 4 3

CONTENTS

Acknowledgments

I would like to thank the following professionals for providing insights into the world of biology careers:

Steven Bailey, Curator of Fishes, New England Aquarium, Boston

Shelby Rodney Carter, Assistant Curator, Vice President, Co-Founder of La Guardar Inc. Wildlife Rehabilitation and Education Center

Rick Darke, Curator of Plants, Kennett Square, Pennsylvania

Leon Fager, Threatened and Endangered Species Program Manager, U.S. Forest Service

Michele Graham, Biology Lecturer, California State University, Hayward

Sharon Grata, Medical Laboratory Technician, Johnstown, Pennsylvania

Elizabeth Johnson, Senior Zookeeper, Detroit Zoological Institute

Susan Kelley, Curatorial Associate, Jamaica Plain, Massachusetts

Jenny Montague, Assistant Curator, Marine Mammals, New England Aquarium, Boston

Mary Lee Nitschke, Animal Behaviorist, Animal School, Inc., Beaverton, Oregon

Carin Peterson, Animal Curator, Austin Zoo

Bobbie Pfeifer, High School Biology Teacher, Topeka, Kansas

Carla Lee Suson, Micro/Molecular Biologist, Kingsville, Texas

Melissa Tippens, Clinical Microbiologist, Acworth, Georgia

Heather Urquhart, Diving Aquarist, New England Aquarium, Boston

Terry Wolf, Wildlife Director, Lion Country Safari, West Palm Beach, Florida

INTRODUCTION

BIOLOGY: A DIVERSE DEGREE

People who become biology majors are as diverse as the wide variety of specialized fields in the biological sciences. And though the number of people entering biology careers each year is growing quickly, so is the number of new fields being added to the list of options.

With so many possibilities available, new biologists will never feel pigeonholed. They can choose a career path suited to their personality and preferred lifestyle. For indoor types there are labs, offices, hospitals, classrooms, museums, and libraries in which to work. Those who prefer the out-of-doors can opt for field work at sea, in a tropical rain forest, a botanical garden, zoo, or aquarium.

Biologists can choose what kinds of systems or groups to focus on as well as the setting in which they work. With a degree in biology you can investigate a particular type or group of organisms, such as animals, bacteria, or plants. Or, you could work with a particular system within an organism, such as cells, tissues, or entire organs.

You could also investigate the interaction between organisms and their environment in a particular area, such as the ocean or a desert. Or you could focus on the chemical, physical, or medical aspects of living things.

Although many biologists are mainly involved in research and development and work in the laboratory or field, you can find many other sectors of science to work in also. There are jobs available in areas such as management, administration, service work, sales, writing, illustrating, or photography.

Biology majors can also use their undergraduate degrees as a stepping stone to graduate work and then careers in university education, medicine, law, and advanced research. A biology major offers much flexibility.

THE ROAD AHEAD

In Part One of this book, you will learn many valuable tips on the job search, especially how to prepare yourself and make a case for the ideal job you are seeking.

In Part Two, you will explore a variety of career paths, many that are open to any biology major, some that are more defined, and still others that require further education or training, master's degrees, and often doctorates. Chapter 9 will give you a broad overview of the various paths; the remaining chapters will help you narrow those paths.

Once you've found the path you want to follow, you'll realize how important your biology degree is in reaching your ultimate destination.

PART ONE

THE JOB SEARCH

CHAPTER ONE

THE SELF-ASSESSMENT

elf-assessment is the process by which you begin to acknowledge your own particular blend of education, experiences, values, needs, and goals. It provides the foundation for career planning and the entire job search process. Self-assessment involves looking inward and asking yourself what can sometimes prove to be difficult questions. This self-examination should lead to an intimate understanding of your personal traits, your personal values, your consumption patterns and economic needs, your longer-term goals, your skill base, your preferred skills, and your under-developed skills.

You come to the self-assessment process knowing yourself well in some of these areas, but you may still be uncertain about other aspects. You may be well aware of your consumption patterns, but have you spent much time specifically identifying your longer-term goals or your personal values as they relate to work? No matter what level of self-assessment you have undertaken to date, it is now time to clarify all of these issues and questions as they relate to the job search.

The knowledge you gain in the self-assessment process will guide the rest of your job search. In this book, you will learn about all of the following tasks:

- Writing resumes
- Exploring possible job titles
- Identifying employment sites
- Networking
- Interviewing
- Following up
- Evaluating job offers

In each of these steps, you will rely on and return often to the understanding gained through your self-assessment. Any individual seeking employment must be able and willing to express these facets of his or her personality to recruiters and interviewers throughout the job search. This communication allows you to show the world who you are so that together with employers you can determine whether there will be a workable match with a given job or career path.

HOW TO CONDUCT A SELF-ASSESSMENT

The self-assessment process goes on naturally all the time. People ask you to clarify what you mean, or you make a purchasing decision, or you begin a new relationship. You react to the world and the world reacts to you. How you understand these interactions and any changes you might make because of them are part of the natural process of self-discovery. There is, however, a more comprehensive and efficient way to approach self-assessment with regard to employment.

Because self-assessment can become a complex exercise, we have distilled it into a seven-step process that provides an effective basis for undertaking a job search. The seven steps include the following:

1. Understanding your personal traits

2. Identifying your personal values

3. Calculating your economic needs

4. Exploring your longer-term goals

5. Enumerating your skill base

6. Recognizing your preferred skills

7. Assessing skills needing further development

As you work through your self-assessment, you might want to create a worksheet similar to the one shown in Exhibit 1.1. Or you might want to keep a journal of the thoughts you have as you undergo this process. There will be many opportunities to revise your self-assessment as you start down the path of seeking a career.

STEP 1 Understanding Your Personal Traits

Each person has a unique personality that he or she brings to the job search process. Gaining a better understanding of your personal traits can help you

Exhibit 1.1

Self-Assessment Worksheet

STEP 1. Understand Your Personal Traits
The personal traits that describe me are:
(Include all of the words that describe you.)

The ten personal traits that most accurately describe me are: *(List these ten traits.)*

STEP 2. Identify Your Personal Values
Working conditions that are important to me include: *(List working conditions that would have to exist for you to accept a position.)*

The values that go along with my working conditions are:
(Write down the values that correspond to each working condition.)

Some additional values I've decided to include are: *(List those values you identify as you conduct this job search.)*

STEP 3. Calculate Your Economic Needs
My estimated minimum annual salary requirement is: *(Write the salary you have calculated based on your budget.)*

Starting salaries for the positions I'm considering are: *(List the name of each job you are considering and the associated starting salary.)*

STEP 4. Explore Your Longer-Term Goals
My thoughts on longer-term goals right now are: *(Jot down some of your longer-term goals as you know them right now.)*

STEP 5. Enumerate Your Skill Base
The general skills I possess are: *(List the skills that underlie tasks you are able to complete.)*

The specific skills I possess are:
(List more technical or specific skills that you possess and indicate your level of expertise.)

General and specific skills that I want to promote to employers for the jobs I'm considering are:
(List general and specific skills for each type of job you are considering.)

STEP 6. Recognize Your Preferred Skills
Skills that I would like to use on the job include:
(List skills that you hope to use on the job, and indicate how often you'd like to use them.)

STEP 7. Assess Skills Needing Further Development
Some skills that I'll need to acquire for the jobs I'm considering include:
(Write down skills listed in job advertisements or job descriptions that you don't currently possess.)

I believe I can build these skills by:
(Describe how you plan to acquire these skills.)

evaluate job and career choices. Identifying these traits, then finding employment that allows you to draw on at least some of them can create a rewarding and fulfilling work experience. If potential employment doesn't allow you to use these preferred traits, it is important to decide whether you can find other ways to express them or whether you would be better off not considering this type of job. Interests and hobbies pursued outside of work hours can be one way to use personal traits you don't have an opportunity to draw on in your work. For example, if you consider yourself an outgoing person and the kinds of jobs you are examining allow little contact with other people, you may be able to achieve the level of interaction that is comfortable for you outside of your work setting. If such a compromise seems impractical or otherwise unsatisfactory, you probably should explore only jobs that provide the interaction you want and need on the job.

Many young adults who are not very confident about their attractiveness to employers will downplay their need for income. They will say, "Money is not all that important if I love my work." But if you begin to document exactly what you need for housing, transportation, insurance, clothing, food, and utilities, you will begin to understand that some jobs cannot meet your financial needs and it doesn't matter how wonderful the job is. If you have to worry each payday about bills and other financial obligations, you won't be very effective on the job. Begin now to be honest with yourself about your needs.

Inventorying Your Personal Traits. Begin the self-assessment process by creating an inventory of your personal traits. Using the list in Exhibit 1.2, decide which of these personal traits describe you.

Exhibit 1.2

Accurate	Cooperative	Flexible
Active	Courageous	Formal
Adaptable	Critical	Friendly
Adventurous	Curious	Future-oriented
Affectionate	Daring	Generous
Aggressive	Decisive	Gentle
Ambitious	Deliberate	Good-natured
Analytical	Detail-oriented	Helpful
Appreciative	Determined	Honest
Artistic	Discreet	Humorous
Brave	Dominant	Idealistic
Businesslike	Eager	Imaginative
Calm	Easygoing	Impersonal
Capable	Efficient	Independent
Caring	Emotional	Individualistic
Cautious	Empathetic	Industrious
Cheerful	Energetic	Informal
Clean	Excitable	Innovative
Competent	Expressive	Intellectual
Confident	Extroverted	Intelligent
Conscientious	Fair-minded	Introverted
Conservative	Farsighted	Intuitive
Considerate	Feeling	Inventive
Cool	Firm	Jovial

Just	Poised	Sensitive
Kind	Polite	Serious
Liberal	Practical	Sincere
Likable	Precise	Sociable
Logical	Principled	Spontaneous
Loyal	Private	Strong
Mature	Productive	Strong-minded
Methodical	Progressive	Structured
Meticulous	Quick	Subjective
Mistrustful	Quiet	Tactful
Modest	Rational	Thorough
Motivated	Realistic	Thoughtful
Objective	Receptive	Tolerant
Observant	Reflective	Trusting
Open-minded	Relaxed	Trustworthy
Opportunistic	Reliable	Truthful
Optimistic	Reserved	Understanding
Organized	Resourceful	Unexcitable
Original	Responsible	Uninhibited
Outgoing	Reverent	Verbal
Patient	Sedentary	Versatile
Peaceable	Self-confident	Wholesome
Personable	Self-controlled	Wise
Persuasive	Self-disciplined	
Pleasant	Sensible	

Focusing on Selected Personal Traits. Of all the traits you identified from the list in Exhibit 1.2, select the ten you believe most accurately describe you. If you are having a difficult time deciding, think about which words people who know you well would use to describe you. Keep track of these ten traits.

Considering Your Personal Traits in the Job Search Process. As you begin exploring jobs and careers, watch for matches between your personal traits and the job descriptions you read. Some jobs will require many personal traits you know you possess, and others will not seem to match those traits.

• •

Working as a high school biology teacher, for example,
will draw upon not only your knowledge of the subject
area but also your ability to communicate, work with

others, inspire trust and confidence, and motivate students. Teaching is essentially outer-directed and being able to create methods to stimulate, encourage, and guide students would be far more important personal traits for success than the traits you'd need to conduct your own research, for example. Although both the high school teacher and the researcher might share the same love of the subject matter, the qualities they need to function in their professions differ greatly. Researchers often work autonomously and require more inner-directed qualities such as self-motivation, time management skills, and the ability to think analytically.

....

Your ability to respond to changing conditions, decision-making ability, productivity, creativity, and verbal skills all have a bearing on your success in and enjoyment of your work life. To better guarantee success, be sure to take the time needed to understand these traits in yourself.

STEP 2   Identifying Your Personal Values

Your personal values affect every aspect of your life, including employment, and they develop and change as you move through life. Values can be defined as principles that we hold in high regard, qualities that are important and desirable to us. Some values aren't ordinarily connected to work (love, beauty, color, light, marriage, family, or religion), and others are (autonomy, cooperation, effectiveness, achievement, knowledge, and security). Our values determine, in part, the level of satisfaction we feel in a particular job.

Defining Acceptable Working Conditions. One facet of employment is the set of working conditions that must exist for someone to consider taking a job.

Each of us would probably create a unique list of acceptable working conditions, but items that might be included on many people's lists are the amount of money you would need to be paid, how far you are willing to drive or travel, the amount of freedom you want in determining your own schedule, whether you would be working with people or data or things, and the types of tasks you would be willing to do. Your conditions might include statements of working conditions you will *not* accept; for example, you might not be willing to work at night or on weekends or holidays.

Exhibit 1.3

Work Values

Achievement	Development	Physical activity
Advancement	Effectiveness	Power
Adventure	Excitement	Precision
Attainment	Fast pace	Prestige
Authority	Financial gain	Privacy
Autonomy	Helping	Profit
Belonging	Humor	Recognition
Challenge	Improvisation	Risk
Change	Independence	Security
Communication	Influencing others	Self-expression
Community	Intellectual stimulation	Solitude
Competition	Interaction	Stability
Completion	Knowledge	Status
Contribution	Leading	Structure
Control	Mastery	Supervision
Cooperation	Mobility	Surroundings
Creativity	Moral fulfillment	Time freedom
Decision making	Organization	Variety

If you were offered a job tomorrow, what conditions would have to exist for you to realistically consider accepting the position? Take some time and make a list of these conditions.

Realizing Associated Values. Your list of working conditions can be used to create an inventory of your values relating to jobs and careers you are exploring. For example, if one of your conditions stated that you wanted to earn at least $25,000 per year, the associated value would be financial gain. If another condition was that you wanted to work with a friendly group of people, the value that goes along with that might be belonging or interaction with people. Exhibit 1.3 provides a list of commonly held values that relate to the work environment; use it to create your own list of personal values.

Relating Your Values to the World of Work. As you read the job descriptions in this book and in other suggested resources, think about the values associated with each position.

....

> For example, in pharmaceutical sales, your duties may
> include calling on clients; explaining products you offer;
> arranging delivery; and providing follow-up services after
> the sale. Associated qualities include knowledge, mastery,
> competition, and variety.

....

If you were thinking about a career in this field, or any other field you're exploring, at least some of the associated values should match those you extracted from your list of working conditions. Take a second look at any values that don't match up. How important are they to you? What will happen if they are not satisfied on the job? Can you incorporate those personal values elsewhere? Your answers need to be brutally honest. As you continue your exploration, be sure to add to your list any additional values that occur to you.

STEP 3   Calculating Your Economic Needs

Each of us grew up in an environment that provided for certain basic needs, such as food and shelter, and, to varying degrees, other needs that we now consider basic, such as cable TV, reading materials, or an automobile. Needs such as privacy, space, and quiet, which at first glance may not appear to be monetary needs, may add to housing expenses and so should be considered as you examine your economic needs. For example, if you place a high value on a large, open living space for yourself, it would be difficult to satisfy that need without an associated high housing cost, especially in a densely populated city environment.

As you prepare to move into the world of work and become responsible for meeting your own basic needs, it is important to consider the salary you will need to be able to afford a satisfying standard of living. The three-step process outlined here will help you plan a budget, which in turn will allow you to evaluate the various career choices and geographic locations you are considering. The steps include (1) developing a realistic budget, (2) examining starting salaries, and (3) using a cost-of-living index.

Developing a Realistic Budget. Each of us has certain expectations for the kind of lifestyle we want to maintain. In order to begin the process of defining your economic needs, it will be helpful to determine what you expect to spend on routine monthly expenses. These expenses include housing, food, transportation, entertainment, utilities, loan repayments, and revolving charge accounts. A worksheet that details many of these expenses is shown in Exhibit 1.4. You may not currently spend for certain items, but you probably

Exhibit 1.4

Estimated Monthly Expenses Worksheet

		Could Reduce Spending? (Yes/No)
Cable	$ _____	_____
Child care	_____	_____
Clothing	_____	_____
Educational loan repayment	_____	_____
Entertainment	_____	_____
Food	_____	_____
At home	_____	_____
Meals out	_____	_____
Gifts	_____	_____
Housing		
Rent/mortgage	_____	_____
Insurance	_____	_____
Property taxes	_____	_____
Medical insurance	_____	_____
Reading materials		
Newspapers	_____	_____
Magazines	_____	_____
Books	_____	_____
Revolving loans/charges	_____	_____
Savings	_____	_____
Telephone	_____	_____
Transportation		
Auto payment	_____	_____
Insurance	_____	_____
Parking	_____	_____
Gasoline	_____	_____
or		
Cab/train/bus fare	_____	_____
Utilities		
Electric	_____	_____
Gas	_____	_____
Water/sewer	_____	_____
Vacations	_____	_____
Miscellaneous expense 1	_____	_____
Expense: _____		
Miscellaneous expense 2	_____	_____
Expense: _____		

continued

continued

Miscellaneous expense 3 _____ _____
Expense: _____
TOTAL MONTHLY EXPENSES: _____
YEARLY EXPENSES (Monthly expenses x 12): _____
INCREASE TO INCLUDE TAXES (Yearly expenses x 1.35): ___ =
MINIMUM ANNUAL SALARY REQUIREMENT _____

will have to once you begin supporting yourself. As you develop this budget, be generous in your estimates, but keep in mind any items that could be reduced or eliminated. If you are not sure about the cost of a certain item, talk with family or friends who would be able to give you a realistic estimate.

If this is new or difficult for you, start to keep a log of expenses right now. You may be surprised at how much you actually spend each month for food or stamps or magazines. Household expenses and personal grooming items can often loom very large in a budget, as can auto repairs or home maintenance.

Income taxes must also be taken into consideration when examining salary requirements. State and local taxes vary by location, so it is difficult to calculate exactly the effect of taxes on the amount of income you need to generate. To roughly estimate the gross income necessary to generate your minimum annual salary requirement, multiply the minimum salary you have calculated (see Exhibit 1.4) by a factor of 1.35. The resulting figure will be an approximation of what your gross income would need to be, given your estimated expenses.

Examining Starting Salaries. Starting salaries for each of the career tracks are provided throughout this book. These salary figures can be used in conjunction with the cost-of-living index (discussed in the next section) to determine whether you would be able to meet your basic economic needs in a given geographic location.

Using a Cost-of-Living Index. If you are thinking about trying to get a job in a geographic region other than the one where you now live, understanding differences in the cost of living will help you come to a more informed decision about making a move. By using a cost-of-living index, you can compare salaries offered and the cost of living in different locations with what you know about the salaries offered and the cost of living in your present location.

Many variables are used to calculate the cost-of-living index, including housing expenses, groceries, utilities, transportation, health care, clothing, entertainment, local income taxes, and local sales taxes. Cost-of-living indices can be found in many resources, such as *Equal Employment Opportunity Bimonthly, Places Rated Almanac,* or *The Best Towns in America.* They are constantly being recalculated based on changes in costs.

....

If you lived in Cleveland, Ohio, for example, and you were interested in working as a sales representative for a biotechnology firm, you would earn, say, on average $20,784 annually. But let's say you're also thinking about moving to either New York, Los Angeles, or Denver. You know you can live on $20,784 in Cleveland, but you want to be able to equate that salary in other locations you're considering. How much will you need to earn in those locations to do this? Figuring the cost of living for each city will show you.

Let's walk through this example. In any cost-of-living index, the number 100 represents the national average cost of living, and each city is assigned an index number based on current prices in that city for the items included in the index (housing, food, etc.). In the index used here, New York was assigned the number 213.3, Los Angeles' index was 124.6, Denver's was 100.0, and Cleveland's index was 114.3. In other words, it costs more than twice as much to live in New York than it does in Denver. You can set up a table to determine exactly how much you would have to earn in each of these cities to have the same buying power that you have in Cleveland.

Job: Sales representative

CITY	INDEX	EQUIVALENT SALARY
$\dfrac{\text{New York}}{\text{Cleveland}}$	$\dfrac{213.3}{114.3}$	$\times \$20{,}784 = \$38{,}785$ in New York
$\dfrac{\text{Los Angeles}}{\text{Cleveland}}$	$\dfrac{124.6}{114.3}$	$\times \$20{,}784 = \$22{,}656$ in Los Angeles
$\dfrac{\text{Denver}}{\text{Cleveland}}$	$\dfrac{100.0}{114.3}$	$\times \$20{,}784 = \$18{,}199$ in Denver

You would have to earn $38,785 in New York, $22,656 in Los Angeles, and $18,199 in Denver to match the buying power of $20,784 in Cleveland.

If you would like to determine whether it's financially worthwhile to make any of these moves, one more piece of information is needed: the salaries of sales representatives in these other cities. The *American Salaries and Wages Survey* (3rd edition) reports the following average salary information for sales representatives:

Region	Annual Salary	Salary Equivalent to Ohio	Change in Buying Power
Mid Atlantic (including New York)	$29,030	$38,785	−$9,755
West (including Los Angeles)	$23,070	$22,656	+$ 414
Mountain Plains (including Denver)	$22,862	$18,199	+$3,863
Midwest (including Cleveland)	$20,784	—	—

If you moved to New York City and secured employment as a sales representative for a biotechnology firm, you would not be able to maintain a lifestyle similar to the one you led in Cleveland; in fact, you would have to add more than fifty percent to your income to maintain a similar lifestyle in New York. The same would not be true for a move to Los Angeles or Denver. You would increase your buying power given the rate of pay and cost of living in these cities.

••

You can work through a similar exercise for any type of job you are considering and for many locations when current salary information is available. It will be worth your time to undertake this analysis if you are seriously considering a relocation. By doing so you will be able to make an informed choice.

STEP 4 Exploring Your Longer-Term Goals

There is no question that when we first begin working, our goals are to use our skills and education in a job that will reward us with employment, income, and status relative to the preparation we brought with us to this position. If we are not being paid as much as we feel we should for our level of education, or if job demands don't provide the intellectual stimulation we had hoped for, we experience unhappiness and as a result often seek other employment.

Most jobs we consider "good" are those that fulfill our basic "lower-level" needs of security, food, clothing, shelter, income, and productive work. But even when our basic needs are met and our jobs are secure and productive, we as individuals are constantly changing. As we change, the demands and expectations we place on our jobs may change. Fortunately, some jobs grow and change with us, and this explains why some people are happy throughout many years in a job.

But more often people are bigger than the jobs they fill. We have more goals and needs than any job could fulfill. These are "higher-level" needs of self-esteem, companionship, affection, and an increasing desire to feel we are employing ourselves in the most effective way possible. Not all of these higher-level needs can be fulfilled through employment, but for as long as we are employed, we increasingly demand that our jobs play their part in moving us along the path to fulfillment.

Another obvious but important fact is that we change as we mature. Although our jobs also have the potential for change, they may not change as frequently or as markedly as we do. There are increasingly fewer one-job, one-employer careers; we must think about a work future that may involve voluntary or forced moves from employer to employer. Because of that very real possibility, we need to take advantage of the opportunities in each position we hold to acquire skills and competencies that will keep us viable and attractive as employees in a job market that is not only increasingly technology/computer dependent, but also is populated with more and more small, self-transforming organizations rather than the large, seemingly stable organizations of the past.

It may be difficult in the early stages of the job search to determine whether the path you are considering can meet these longer-term goals. Reading about career paths and individual career histories in your field can be very helpful in this regard. Meeting and talking with individuals farther along in their careers can be enlightening as well. Older workers can provide valuable guidance on "self-managing" your career, which will become an increasingly valuable skill in the future. Some of these ideas may seem remote as you read this now, but you should be able to appreciate the need to ensure that you are growing, developing valuable new skills, and researching other employers who might be interested in your particular skills package.

••

> If you are considering a career as a curator in an aquar-
> ium, you would gain a better perspective on this career
> if you talked to an entry-level aquarist, a more experi-
> enced trainer or assistant curator, and finally a senior or
> chief curator, or director or department head who has a
> considerable work history in the curatorial field. Each
> will have a different perspective, unique concerns, and
> an individual set of value priorities.

••

STEP 5 Enumerating Your Skill Base

In terms of the job search, skills can be thought of as capabilities that can be developed in school, at work, or by volunteering and then used in specific job settings. Many studies have documented the kinds of skills that employers seek in entry-level applicants. For example, some of the most desired skills for individuals interested in the teaching profession include the ability to interact effectively with students one on one, to manage a classroom, to adapt to varying situations as necessary, and to get involved in school activities. Business employers have also identified important qualities, including enthusiasm for the employer's product or service, a businesslike mind, the ability to follow written or verbal instructions, the ability to demonstrate self-control, the confidence to suggest new ideas, the ability to communicate with all members of a group, awareness of cultural differences, and loyalty, to name just a few. You will find that many of these skills are also in the repertoire of qualities demanded in your college major.

In order to be successful in obtaining any given job, you must be able to demonstrate that you possess a certain mix of skills that will allow you to carry out the duties required by that job. This skill mix will vary a great deal from job to job; to determine the skills necessary for the jobs you are seeking, you can read job advertisements or more generic job descriptions, such as those found later in this book. If you want to be effective in the job search, you must directly show employers that you possess the skills needed to be successful in filling the position. These skills will initially be described on your resume and then discussed again during the interview process.

Skills are either general or specific. General skills are those that are developed throughout the college years by taking classes, being employed, and getting involved in other related activities such as volunteer work or campus organizations. General skills include the ability to read and write, to perform computations, to think critically, and to communicate effectively. Specific skills are also acquired on the job and in the classroom, but they allow you to complete tasks that require specialized knowledge. Computer programming, drafting, language translating, and copyediting are just a few examples of specific skills that may relate to a given job.

In order to develop a list of skills relevant to employers, you must first identify the general skills you possess, then list specific skills you have to offer, and, finally, examine which of these skills employers are seeking.

Identifying Your General Skills. Because you possess or will possess a college degree, employers will assume that you can read and write, perform certain basic computations, think critically, and communicate effectively. Employers will want to see that you have acquired these skills, and they will want to know which additional general skills you possess.

One way to begin identifying skills is to write an experiential diary. An experiential diary lists all the tasks you were responsible for completing for each job you've held and then outlines the skills required to do those tasks. You may list several skills for any given task. This diary allows you to distinguish between the tasks you performed and the underlying skills required to complete those tasks. Here's an example:

Tasks	Skills
Answering telephone	Effective use of language, clear diction, ability to direct inquiries, ability to solve problems
Waiting on tables	Poise under conditions of time and pressure, speed, accuracy, good memory, simultaneous completion of tasks, sales skills

For each job or experience you have participated in, develop a worksheet based on the example shown here. On a resume, you may want to describe these skills rather than simply listing tasks. Skills are easier for the employer to appreciate, especially when your experience is very different from the employment you are seeking. In addition to helping you identify general skills, this experiential diary will prepare you to speak more effectively in an interview about the qualifications you possess.

Identifying Your Specific Skills. It may be easier to identify your specific skills because you can definitely say whether you can speak other languages, program a computer, draft a map or diagram, or edit a document using appropriate symbols and terminology.

Using your experiential diary, identify the points in your history where you learned how to do something very specific, and decide whether you have a beginning, intermediate, or advanced knowledge of how to use that particular skill. Right now, be sure to list *every* specific skill you have, and don't consider whether you like using the skill. Write down a list of specific skills you have acquired and the level of competence you possess—beginning, intermediate, or advanced.

Relating Your Skills to Employers. You probably have thought about a couple of different jobs you might be interested in obtaining, and one way to begin relating the general and specific skills you possess to a potential employer's needs is to read actual advertisements for these types of positions (see Part Two for resources listing actual job openings).

••••••••••••••••••••••••••••••••••••••

For example, you might be interested in a career as an animal behaviorist. A typical job listing might read, "Requires 3 to 5 years of experience, organizational and interpersonal skills, imagination, drive, and the ability to work under pressure." If you then used any one of a number of general sources of information that describe the job of animal behaviorist, you would find additional information. Depending on the setting in which they work, animal behaviorists also develop training programs, methods, and schedules; teach animal trainers; advise and consult with animal handlers; conduct research; provide information to the public; and must be thoroughly knowledgeable about the animal world.

Begin building a comprehensive list of required skills with the first job description you read. Exploring advertisements for and descriptions of several types of related positions will reveal an important core of skills necessary for obtaining the type of work you're interested in. In building this list, include both general and specific skills.

On separate sheets of paper, try to generate a comprehensive list of required skills for at least one job you are considering.

Following is a sample list of skills needed to be successful as an animal behaviorist. These items were extracted from general resources and actual job listings.

The list of general skills that you develop for a given career path would be valuable for any number of jobs you might apply for. Many of the specific skills would also be transferable to other types of positions. For example, the ability to solve problems would be a necessary skill for animal behaviorists, and it would also be important for curators working in a zoo.

Job: Animal behaviorist

General Skills	**Specific Skills**
Disseminate information	Write articles, books, manuals
Have a specific body of knowledge	Speak publicly
Gather information	Teach
Writing	Write letters and memos
Work well with people	Write grants
Work well with animals	Propose projects
Exhibit creativity	Conduct research
Observation skills	Analyze research data
Analytical thinking	Present exhibitions
Problem solving	Demonstrate techniques
Evaluation skills	Develop specific training methods

Now review the list of skills you developed and check off those skills that *you know you possess* and that are required for jobs you are considering. You should refer to these specific skills on the resume that you write for this type of job. See Chapter 2 for details on resume writing.

STEP 6 Recognizing Your Preferred Skills

In the previous section you developed a comprehensive list of skills that relate to particular career paths that are of interest to you. You can now relate these to skills that you prefer to use. We all use a wide range of skills (some researchers say individuals have a repertoire of about 500 skills), but we may not be particularly interested in using all of them in our work. There may be some skills that come to us more naturally or that we use successfully time and time again and that we want to continue to use; these are best described as our preferred skills. For this exercise use the list of skills that you developed for the previous section and decide which of them you are *most interested in using* in future work and how often you would like to use them. You might be interested in using some skills only occasionally, while others you would like to use more regularly. You probably also have skills that you hope you can use constantly.

As you examine job announcements, look for matches between this list of preferred skills and the qualifications described in the advertisements. These skills should be highlighted on your resume and discussed in job interviews.

STEP 7 Assessing Skills Needing Further Development

Previously you developed a list of general and specific skills required for given positions. You already possess some of these skills; those that remain to be developed are your underdeveloped skills.

If you are just beginning the job search, there may be gaps between the qualifications required for some of the jobs being considered and skills you possess. These are your underdeveloped skills. The thought of having to admit to and talk about these underdeveloped skills, especially in a job interview, is a frightening one. One way to put a healthy perspective on this subject is to target and relate your exploration of underdeveloped skills to the types of positions you are seeking. Recognizing these shortcomings and planning to overcome them with either on-the-job training or additional formal education can be a positive way to address the concept of underdeveloped skills.

On your worksheet or in your journal, make a list of up to five general or specific skills required for the positions you're interested in that you *don't currently possess*. For each item list an idea you have for specific action you could take to acquire that skill. Do some brainstorming to come up with possible actions. If you have a hard time generating ideas, talk to people currently working in this type of position, professionals in your college career services office, trusted friends, family members, or members of related professional associations.

If, for example, you are interested in a job for which you don't have some specific required experience, you could locate training opportunities such as classes or workshops offered through a local college or university, community college, or club or association that would help you build the level of expertise you need for the job.

Many excellent jobs in today's economy demand computer skills you probably already have. Most graduates are not so lucky and have to acquire these skills—often before an employer will give their application serious consideration. So, what can you do if you find there are certain skills you're missing? If you're still in school, try to fill the gaps in your knowledge before you graduate. If you've already graduated, look at evening programs, continuing education courses, or tutorial programs that may be available commercially. Developing a modest level of expertise will encourage you to be more confident in suggesting to potential employers that you can continue to add to your skill base on the job.

In Chapter 5 on interviewing we will discuss in detail how to effectively address questions about underdeveloped skills. Generally speaking, though, employers want genuine answers to these types of questions. They want you to reveal "the real you," and they also want to see how you answer difficult questions. In taking the positive, targeted approach discussed above, you show the employer that you are willing to continue to learn and that you have a plan for strengthening your job qualifications.

USING YOUR SELF-ASSESSMENT

Exploring entry-level career options can be an exciting experience if you have good resources available and will take the time to use them. Can you effectively complete the following tasks?

1. Understand and relate your personality traits to career choices.

2. Define your personal values.

3. Determine your economic needs.

4. Explore longer-term goals.

5. Understand your skill base.

6. Recognize your preferred skills.

7. Express a willingness to improve on your underdeveloped skills.

If so, then you can more meaningfully participate in the job search process by writing a more effective resume, finding job titles that represent work you are interested in doing, locating job sites that will provide the opportunity for you to use your strengths and skills, networking in an informed way, participating in focused interviews, getting the most out of follow-up contacts, and evaluating job offers to find those that create a good match between you and the employer.

The remaining chapters guide you through these next steps in the job search process. For many job seekers, this process can take anywhere from three months to a year to implement. The time you will need to put into your job search will depend on the type of job you want and the geographic location where you'd like to work. Think of your effort as a job in itself, requiring you to set aside time each week to complete the needed work. Carefully undertaken efforts may reduce the time you need for your job search.

CHAPTER TWO

THE RESUME AND COVER LETTER

T he task of writing a resume may seem overwhelming if you are unfamiliar with this type of document, but there are some easily understood techniques that can and should be used. This section was written to help you understand the purpose of the resume, the different types of resume formats available, and how to write the sections of information traditionally found on a resume. We will present examples and explanations that address questions frequently posed by people writing their first resume or updating an old resume.

Even within the formats and suggestions given below, however, there are infinite variations. True, most resumes follow one of the outlines suggested below, but you should feel free to adjust the resume to suit your needs and make it expressive of your life and experience.

WHY WRITE A RESUME?

The purpose of a resume is to convince an employer that you should be interviewed. You'll want to present enough information to show that you can make an immediate and valuable contribution to an organization. A resume is not an in-depth historical or legal document; later in the job search process you'll be asked to document your entire work history on an application form and attest to its validity. The resume should, instead, highlight relevant information pertaining directly to the organization that will receive the document or the type of position you are seeking.

We will discuss four types of resumes in this chapter: chronological resume, functional resume, targeted resume, and the broadcast letter. The reasons for using one type of resume over another and the typical format for each are addressed in the following sections.

THE CHRONOLOGICAL RESUME

The chronological resume is the most common of the various resume formats and therefore the format that employers are most used to receiving. This type of resume is easy to read and understand because it details the chronological progression of jobs you have held. (See Exhibit 2.1.) It begins with your most recent employment and works back in time. If you have a solid work history or have experience that provided growth and development in your duties and responsibilities, a chronological resume will highlight these achievements. The typical elements of a chronological resume include the heading, a career objective, educational background, employment experience, activities, and references.

The Heading

The heading consists of your name, address, and telephone number. Recently it has come to include fax numbers and electronic mail addresses as well. We suggest that you spell out your full name and type it in all capital letters in bold type. After all, you are the focus of the resume! If you have a current as well as a permanent address and you include both in the heading, be sure to indicate until what date your current address will be valid. Don't forget to include the zip code with your address and the area code with your telephone number.

The Objective

As you formulate the wording for this part of your resume, keep the following points in mind.

The Objective Focuses the Resume. Without a doubt this is the most challenging part of the resume for most resume writers. Even for individuals who have quite firmly decided on a career path, it can be difficult to encapsulate all they want to say in one or two brief sentences. For job seekers who are unfocused or unclear about their intentions, trying to write this section can inhibit the entire resume writing process.

Recruiters tell us, time and again, that the objective creates a frame of reference for them. It helps them see how you express your goals and career

Exhibit 2.1

Chronological Resume

REESE CONNORS

188 Beacon Street
Apt # 12
Boston, MA 02125
(617) 555-3455

OBJECTIVE

A position as an aquarist or trainer at an aquarium in California, working with marine mammals.

EDUCATION

Bachelor of Science Degree in Biology
Salem State College, Salem, Massachusetts, May 1999
Concentration: Marine Biology
Minor: Chemistry
Overall GPA: 3.2 on a 4.0 scale

EXPERIENCE

Internship Diving Aquarist (Junior)
187,000-gallon, Giant Ocean Tank Caribbean Coral Reef Exhibit
New England Aquarium, Boston, Massachusetts
1996 to Present
Year-to-year internship, twenty hours a week, helping maintain the tank and participating in collecting trips.

Internship Aquarist-in-Training
Penguin Exhibit
New England Aquarium, Boston, Massachusetts
1995–96
Nine-month program, assisting in the penguin colony, feeding the penguins, banding them, participating in presentations, and caring for the tank.

Volunteer Junior Keeper/Petting Zoo
Franklin Park Zoo, Boston, Massachusetts
Summer of 1995
A volunteer position three days a week, working in the petting

zoo, feeding and bathing the animals, and assisting visitors, including children and their parents. Responsible also for ensuring the safety of visitors and animals.

ADDITIONAL QUALIFICATIONS
Advanced PADI SCUBA Diving Certificate

REFERENCES
Both personal and professional references are available upon request.

focus. In addition, the statement may indicate in what ways you can immediately benefit an organization. Given the importance of the objective, every point covered in the resume should relate to it. If information doesn't relate, it should be omitted. With the word processing technology available today, each resume can and should be tailored for individual employers or specific positions that are available.

Choose an Appropriate Length. Because of the brevity necessary for a resume, you should keep the objective as short as possible. Although objectives of only four or five words often don't show much direction, objectives that take three full lines would be viewed as too wordy and might possibly be ignored.

Consider Which Type of Objective Statement You Will Use. There are many ways to state an objective, but generally there are four forms this statement can take: (1) a very general statement; (2) a statement focused on a specific position; (3) a statement focused on a specific industry; or (4) a summary of your qualifications. In our contacts with employers, we often hear that many resumes don't exhibit any direction or career goals, so we suggest avoiding general statements when possible.

1. General Objective Statement. General objective statements look like the following:

- An entry-level educational programming coordinator position
- An entry-level marketing position

This type of objective would be useful if you know what type of job you want but you're not sure which industries interest you.

2. Position-Focused Objective. Following are examples of objectives focusing on a specific position:

- To obtain the position of director of public information at the State Council for Environmental Quality
- To obtain a position as assistant town manager

When a student applies for an advertised job opening, this type of focus can be very effective. The employer knows that the applicant has taken the time to tailor the resume specifically for this position.

3. Industry-Focused Objective. Focusing on a particular industry in an objective could be stated as follows:

- To begin a career as a sales representative in the cruise line industry

4. Summary of Qualifications Statement. The summary of qualifications can be used instead of an objective or in conjunction with an objective. The purpose of this type of statement is to highlight relevant qualifications gained through a variety of experiences. This type of statement is often used by individuals with extensive and diversified work experience. An example of a qualifications statement follows:

··

A degree in biology and four years of progressively increasing responsibilities in the curatorial department of a major aquarium have prepared me for a career as assistant curator in an institution that values hands-on involvement and thoroughness.

··

Support Your Objective. A resume that contains any one of these types of objective statements should then go on to demonstrate why you are qualified to get the position. Listing academic degrees can be one way to indicate qualifications. Another demonstration would be in the way previous experiences, both volunteer and paid, are described. Without this kind of documentation in the body of the resume, the objective looks unsupported. Think of the resume as telling a connected story about you. All the elements should work together to form a coherent picture that ideally should relate to your statement of objective.

Education

This section of your resume should indicate the exact name of the degree you will receive or have received, spelled out completely with no abbreviations. The degree is generally listed after the objective, followed by the institution name and address, and then the month and year of graduation. This section could also include your academic minor, grade point average (GPA), and appearance on the Dean's or President's List.

If you have enough space, you might want to include a section listing courses related to the field in which you are seeking work. The best use of a "related courses" section would be to list some course work that is not traditionally associated with the major. Perhaps you took several computer courses outside your degree that will be helpful and related to the job prospects you are entertaining. Several education section examples are shown here:

. . . .

❑ **Bachelor of Science Degree in Biology**
  University of Florida, Gainesville, Florida, June 1999
  Concentration: Botany

❑ **Bachelor of Science Degree in Biology**
  Tufts University, Medford, Massachusetts, May 1999
  Minor: Marine Biology

❑ **Bachelor of Arts Degree in Secondary Education**
  University of New Mexico, Albuquerque, New
      Mexico, June 1999
  Concentration: Biology

  An example of a format for a related course section follows:

RELATED COURSES	
Chemistry	Psychology
Taxonomy	Ecology
Oceanography	Research Methods

. . . .

Experience

The experience section of your resume should be the most substantial part and should take up most of the space on the page. Employers want to see what kind of work history you have. They will look at your range of experiences, longevity in jobs, and specific tasks you are able to complete. This section may also be called "work experience," "related experience," "employment history," or "employment." No matter what you call this section, some important points to remember are the following:

1. **Describe your duties** as they relate to the position you are seeking.

2. **Emphasize major responsibilities** and indicate increases in responsibility. Include all relevant employment experiences: summer, part-time, internships, cooperative education, or self-employment.

3. **Emphasize skills,** especially those that transfer from one situation to another. The fact that you coordinated a student organization, chaired meetings, supervised others, and managed a budget leads one to suspect that you could coordinate other things as well.

4. **Use descriptive job titles** that provide information about what you did. A "Student Intern" should be more specifically stated as, for example, "Magazine Operations Intern." "Volunteer" is also too general; a title like "Peer Writing Tutor" would be more appropriate.

5. **Create word pictures** by using active verbs to start sentences. Describe *results* you have produced in the work you have done.

A limp description would say something like the following: "My duties included helping with production, proofreading, and editing. I used a word processing package to alter text." An action statement would be stated as follows: "Coordinated and assisted in the creative marketing of brochures and seminar promotions, becoming proficient in WordPerfect."

Remember, an accomplishment is simply a result, a final measurable product that people can relate to. A duty is not a result, it is an obligation—every job holder has duties. For an effective resume, list as many results as you can. To make the most of the limited space you have and to give your description impact, carefully select appropriate and accurate descriptors from the list of action words in Exhibit 2.2.

Here are some traits that employers tell us they like to see:

❑ Teamwork

❑ Energy and motivation

❑ Learning and using new skills

❑ Demonstrated versatility

❑ Critical thinking

❑ Understanding how profits are created

Exhibit 2.2

Resume Action Verbs

Achieved	Established	Operated
Acted	Estimated	Organized
Administered	Evaluated	Participated
Advised	Examined	Performed
Analyzed	Explained	Planned
Assessed	Facilitated	Predicted
Assisted	Finalized	Prepared
Attained	Generated	Presented
Balanced	Handled	Processed
Budgeted	Headed	Produced
Calculated	Helped	Projected
Collected	Identified	Proposed
Communicated	Illustrated	Provided
Compiled	Implemented	Qualified
Completed	Improved	Quantified
Composed	Increased	Questioned
Conceptualized	Influenced	Realized
Condensed	Informed	Received
Conducted	Initiated	Recommended
Consolidated	Innovated	Recorded
Constructed	Instituted	Reduced
Controlled	Instructed	Reinforced
Converted	Integrated	Reported
Coordinated	Interpreted	Represented
Corrected	Introduced	Researched
Created	Learned	Resolved
Decreased	Lectured	Reviewed
Defined	Led	Scheduled
Demonstrated	Maintained	Selected
Designed	Managed	Served
Determined	Mapped	Showed
Developed	Marketed	Simplified
Directed	Met	Sketched
Documented	Modified	Sold
Drafted	Monitored	Solved
Edited	Negotiated	Staffed
Eliminated	Observed	Streamlined
Ensured	Obtained	Studied

continued

continued		
Submitted	Tabulated	Updated
Summarized	Tested	Verified
Systematized	Transacted	

❑ Displaying organizational acumen

❑ Communicating directly and clearly, in both writing and speaking

❑ Risk taking

❑ Willingness to admit mistakes

❑ Manifesting high personal standards

SOLUTIONS TO FREQUENTLY ENCOUNTERED PROBLEMS

Repetitive Employment with the Same Employer

EMPLOYMENT: The Foot Locker, Portland, Oregon. Summer 1995, 1996, 1997. Initially employed in high school as salesclerk. Due to successful performance, asked to return next two summers at higher pay with added responsibility. Ranked as the #2 salesperson the first summer and #1 the next two summers. Assisted in arranging eye-catching retail displays; served as manager of other summer workers during owner's absence.

A Large Number of Jobs

EMPLOYMENT: Recent Hospitality Industry Experience: Affiliated with four upscale hotel/restaurant complexes (September 1995–February 1998), where I worked part- and full-time as a waiter, bartender, disc jockey, and bookkeeper to produce income for college.

Several Positions with the Same Employer

EMPLOYMENT: Coca-Cola Bottling Co., Burlington, Vermont, 1995–98. In four years, I received three promotions, each with increased pay and responsibility.

Summer Sales Coordinator: Promoted to hire, train, and direct efforts of add-on staff of 15 college-age route salespeople hired to meet summer peak demand for product.

Sales Administrator: Promoted to run home office sales desk, managing accounts and associated delivery schedules for professional sales force of ten people. Intensive phone work, daily interaction with all personnel, and strong knowledge of product line required.

Route Salesperson: Summer employment to travel and tourism industry sites using Coke products. Met specific schedule demands, used good communication skills with wide variety of customers, and demonstrated strong selling skills. Named salesperson of the month for July and August of that year.

QUESTIONS RESUME WRITERS OFTEN ASK

How Far Back Should I Go in Terms of Listing Past Jobs?

Usually, listing three or four jobs should suffice. If you did something back in high school that has a bearing on your future aspirations for employment, by all means list the job. As you progress through your college career, high school jobs may be replaced on the resume by college employment.

Should I Differentiate Between Paid and Nonpaid Employment?

Most employers are not initially concerned about how much you were paid. They are anxious to know how much responsibility you held in your past employment. There is no need to specify that your work was volunteer if you had significant responsibilities.

How Should I Represent My Accomplishments or Work-Related Responsibilities?

Succinctly, but fully. In other words, give the employer enough information to arouse curiosity, but not so much detail that you leave nothing to the imagination. Besides, some jobs merit more lengthy explanations than others. Be sure to convey any information that can give an employer a better understanding of the depth of your involvement at work. Did you supervise others? How many? Did your efforts result in a more efficient operation? How much did you increase efficiency? Did you handle a budget? How much? Were you promoted in a short time? Did you work two jobs at once or 15 hours per week after high school? Where appropriate, quantify.

Should the Work Section Always Follow the Education Section on the Resume?

Always lead with your strengths. If your education closely relates to the employment you now seek, put this section after the objective. Or, if you are weak on the academic side but have a surplus of good work experiences, consider reversing the order of your sections to lead with employment, followed by education.

How Should I Present My Activities, Honors, Awards, Professional Societies, and Affiliations?

This section of the resume can add valuable information for an employer to consider if used correctly. The rule of thumb for information in this section is to include only those activities that are in some way relevant to the objective stated on your resume. If you can draw a valid connection between your activities and your objective, include them; if not, leave them out.

Granted, this is hard to do. Playing center on the championship basketball team or serving as coordinator of the biggest homecoming parade ever held are roles that have meaning for you and represent personal accomplishments you'd like to share. But the resume is a brief document, and the information you provide on it should help the employer make a decision about your job eligibility. Including personal details can be confusing and could hurt your candidacy. Limiting your activity list to a few very significant experiences can be very effective.

If you are applying for a position as a safety officer, your certificate in Red Cross lifesaving skills or CPR would be related and valuable. You would want to include it. If, however, you are applying for a job as a junior account executive in an advertising agency, that information would be unrelated and superfluous. Leave it out.

Professional affiliations and honors should *all* be listed; especially important are those related to your job objective. Social clubs and activities need not be a part of your resume unless you hold a significant office or you are looking for a position related to your membership. Be aware that most prospective employers' principal concerns are related to your employability, not your social life. If you have any, publications can be included as an addendum to your resume.

The focus of the resume is your experience and education. It is not necessary to describe your involvement in activities. However, if your resume needs to be lengthened, this section provides the freedom either to expand on or mention only briefly the contributions you have made. If you have made significant contributions (e.g., an officer of an organization or a particularly long tenure with a group), you may choose to describe them in more detail. It is not always necessary to include the dates of your memberships with your activities the way you would include job dates.

There are a number of different ways in which to present additional information. You may give this section a number of different titles. Assess what you want to list, and then use an appropriate title. Do not use extracurricular activities. This terminology is scholastic, not professional, and therefore not appropriate. The following are two examples:

❑ ACTIVITIES: Society for Technical Communication, Student
                Senate, Student Admissions Representative, Senior
                Class Officer

❑ ACTIVITIES:
  • Society for Technical Communication, Member
  • Student Senator
  • Student Admissions Representative
  • Senior Class Officer

The position you are looking for will determine what you should or should not include. *Always* look for a correlation between the activity and the prospective job.

How Should I Handle References?

The use of references is considered a part of the interview process, and they should never be listed on a resume. You would always provide references to a potential employer if requested to, so it is not even necessary to include this section on the resume if room does not permit. If space is available, it is acceptable to include one of the following statements:

❑ REFERENCES: Furnished upon request.

❑ REFERENCES: Available upon request.

Individuals used as references must be protected from unnecessary contacts. By including names on your resume, you leave your references unprotected. Overuse and abuse of your references will lead to less-than-supportive comments. Protect your references by giving out their names only when you are being considered seriously as a candidate for a given position.

THE FUNCTIONAL RESUME

The functional resume departs from a chronological resume in that it organizes information by specific accomplishments in various settings: previous jobs, volunteer work, associations, etc. This type of resume permits you to stress the substance of your experiences rather than the position titles you have held. (See Exhibit 2.3.) You should consider using a functional resume if you have held a series of similar jobs that relied on the same skills or abilities.

Exhibit 2.3

Functional Resume

SUSAN VICKERS

Hampton Hall, Rm 620
University of Wisconsin
Madison, WI 53705
(608) 555-1222
(Until May 1999)

32 Warren Street
Watertown, MA 02472
(617) 555-1439

OBJECTIVE
An entry-level curatorial or educator position in a botanical garden that allows me to show my initiative and my knowledge of botany and horticulture.

CAPABILITIES
- Knowledge of Botany
- Plant Identification
- Labeling and Mapping
- Photography
- Strong People Skills
- Lecturing

SELECTED ACCOMPLISHMENTS
Visitor Education Through a college work-study program I achieved four years of progressively more challenging outreach duties in the education department of a major botanical garden. Created copy and designed layout for promotional material for major exhibits. Prepared lectures and offered classes in gardening as part of the public program for visitors. Selected slides, photographs, and line drawings for catalogs.
Team Player Collaborated with co-workers and professionals in other departments including the curatorial staff and the research department.
Horticulture Part-time summer job in local florist shop. Worked with customers. Helped owner order flowers and make flower arrangements. Scheduled deliveries.

AWARDS
Dean's List (six semesters)
Graduated with Honors

EMPLOYMENT HISTORY
Boerner Botanical Gardens, Milwaukee County Parks
    Department
Hales Corners, Wisconsin. Work-study 1995–99
Waltham Florists, Waltham, Massachusetts. Part-time 1995

EDUCATION
Bachelor of Science in Science Education
Double major: Botany and Education
University of Massachusetts, Amherst, Massachusetts, June 1999

REFERENCES
Provided upon request.

The Objective

A functional resume begins with an objective that can be used to focus the contents of the resume.

Specific Accomplishments

Specific accomplishments are listed on this type of resume. Examples of the types of headings used to describe these capabilities might include sales, counseling, teaching, communication, production, management, marketing, or writing. The headings you choose will directly relate to your experience and the tasks that you carried out. Each accomplishment section contains statements related to your experience in that category, regardless of when or where it occurred. Organize the accomplishments and the related tasks you describe in their order of importance as related to the position you seek.

Experience or Employment History

Your actual work experience is condensed and placed after the specific accomplishments section. It simply lists dates of employment, position titles, and employer names.

Education

The education section of a functional resume is identical to that of the chronological resume, but it does not carry the same visual importance because it is placed near the bottom of the page.

References

Because actual reference names are never listed on a resume, this section is optional if space does not permit.

THE TARGETED RESUME

The targeted resume focuses on specific work-related capabilities you can bring to a given position within an organization. (See Exhibit 2.4.) It should be sent to an individual within the organization who makes hiring decisions about the position you are seeking.

The Objective

The objective in this type of resume should be targeted to a specific career or position. It should be supported by the capabilities, accomplishments, and achievements documented in the resume.

Exhibit 2.4

Targeted Resume

JAMES PARKER

Oakley Hall, Room 325   7890 Congress Ave
University of Texas   Houston, TX 77090
Richardson, TX 75204   (281) 555-9076
(214) 555-0967
(Until May 1999)

JOB TARGET
A position as a clinical microbiologist within a hospital laboratory.

CAPABILITIES
- Receiving and logging specimens
- Setting up specimens in nutritive media
- Incubating specimens
- Examining and recording Gram stains
- Isolating pathogens for identification
- Entering results into the computer

- Familiar with a variety of computer software

ACHIEVEMENTS
- Set up new computerized tracking technique
- Co-wrote two articles for professional journals
- Graduated with Honors

WORK HISTORY

1997–present   Chemical Technician, ACOM Chemical Co., Dallas, Texas
- Internship, lab work testing new drugs

1996–97   Research Technician, University of Texas Medical School
- Work-Study position, maintaining equipment and logging data

EDUCATION

1997
Bachelor of Arts in Microbiology
Minor in Chemistry
University of Texas

1999
Master of Medical Science (MMSc)
University of Texas

Capabilities

Capabilities should be statements that illustrate tasks you believe you are capable of, based on your accomplishments, achievements, and work history. Each should relate to your targeted career or position. You can stress your qualifications rather than your employment history. This approach may require research to obtain an understanding of the nature of the work involved and the capabilities necessary to carry out that work.

Accomplishments/Achievements

This section relates the various activities you have been involved in to the job market. These experiences may include previous jobs, extracurricular activities at school, internships, and part-time summer work.

Experience

Your work history should be listed in abbreviated form and may include position title, employer name, and employment dates.

Education

Because this type of resume is directed toward a specific job target and an individual's related experience, the education section is not prominently located at the top of the resume as is done on the chronological resume.

THE BROADCAST LETTER

The broadcast letter is used by some job seekers in place of a resume and cover letter. (See Exhibit 2.5.) The purpose of this type of document is to

---

Exhibit 2.5

Broadcast Letter

PAUL WARWICK
456 Jefferson Avenue
Chicago, Illinois 60615
(773) 555-2238

June 8, 1999
Ms. Mary Gordon
Personnel Director
San Clemente School District
3444 Woodside Road
San Clemente, CA 92672

Dear Ms. Gordon,

I am writing to you because your school district may be in need of a high school biology teacher with a specialization in botany. With my bachelor's degree from the University of Chicago and my four years of progressively increasing experience at a local high school in Chicago, I have had the opportunity to work with a cross-section of students with a range of educational needs. I am able to adapt to different environments and put my skills and abilities to immediate use. Some high-lights of my experience that might interest you include:

- During college I volunteered more than 400 hours in the curatorial department of a local botanical garden.

- During my student teaching I worked with a special class of "underachievers" in a public school and was able to see a marked improvement in their grades by the end of the term.

- I was promoted to head of the biology department after teaching three years at the Chicago Heights High School.

- I ran a community gardening program through the Cooperative Extension Program, which involved answering questions and identifying plants and their diseases.

I received my B.Ed. in Education in 1994 from the University of Chicago and my teaching credentials the same year.

It would be a pleasure to review my qualifications with you in a telephone interview at some mutually convenient time. I will call your office at the end of next week to make arrangements. I look forward to discussing career opportunities with the San Clemente School District.

Sincerely,

Paul Warwick

---

make a number of potential employers aware of the availability and expertise of the job seeker. Because the broadcast letter is mass-mailed (500 to 600 employers), the amount of work required may not be worth the return for many people. If you choose to mail out a broadcast letter, you can expect to receive a response from 2 to 5 percent, at best, of the organizations that receive your letter.

This type of document is most often used by individuals who have an extensive and quantifiable work history. College students often do not have the credentials and work experience to support using a broadcast letter, and most will find it difficult to effectively quantify a slim work history.

A broadcast letter is generally four paragraphs (one page) long. The first paragraph should immediately gain the attention of the reader and state some unusual accomplishment or skill that would be of benefit to the organization. It also states the reason for the letter. Details of the sender's work history are revealed in the third paragraph. These can appear in paragraph form or as a bulleted list. Education and other qualifications or credentials are then described. Finally, the job seeker indicates what he or she will do to follow up on the letter, which usually is a follow-up call one to two weeks after the letter is sent.

RESUME PRODUCTION AND OTHER TIPS

If you have the option and convenience of using a laser printer, you may want to initially produce a limited number of copies in case you want or need to make changes on your resume.

Resume paper color should be carefully chosen. You should consider the types of employers who will receive your resume and the types of positions for which you are applying. Use white or ivory paper for traditional or conservative employers or for higher-level positions.

Black ink on sharply white paper can be harsh on the reader's eyes. Think about an ivory or cream paper that will provide less contrast and be easier to read. Pink, green, and blue tints should generally be avoided.

Many resume writers buy packages of matching envelopes and cover sheet stationery that, although not absolutely necessary, does convey a professional impression.

If you'll be producing many cover letters at home, be sure you have high-quality printing equipment, whether it be computerized or standard typewriter equipment. Learn standard envelope formats for business and retain a copy of every cover letter you send out. You can use it to take notes of any telephone conversations that may occur.

If attending a job fair, women generally can fold their resume in thirds lengthwise and find it fits into a clutch bag or envelope-style purse. Both men and women will have no trouble if they carry a briefcase. For men without a briefcase, carry the resume in a nicely covered legal-size pad holder or fold it in half lengthwise and place it inside your suitcoat pocket, taking care it doesn't "float" outside your collar.

THE COVER LETTER

The cover letter provides you with the opportunity to tailor your resume by telling the prospective employer how you can be a benefit to the organization. It will allow you to highlight aspects of your background that are not already discussed in your resume and that might be especially relevant to the organization you are contacting or to the position you are seeking. Every resume should have a cover letter enclosed when you send it out. Unlike the resume, which may be mass-produced, a cover letter is most effective when it is individually typed and focused on the particular requirements of the organization in question.

A good cover letter should supplement the resume and motivate the reader to review the resume. The format shown in Exhibit 2.6 is only a suggestion to help you decide what information to include in writing a cover letter.

Exhibit 2.6

Cover Letter Format

Your Street Address
Your Town, State, Zip
Phone Number
Date
Name
Title
Organization
Address

Dear _____:

First Paragraph. In this paragraph state the reason for the letter, name the specific position or type of work you are applying for, and indicate from which resource (career development office, newspaper, contact, employment service) you learned of the opening. The first paragraph can also be used to inquire about future openings.

continued

---

continued

Second Paragraph. Indicate why you are interested in the position, the company, its products or services, and what you can do for the employer. If you are a recent graduate, explain how your academic background makes you a qualified candidate. Try not to repeat the same information found in the resume.

Third Paragraph. Refer the reader to the enclosed resume for more detailed information.

Fourth Paragraph. In this paragraph say what you will do to follow up on your letter. For example, state that you will call by a certain date to set up an interview or to find out if the company will be recruiting in your area. Finish by indicating your willingness to answer any questions they may have. Be sure you have provided your phone number.

Sincerely,

Type your name

Enclosure

Begin the cover letter with your street address 12 lines down from the top. Leave three to five lines between the date and the name of the person to whom you are addressing the cover letter. Make sure you leave one blank line between the salutation and the body of the letter and between paragraphs. After typing "Sincerely," leave four blank lines and type your name. This should leave plenty of room for your signature. A sample cover letter is shown in Exhibit 2.7.

The following guidelines will help you write good cover letters:

1. Be sure to type your letter; ensure there are no misspellings.

2. Avoid unusual typefaces, such as script.

3. Address the letter to an individual, using the person's name and title. To obtain this information, call the company. If answering a blind

EXHIBIT 2.7

Sample Cover Letter

RICHARD STERN
435 NE 45 Court
Fort Lauderdale, FL 33309
(954) 555-2213

April 25, 1999

Peter Schreiber
Director of Personnel
Sea World
P.O. Box 555
Orlando, FL 31455

Dear Mr. Schreiber,

In May of 1999 I will graduate from the University of Miami with a Bachelor of Science degree in biology. I read of your opening for an assistant trainer experienced with marine mammals in the Sunday, April 24 *Orlando Sentinel.* I am very interested in that possibility and want to explore the opportunity for employment with Sea World.

The ad indicated you were looking for hard-working individuals with good communication skills, who also have experience in training, medical, show, and research behaviors. I believe I possess those skills. During the summers while in college I worked at the Miami Seaquarium in several capacities, including an internship working with sea lions and a stint as an aquarist-in-training, maintaining the tank.

Through my work there, I learned the importance of possessing good observation skills and maintaining a positive attitude with co-workers and visitors.

In addition to the various animal behavior courses in my academic program, I felt it important to enroll in some history, anthropology, and psychology courses, focusing particularly on training module design and methods. These courses helped me become comfortable with understanding marine mammals, as well as honing my research skills. These accomplishments I believe

continued

continued

will help me to represent Sea World in a professional and enthusiastic manner.

I would like to meet with you to discuss how my education and experience would be consistent with your needs. I will contact your office next week to discuss the possibility of an interview. In the meantime, if you have any questions or require additional information, please contact me at my home, (954) 555-2213, or via e-mail at RStern@theonramp.com.

Sincerely,

Richard Stern
Enclosure

newspaper advertisement, address the letter "To Whom It May Concern" or omit the salutation.

4. Be sure your cover letter directly indicates the position you are applying for and tells why you are qualified to fill it.

5. Send the original letter, not a photocopy, with your resume. Keep a copy for your records.

6. Make your cover letter no more than one page.

7. Include a phone number where you can be reached.

8. Avoid trite language and have someone read it over to react to its tone, content, and mechanics.

9. For your own information, record the date you send out each letter and resume.

CHAPTER THREE

RESEARCHING CAREERS

· ·

One common question a career counselor encounters is "What can I do with my degree?" Biology majors have narrowed their interests a little more successfully than some other college majors, but still, all the choices—and there are many—are not immediately obvious. Biology graduates often struggle with this problem, because unlike their fellow students in more narrowly defined fields, such as accounting, theater, music, or health and physical education, there is real confusion about just what kinds of jobs, other than the obvious route of teaching, they can do with their degrees. Accounting majors become accountants; computer science majors can work as data analysts. What jobs are open to biology majors?

· ·

WHAT DO THEY CALL THE JOB YOU WANT?

There is every reason to be unaware. One reason for confusion is perhaps a mistaken assumption that a college education provides job training. In most cases it does not. Of course, applied fields such as engineering, management, or education provide specific skills for the workplace, whereas most liberal arts degrees simply provide an education. A liberal arts education exposes you to numerous fields of study and teaches you quantitative reasoning, critical thinking, writing, and speaking, all of which can be successfully applied to a number of different job fields. But it still remains up to you to choose a job field and to learn how to articulate the benefits of your education in a way the employer will appreciate.

As indicated in Chapter 1 on self-assessment, your first task is to understand and value what parts of that education you enjoyed and were good at and would continue to enjoy in your life's work. Did your writing courses encourage you in your ability to express yourself in writing? Did you enjoy the research process, and did you find your work was well received? Did you enjoy any of your required quantitative subjects like algebra or calculus?

The answers to questions such as these provide clues to skills and interests you bring to the employment market over and above the credential of your degree. In fact, it is not an overstatement to suggest that most employers who demand a college degree immediately look beyond that degree to you as a person and your own individual expression of what you like to do and think you can do for them, regardless of your major.

COLLECTING JOB TITLES

The world of employment is a big place, and even seasoned veterans of the job hunt can be surprised about what jobs are to be found in what organizations. You need to become a bit of an explorer and adventurer and be willing to try a variety of techniques to begin a list of possible occupations that might use your talents and education. Once you have a list of possibilities that you are interested in and qualified for, you can move on to find out what kinds of organizations have these job titles.

Not every employer seeking to hire a molecular biologist may be equally desirable to you. Some employment environments may be more attractive to you than others. A molecular biologist wanting to work with DNA molecules could do that for a large hospital, a private research lab, a university medical school, or a private pharmaceutical or chemical company.

Each of these environments presents a different "culture" with associated norms in the pace of work, the subject matter of interest, and the backgrounds of its employees. Although the job titles may be the same, not all locations may present the same "fit" for you.

If you majored in biology and enjoyed the classroom laboratory work you might have done as part of your degree and have developed some strong research skills, you might naturally think about private research labs. But biology majors with these same skills and interests might go on to train others in their skills, or work as researchers for nonprofit agencies or technicians for teaching hospitals and university medical schools. Each of these job titles can also be found in a number of different settings.

....

Take training, for example. Trainers write policy and procedural manuals and actively teach to assist all levels of employees in mastering various tasks and work-related systems. Trainers exist in all large corporations, banks, consumer goods manufacturers, medical diagnostic equipment firms, sales organizations, and any organization that has processes or materials that need to be presented to and learned by the staff.

In reading job descriptions or want ads for any of these positions, you would find your four-year degree a "must." However, the academic major might be less important than your own individual skills in critical thinking, analysis, report writing, public presentations, and interpersonal communication. Even more important than thinking or knowing you have certain skills is your ability to express those skills concretely and the examples you use to illustrate them to an employer.

The best beginning to a job search is to create a list of job titles you might want to pursue, learn more about the nature of the jobs behind those titles, and then discover what kinds of employers hire for those positions. In the following section we'll teach you how to build a job title directory to use in your job search.

Developing a Job Title Directory That Works for You

A job title directory is simply a complete list of all the job titles you are interested in, are intrigued by, or think you are qualified for. Combining the understanding gained through self-assessment with your own individual interests and the skills and talents you've acquired with your degree, you'll soon start to read and recognize a number of occupational titles that seem right for you. There are several resources you can use to develop your list, including computer searches, books, and want ads.

Computerized Interest Inventories. One way to begin your search is to identify a number of jobs that call for your degree and the particular skills and interests you identified as part of the self-assessment process. There are excellent interactive computer career guidance programs on the market to help you produce such selected lists of possible job titles. Most of these are available at high schools and colleges and at some larger town and city libraries. Two of the industry leaders are SIGI and DISCOVER. Both allow you to enter interests, values, educational background, and other information to produce lists of possible occupations and industries. Each of the resources listed here will produce different job title lists. Some job titles will appear again and again, while others will be unique to a particular source. Investigate them all!

Reference Books. Books on the market that may be available through your local library, bookstore, or career counseling office also suggest various occupations related to a number of majors. The following are only two of the many good books on the market: *Occupational Outlook Handbook* and *Occupational Projections and Training Data*, both put out annually by the U.S. Department of Labor, Bureau of Labor Statistics. The *OOH* describes hundreds of job titles under several broad categories such as Executive, Administrative, and Managerial Occupations and also identifies those jobs by their *Dictionary of Occupational Titles* (*DOT*) code. (See following discussion.)

••••••••••••••••••••••••••••••••••••••

For biology majors more than two dozen related job titles are listed throughout various sections of the *OOH*. Some are familiar ones such as the generic "biologist" or "botanist." Others might be new to you, such as ethologist or limnologist. Biologist is a broad term and biologists are further classified by the type of organism they study or by the specific activity they perform.

The *Occupational Projections and Training Data* is another good resource that essentially allows job seekers to compare 500 occupations on factors such as job openings, earnings, and training requirements.

So, if as a biology major you discover ecologist as a job title in the *OOH*, you can then go to the *Occupational Projections and Training Data* and compare it with scores of jobs related to that title. This source adds some

depth by presenting statistics in a number of different occupations within that field.

·····································

Each job title deserves your consideration. Like the layers of an onion, the search for job titles can go on and on! As you spend time doing this activity, you are actually learning more about the value of your degree. What's important in your search at this point is not to become critical or selective, but rather to develop as long a list of possibilities as you can. Every source used will help you add new and potentially exciting jobs to your growing list.

Want Ads. It has been well publicized that newspaper want ads represent only about 10 to 15 percent of the current job market. Nevertheless, the Sunday want ads can be a great help to you in your search. Although they may not be the best place to look for a job, they can teach the job seeker much about the job market and provide a good education in job descriptions, duties and responsibilities, active industries, and some indication of the volume of job traffic. For our purposes they are a good source for job titles to add to your list.

Read the Sunday want ads in a major market newspaper for several Sundays in a row. Circle and then cut out any and all ads that interest you and seem to call for something close to your education and experience. Remember, because want ads are written for what an organization *hopes* to find, you don't have to meet absolutely every criterion. However, if certain requirements are stated as absolute minimums and you cannot meet them, it's best not to waste your time.

A recent examination of *The Boston Sunday Globe* reveals the following possible occupations for a liberal arts major with some computer skills and limited prior work experience. (This is only a partial list of what was available.)

❑ Admissions representative	❑ Technical writer
❑ Salesperson	❑ Personnel trainee
❑ Compliance director	❑ GED examiner
❑ Assistant principal gifts writer	❑ Direct mail researcher
❑ Public relations officer	❑ Associate publicist

After performing this exercise for a few Sundays, you'll find you have collected a new library of job titles.

The Sunday want ad exercise is important because these jobs are out in the marketplace. They truly exist, and people with your qualifications are being sought to apply. What's more, many of these advertisements describe the duties and responsibilities of the job advertised and give you a beginning sense of the challenges and opportunities such a position presents. Some will indicate salary, and that will be helpful as well. This information will better define the jobs for you and provide some good material for possible interviews in that field.

Exploring Job Descriptions

Once you've arrived at a solid list of possible job titles that interest you and for which you believe you are somewhat qualified, it's a good idea to do some research on each of these jobs. The preeminent source for such job information is the *Dictionary of Occupational Titles,* or *DOT.* This directory lists every conceivable job and provides excellent up-to-date information on duties and responsibilities, interactions with associates, and day-to-day assignments and tasks. These descriptions provide a thorough job analysis, but they do not consider the possible employers or the environments in which this job may be performed. So, although a position as public relations officer may be well defined in terms of duties and responsibilities, it does not explain the differences in doing public relations work in a college or a hospital or a factory or a bank. You will need to look somewhere else for work settings.

Learning More About Possible Work Settings

After reading some job descriptions, you may choose to edit and revise your list of job titles once again, discarding those you feel are not suitable and keeping those that continue to hold your interest. Or you may wish to keep your list intact and see where these jobs may be located. For example, if you are interested in public relations and you appear to have those skills and the requisite education, you'll want to know what organizations do public relations. How can you find that out? How much income does someone in public relations make a year and what is the employment potential for the field of public relations?

To answer these and many other good questions about your list of job titles, we recommend you try any of the following resources: *Careers Encyclopedia, Career Information Center, College to Career: The Guide to Job Opportunities,* and the *Occupational Outlook Handbook.* Each of these books, in a different way, will help to put the job titles you have selected into an employer context. *VGM's Handbook of Business and Management Careers* contains detailed career descriptions for more than fifty fields. Entries include complete information on duties and responsibilities for individual careers and detailed entry-level requirements. There is information on working conditions and promotional opportunities as well. Salary ranges and career outlook projections are also provided. Perhaps the most extensive discussion is found in the *Occupational Outlook Handbook,* which gives a thorough presentation of the nature of the work, the working conditions, employment statistics, training, other qualifications, and advancement possibilities as well as job outlook and earnings. Related occupations are also detailed, and a select bibliography is provided to help you find additional information.

Continuing with our public relations example, your search through these reference materials would teach you that the public relations jobs you find attractive are available in larger hospitals, financial institutions, most corporations (both consumer goods and industrial goods), media organizations, and colleges and universities.

Networking to Get the Complete Story

You now have not only a list of job titles but also, for each of these job titles, a description of the work involved and a general list of possible employment settings in which to work. You'll want to do some reading and keep talking to friends, colleagues, teachers, and others about the possibilities. Don't neglect to ask if the career office at your college maintains some kind of alumni network. Often such alumni networks will connect you with another graduate from the college who is working in the job title or industry you are seeking information about. These career networkers offer what assistance they can. For some it is a full day "shadowing" the alumnus as he or she goes about the job. Others offer partial day visits, tours, informational interviews, resume reviews, job postings, or, if distance prevents a visit, telephone interviews. As fellow graduates, they'll be frank and informative about their own jobs and prospects in their field.

Take them up on their offer and continue to learn all you can about your own personal list of job titles, descriptions, and employment settings. You'll probably continue to edit and refine this list as you learn more about the realities of the job, the possible salary, advancement opportunities, and supply and demand statistics.

In the next section we'll describe how to find the specific organizations that represent these industries and employers so that you can begin to make contact.

WHERE ARE THESE JOBS, ANYWAY?

Having a list of job titles that you've designed around your own career interests and skills is an excellent beginning. It means you've really thought about who you are and what you are presenting to the employment market. It has caused you to think seriously about the most appealing environments to work in, and you have identified some employer types that represent these environments.

The research and the thinking that you've done this far will be used again and again. It will be helpful in writing your resume and cover letters, in talking about yourself on the telephone to prospective employers, and in answering interview questions.

Now is a good time to begin to narrow the field of job titles and employment sites down to some specific employers to initiate the employment contact.

Finding Out Which Employers Hire People Like You

This section will provide tips, techniques, and specific resources for developing an actual list of specific employers that can be used to make contacts. It is only an outline that you must be prepared to tailor to your own particular needs and according to what you bring to the job search. Once again, it is important to stress the need to communicate with others along the way exactly what you're looking for and what your goals are for the research you're doing. Librarians, employers, career counselors, friends, friends of friends, business contacts, and bookstore staff will all have helpful information on geographically specific and new resources to aid you in locating employers who'll hire you.

Identifying Information Resources

Your interview wardrobe and your new resume may have put a dent in your wallet, but the resources you'll need to pursue your job search are available for free (although you might choose to copy materials on a machine instead of taking notes by hand). The categories of information detailed here are not hard to find and are yours for the browsing.

Numerous resources described in this section will help you identify actual employers. Use all of them or any others that you identify as available in your geographic area. As you become experienced in this process, you'll quickly figure out which information sources are helpful and which are not. If you live in a rural area, a well-planned day trip to a major city that includes a college career office, a large college or city library, state and federal employment centers, a chamber of commerce office, and a well-stocked bookstore can produce valuable results.

There are many excellent resources available to help you identify actual job sites. They are categorized into employer directories (usually indexed by product lines and geographic location), geographically based directories (designed to highlight particular cities, regions, or states), career-specific directories (e.g., *Sports Market Place,* which lists tens of thousands of firms involved with sports), periodicals and newspapers, targeted job posting publications, and videos. This is by no means meant to be a complete list of resources, but rather a starting point for identifying useful resources.

Working from the more general references to highly specific resources, we will provide a basic list to help you begin your search. Many of these you'll find easily available. In some cases reference librarians and others will suggest even better materials for your particular situation. Start to create your own customized bibliography of job search references. Use copying services to save time and to allow you to carry away information about organization mission, location, company officers, phone numbers, and addresses.

Employer Directories. There are many employer directories available to give you the kind of information you need for your job search. Some of our favorites are listed here, but be sure to ask the professionals you are working with to make additional suggestions.

- *America's Corporate Families* identifies many major U.S. ultimate parent companies and displays corporate family linkage of subsidiaries and divisions. Businesses can be identified by their industrial code.

- *Million Dollar Directory: America's Leading Public and Private Companies* lists about 160,000 companies.

- *Moody's* various manuals are intended as guides for investors, so they contain a history of each company. Each manual contains a classification of companies by industries and products.

- *Standard and Poor's Register of Corporations* contains listings for 45,000 businesses, some of which are not listed in the *Million Dollar Directory.*

- *Job Seekers Guide to Private and Public Companies* profiles 15,000 employers in four volumes, each covering a different geographic region. Company entries include contact information, business descriptions, and application procedures.

- *The Career Guide: Dun's Employment Opportunities Directory* lists more than 5,000 large organizations, including hospitals and local governments. Profiles include an overview and history of the employer as well as opportunities, benefits, and contact names. It contains geographic and industrial indexes and indexes by discipline or internship availability. This guide also includes a state-by-state list of professional personnel consultants and their specialties.

❑ *Professional's Job Finder/Government Job Finder/Non-Profits Job Finder* are specific directories of job services, salary surveys, and periodical listings in which advertisements for jobs in the professional, government, or not-for-profit sector are found.

❑ *Opportunities in Nonprofit Organizations* is a VGM career series edition that opens up the world of not-for-profit by helping you match your interest profile to the aims and objectives of scores of nonprofit employers in business, education, health and medicine, social welfare, science and technology, and many others. There is also a special section on fund-raising and development career paths.

❑ *The 100 Best Companies to Sell For* lists companies by industry and provides contact information and describes benefits and corporate culture.

❑ *The 100 Best Companies to Work For in America* rates organizations on several factors including opportunities, job security, and pay.

❑ *Companies That Care* lists organizations that the authors believe are family-friendly. One index organizes information by state.

❑ *Infotrac CD-ROM Business Index* covers business journals and magazines as well as news magazines and can provide information on public and private companies.

❑ *ABI/Inform On Disc* (CD-ROM) indexes articles in more than 800 journals.

Geographically Based Directories. The Job Bank series published by Bob Adams, Inc. contains detailed entries on each area's major employers, including business activity, address, phone number, and hiring contact name. Many listings specify educational backgrounds being sought in potential employees. Each volume contains a solid discussion of each city's or state's major employment sectors. Organizations are also indexed by industry. Job Bank volumes are available for the following places: Atlanta, Boston, Chicago, Denver, Dallas–Ft. Worth, Florida, Houston, Ohio, St. Louis, San Francisco, Seattle, Los Angeles, New York, Detroit, Philadelphia, Minneapolis, the Northwest, and Washington, D.C.

National Job Bank lists employers in every state, along with contact names and commonly hired job categories. Included are many small companies often overlooked by other directories. Companies are also indexed by industry. This publication provides information on educational backgrounds sought and lists company benefits.

Career-Specific Directories. VGM publishes a number of excellent series detailing careers for college graduates. In the *Professional Career Series* are guides to careers in the following fields, among others:

- Advertising
- Communications
- Business
- Computers
- Health Care
- High Tech

Each provides an excellent discussion of the industry, educational requirements for jobs, salary ranges, duties, and projected outlooks for the field.

Another VGM series, *Opportunities In . . .,* has an equally wide range of titles relating to specific majors, such as the following:

- *Opportunities in Banking*
- *Opportunities in Insurance*
- *Opportunities in Federal Government*
- *Opportunities in Government Service*
- *Opportunities in Journalism*
- *Opportunities in Law*
- *Opportunities in State and Local Government*
- *Opportunities in Teaching*
- *Opportunities in Nonprofit Organizations*

Periodicals and Newspapers. Several sources are available to help you locate which journals or magazines carry job advertisements in your field. Other resources help you identify opportunities in other parts of the country.

- *Where the Jobs Are: A Comprehensive Directory of 1,200 Journals Listing Career Opportunities* links specific occupational titles to corresponding periodicals that carry job listings for your field.

- *Social & Behavioral Sciences Jobs Handbook* contains a periodicals matrix organized by academic discipline and highlights periodicals containing job listings.

❏ *National Business Employment Weekly* compiles want ads from four regional editions of the *Wall Street Journal.* Most are business and management positions.

❏ *National Ad Search* reprints ads from seventy-five metropolitan newspapers across the country. Although the focus is on management positions, technical and professional postings are also included. *Caution:* Watch deadline dates carefully on listings because deadlines may have already passed by the time the ad is printed.

❏ *The Federal Jobs Digest* and *Federal Career Opportunities* list government positions.

❏ *World Chamber of Commerce Directory* lists addresses for chambers worldwide, state boards of tourism, convention and visitors' bureaus, and economic development organizations.

This list is certainly not exhaustive; use it to begin your job search work.

Targeted Job Posting Publications. Although the resources that follow are national in scope, they are either targeted to one medium of contact (telephone), focused on specific types of jobs, or are less comprehensive than the sources previously listed.

❏ *Job Hotlines USA* pinpoints more than one thousand hard-to-find telephone numbers for companies and government agencies that use prerecorded job messages and listings. Very few of the telephone numbers listed are toll-free, and sometimes recordings are long, so callers beware!

❏ *The Job Hunter* is a national biweekly newspaper listing business, arts, media, government, human services, health, community-related, and student services job openings.

❏ *Current Jobs for Graduates* is a national employment listing for liberal arts professions, including editorial positions, management opportunities, museum work, teaching, and nonprofit work.

❏ *Environmental Opportunities* serves environmental job interests nationwide by listing administrative, marketing, and human resources positions along with education-related jobs and positions directly related to a degree in an environmental field.

❏ *Y National Vacancy List* shows YMCA professional vacancies, including development, administration, programming, membership, and recreation postings.

❑ *ARTSearch* is a national employment service bulletin for the arts, including administration, managerial, marketing, and financial management jobs.

❑ *Community Jobs* is an employment newspaper for the nonprofit sector that provides a variety of listings, including project manager, canvas director, government relations specialist, community organizer, and program instructor.

❑ *College Placement Council Annual: A Guide to Employment Opportunities for College Graduates* is an annual guide containing solid job-hunting information and, more importantly, displaying ads from large corporations actively seeking recent college graduates in all majors. Company profiles provide brief descriptions and available employment opportunities. Contact names and addresses are given. Profiles are indexed by organization name, geographic location, and occupation.

Videos. You may be one of the many job seekers who like to get information via a medium other than paper. Many career libraries, public libraries, and career centers in libraries carry an assortment of videos that will help you learn new techniques and get information helpful in the job search. A small sampling of the multitude of videos now available includes the following:

❑ *The Skills Search* (20 min.) discusses three types of skills important in the workplace, how to present the skills in an interview, and how to respond to problem questions.

❑ *Effective Answers to Interview Questions* (35 min.) presents two real-life job seekers and shows how they realized the true meaning of interview questions and formulated positive answers.

❑ *Employer's Expectations* (33 min.) covers three areas that are important to all employers: appearance, dependability, and skills.

❑ *The Tough New Labor Market of the 1990s* (30 min.) presents labor market facts as well as suggestions on what job seekers should do to gain employment in this market.

❑ *Dialing for Jobs: Using the Phone in the Job Search* (30 min.) describes how to use the phone effectively to gain information and arrange interviews by following two new graduates as they learn and apply techniques.

Locating Information Resources

An essay by John Case that appeared in the *Boston Globe* (August 25, 1993) alerts both new and seasoned job seekers that the job market is changing, and the old guarantees of lifelong employment no longer hold true. Some of our major corporations, which were once seen as the most prestigious of employment destinations, are now laying off thousands of employees. Middle management is especially hard hit in downsizing situations. On the other side of the coin, smaller, more entrepreneurial firms are adding employees and realizing enormous profit margins. The geography of the new job market is unfamiliar, and the terrain is much harder to map. New and smaller firms can mean different kinds of jobs and new job titles. The successful job seeker will keep an open mind about where he or she might find employment and what that employment might be called.

In order to become familiar with this new terrain, you will need to undertake some research, which can be done at any of the following locations:

- Public libraries

- Business organizations

- Employment agencies

- Bookstores

- Career libraries

Each one of these places offers a collection of resources that will help you get the information you need.

As you meet and talk with service professionals at all these sites, be sure to let them know what you're doing. Inform them of your job search, what you've already accomplished, and what you're looking for. The more people who know you're job seeking, the greater the possibility that someone will have information or know someone who can help you along your way.

Public Libraries. Large city libraries, college and university libraries, and even well-supported town library collections contain a variety of resources to help you conduct a job search. It is not uncommon for libraries to have separate "vocational choices" sections with books, tapes, and associated materials relating to job search and selection. Some are now even making resume creation software available for use by patrons.

Some of the publications we name throughout this book are expensive reference items that are rarely purchased by individuals. In addition, libraries carry a wide range of newspapers and telephone yellow pages as well as the usual array of books. If resources are not immediately available, many libraries have loan arrangements with other facilities and can make information available to you relatively quickly.

Take advantage of not only the reference collections, but also the skilled and informed staff. Let them know exactly what you are looking for, and they'll have their own suggestions. You'll be visiting the library frequently, and the reference staff will soon come to know who you are and what you're working on. They'll be part of your job search network!

Business Organizations. Chambers of Commerce, Offices of New Business Development, Councils on Business and Industry, Small Business Administration (SBA) offices, and professional associations can all provide geographically specific lists of companies and organizations that have hiring needs. They also have an array of other available materials, including visitors' guides and regional fact books that provide additional employment information.

These agencies serve to promote local and regional businesses and ensure their survival and success. Although these business organizations do not advertise job openings or seek employees for their members, they may be very aware of staffing needs among their member firms. In your visits to each of these locations, spend some time with the personnel getting to know who they are and what they do. Let them know of your job search and your intentions regarding employment. You may be surprised and delighted at the information they may provide.

Employment Agencies. Employment agencies (including state and federal employment offices), professional "headhunters" or executive search firms, and some private career counselors can provide direct leads to job openings. Don't overlook these resources. If you are mounting a complete job search program and want to ensure that you are covering the potential market for employers, consider the employment agencies in your territory. Some of these organizations work contractually with several specific firms and may have access that is unavailable to you. Others may be particularly well-informed about supply and demand in particular industries or geographic locations.

In the case of professional (commercial) employment agencies, which include those executive recruitment firms labeled "headhunters," you should be cautious about entering into any binding contractual agreement. Before doing so, be sure to get the information you need to decide whether their services can be of use to you. Questions to ask include the following: Who pays the fee when employment is obtained? Are there any other fees or costs associated with this service? What is their placement rate? Can you see a list of previous clients and can you talk to any for references? Do they typically work with entry-level job seekers? Do they tend to focus on particular kinds of employment or industries?

A few cautions are in order, however, when you work with professional agencies. Remember, the professional employment agency is, in most cases, paid by the hiring organization. Naturally, their interest and attention is largely directed to the employer, not to the candidate. Of course, they want to provide good candidates to guarantee future contracts, but they are less interested in the job seeker than the employer.

For teacher candidates there are a number of good placement firms that charge the prospective teacher, not the employer. This situation has evolved over time as a result of supply and demand and financial structuring of most school systems, which cannot spend money on recruiting teachers. Usually these firms charge a nonrefundable administrative fee and, upon successful placement, require a fee based on percentage of salary, which may range from 10 to 20 percent of annual compensation. Often, this can be repaid over a number of months. Check your contract carefully.

State and federal employment offices are no-fee services that maintain extensive "job boards" and can provide detailed specifications for each job advertised and help with application forms. Because government employment application forms are detailed, keep a master copy along with copies of all additional documentation (resumes, educational transcripts, military discharge papers, proof of citizenship, etc.). Successive applications may require separate filings. Visit these offices as frequently as you can because most deal with applicants on a "walk-in" basis and will not telephone prospective candidates or maintain files of job seekers. Check your telephone book for the address of the nearest state and federal offices.

One type of employment service that causes much confusion among job seekers is the outplacement firm. Their advertisements tend to suggest they will put you in touch with the "hidden job market." They use advertising phrases such as "We'll work with you until you get that job" or "Maximize your earnings and career opportunities." In fact, if you read the fine print on these ads, you will notice these firms must state they are "Not an employment agency." These firms are, in fact, corporate and private outplacement counseling agencies whose work involves resume editing, counseling to provide leads for jobs, interview skills training, and all the other aspects of hiring preparation. They do this for a fee, sometimes in the thousands of dollars range, which is paid by you, the client. Some of these firms have good reputations and provide excellent materials and techniques. Most, however, provide a service you as a college student or graduate can receive free from your alma mater or through a reciprocity agreement between your college and a college or university located closer to your current address.

Bookstores. Any well-stocked bookstore will carry some job search books that are worth buying. Some major stores will even have an extensive section devoted to materials, including excellent videos, related to the job search process. Several possibilities are listed in the following sections. You will also find copies of local newspapers and business magazines. The one advantage provided by resources purchased at a bookstore is that you can read and work with the information in the comfort of your own home and do not have to conform to the hours of operation of a library, which can present real difficulties if you are working full time as you seek employment. A few minutes spent browsing in a bookstore might be a beneficial break from your job search activities and turn up valuable resources.

Career Libraries. Career libraries, which are found in career centers at colleges and universities and sometimes within large public libraries, contain a unique blend of the job search resources housed in other settings. In addition, career libraries often purchase a number of job listing publications, each of which targets a specific industry or type of job. You may find job listings specifically for entry-level positions for political science majors. Ask about job posting newsletters or newspapers specifically focused on careers in the area that most interests you. Each center will be unique, but you are certain to discover some good sources of jobs.

Most college career libraries now hold growing collections of video material on specific industries and on aspects of your job search process, including dress and appearance, how to manage the luncheon or dinner interview, how to be effective at a job fair, and many other specific titles. Some larger corporations produce handsome video materials detailing the variety of career paths and opportunities available in their organizations.

Some career libraries also house computer-based career planning and information systems. These interactive computer programs help you to clarify your values and interests and will combine that with your education to provide possible job titles and industry locations. Some even contain extensive lists of graduate school programs.

One specific kind of service a career library will be able to direct you to is computerized job search services. These services, of which there are many, are run by private companies, individual colleges, or consortiums of colleges. They attempt to match qualified job candidates with potential employers. The candidate submits a resume (or an application) to the service. This information (which can be categorized into hundreds of separate "fields" of data) is entered into a computer database. Your information is then compared with the information from employers about what they desire in a prospective employee. If there is a "match" between what they want and what you have indicated you can offer, the job search service or the employer will contact you directly to continue the process.

Computerized job search services can complement an otherwise complete job search program. They are *not*, however, a substitute for the kinds of activities described in this book. They are essentially passive operations that are random in nature. If you have not listed skills, abilities, traits, experiences, or education *exactly* as an employer has listed its needs, there is simply no match.

Consult with the staff members at the career libraries you use. These professionals have been specifically trained to meet the unique needs you present. Often you can just drop in and receive help with general questions, or you may want to set up an appointment to speak one-on-one with a career counselor to gain special assistance.

Every career library is different in size and content, but each can provide valuable information for the job search. Some may even provide some limited counseling. If you have not visited the career library at your college or alma mater, call and ask if these collections are still available for your use. Be sure to ask about other services that you can use as well.

If you are not near your own college as you work on your job search, call the career office and inquire about reciprocal agreements with other colleges that are closer to where you live. Very often your own alma mater can arrange for you to use a limited menu of services at another school. This typically would include access to a career library and job posting information and might include limited counseling.

CHAPTER FOUR

NETWORKING

*N*etworking is the process of deliberately establishing relationships to get career-related information or to alert potential employers that you are available for work. Networking is critically important to today's job seeker for two reasons: it will help you get the information you need, and it can help you find out about *all* of the available jobs.

Getting the Information You Need

Networkers will review your resume and give you candid feedback on its effectiveness. They will talk about the job you are looking for and give you a candid appraisal of how they see your strengths and weaknesses. If they have a good sense of the industry or the employment sector for that job, you'll get their feelings on future trends in the industry as well. Some networkers will be very candid about salaries, job hunting techniques, and suggestions for your job search strategy. Many have been known to place calls right from the interview desk to friends and associates who might be interested in you. Each networker will make his or her own contribution, and each will be valuable.

Because organizations must evolve to adapt to current global market needs, the information provided by decision makers within various organizations will be critical to your success as a new job market entrant. Networking can help you find out about trends currently affecting the industries under your consideration.

Finding Out About All of the Available Jobs

Secondly, not every job that is available at this very moment is advertised for potential applicants to see. This is called the *hidden job market.* Only 15 to

20 percent of all jobs are formally advertised, which means that 80 to 85 percent of available jobs do not appear in published channels. Networking will help you become more knowledgeable about all the employment opportunities available during your job search period.

Although someone you might talk to today doesn't know of any openings within his or her organization, tomorrow or next week or next month an opening may occur. If you've taken the time to show an interest in and knowledge of their organization, if you've shown the company representative how you can help achieve organizational goals and that you can fit into the organization, you'll be one of the first candidates considered for the position.

Networking: A Proactive Approach

Networking is a proactive rather than a reactive approach. You, as a job seeker, are expected to initiate a certain level of activity on your own behalf; you cannot afford to simply respond to jobs listed in the newspaper. Being proactive means building a network of contacts that includes informed and interested decision makers who will provide you with up-to-date knowledge of the current job market and increase your chances of finding out about employment opportunities appropriate for your interests, experience, and level of education.

An old axiom of networking says "You are only two phone calls away from the information you need." In other words, by talking to enough people, you will quickly come across someone who can offer you help. Start with your professors. Each of them probably has a wide circle of contacts. In their work and travel they might have met someone who can help you or direct you to someone who can.

Control and the Networking Process

In deliberately establishing relationships, the process of networking begins with you in control—*you* are contacting specific individuals. As your network expands and you establish a set of professional relationships, your search for information or jobs will begin to move outside of your total control. A part of the networking process involves others assisting you by gathering information for you or recommending you as a possible job candidate. As additional people become a part of your networking system, you will have less knowledge about activities undertaken on your behalf; you will undoubtedly be contacted by individuals whom you did not initially approach. If you want to function effectively in surprise situations, you must be prepared at all times to talk with strangers about the informational or employment needs that motivated you to become involved in the networking process.

PREPARING TO NETWORK

In deliberately establishing relationships, maximize your efforts by organizing your approach. Five specific areas in which you can organize your efforts include reviewing your self-assessment, reviewing your research on job sites and organizations, deciding who it is you want to talk to, keeping track of all your efforts, and creating your self-promotion tools.

Review Your Self-Assessment

Your self-assessment is as important a tool in preparing to network as it has been in other aspects of your job search. You have carefully evaluated your personal traits, personal values, economic needs, longer-term goals, skill base, preferred skills, and underdeveloped skills. During the networking process you will be called upon to communicate what you know about yourself and relate it to the information or job you seek. Be sure to review the exercises that you completed in the self-assessment section of this book in preparation for networking. We've explained that you need to assess what skills you have acquired from your major that are of general value to an employer and to be ready to express those in ways employers can appreciate as useful in their own organizations.

Review Your Research of Job Sites and Organizations

In addition, individuals assisting you will expect that you'll have at least some background information on the occupation or industry of interest to you. Refer to the appropriate sections of this book and other relevant publications to acquire the background information necessary for effective networking. They'll explain how to identify not only the job titles that might be of interest to you, but also what kinds of organizations employ people to do that job. You will develop some sense of working conditions and expectations about duties and responsibilities—all of which will be of help in your networking interviews.

Decide Who It Is You Want to Talk To

Networking cannot begin until you decide who it is that you want to talk to and, in general, what type of information you hope to gain from your contacts. Once you know this, it's time to begin developing a list of contacts. Five useful sources for locating contacts are described here.

College Alumni Network. Most colleges and universities have created a formal network of alumni and friends of the institution who are particularly interested in helping currently enrolled students and graduates of their alma mater gain employment-related information.

••••••••••••••••••••••••••••••••••••••

Because biology is such a diverse degree program, you'll find an abundance of biology graduates spanning the full spectrum of possible employment. Just the diversity alone evidenced by such an alumni list should be encouraging and informative to the biology graduate. Among such a varied group, there are likely to be scores you would enjoy talking with and perhaps could meet.

••••••••••••••••••••••••••••••••••••••

It is usually a simple process to make use of an alumni network. You need only visit the alumni or career office at your college or university and follow the procedure that has been established. Often, you will simply complete a form indicating your career goals and interests and you will be given the names of appropriate individuals to contact. In many cases staff members will coach you on how to make the best use of the limited time these alumni contacts may have available for you.

Alumni networkers may provide some combination of the following services: day-long shadowing experiences, telephone interviews, in-person interviews, information on relocating to given geographic areas, internship information, suggestions on graduate school study, and job vacancy notices.

••••••••••••••••••••••••••••••••••••••

What a valuable experience! Perhaps you are interested in working for a major research lab but you are concerned about your degree preparation and whether your capabilities are up to the requirements of the particular institution. Spending a day with an alumnus who works for a similar enterprise, asking lots of questions about his or her educational training and preparation, will give you a more concrete view of the possibilities for your degree. Observing firsthand how this person does the job will be a far better decision criterion for you than any reading on the subject could possibly provide.

In addition to your own observations, the alumnus will have his or her own perspective on the relevance of your training and will give you realistic and honest feed-back on your job search concerns.

....

Present and Former Supervisors. If you believe you are on good terms with present or former job supervisors, they may be an excellent resource for providing information or directing you to appropriate resources that would have information related to your current interests and needs. Additionally, these supervisors probably belong to professional organizations, which they might be willing to utilize to get information for you.

....

> If, for example, you were interested in working for a private botanical garden and you are currently working as an assistant in a local retail florist shop, talk with your supervisor or the owner. He or she may belong to the Chamber of Commerce, whose director would have information on local nurseries and might also have contacts with the private garden. You would be able to obtain the names and telephone numbers of these people, thus enabling you to begin the networking process.

....

Employers in Your Area. Although you may be interested in working in a geographic location different from the one where you currently reside, don't overlook the value of the knowledge and contacts those around you are able to provide. Use the local telephone directory and newspaper to identify the types of organizations you are thinking of working for or professionals who have the kinds of jobs you are interested in. Recently, a call made to a local hospital's financial administrator for information on working in health care financial administration yielded more pertinent information on training seminars, regional professional organizations, and potential employment sites than a national organization was willing to provide.

Employers in Geographic Areas Where You Hope to Work. If you are thinking about relocating, identifying prospective employers or informational contacts in this new location will be critical to your success. Many resources are available to help you locate contact names. These include the yellow pages directory, the local newspapers, local or state business publications, and local chambers of commerce.

Professional Associations and Organizations. Professional associations and organizations can provide valuable information in several areas: career paths that you may not have considered, qualifications relating to those career choices, publications that list current job openings, and workshops or seminars that will enhance your professional knowledge and skills. They can also be excellent sources for background information on given industries: their health, current problems, and future challenges.

There are several excellent resources available to help you locate professional associations and organizations that would have information to meet your needs. Two especially useful publications are the *Encyclopedia of Associations* and the *National Trade and Professional Associations of the United States*.

Keep Track of All Your Efforts

It can be difficult, almost impossible, to remember all the details related to each contact you make during the networking process, so you will want to develop a record-keeping system that works for you. Formalize this process by using a notebook or index cards to organize the information you gather. Begin by creating a list of the people or organizations you want to contact. Record the contact's name, address, telephone number, and what information you hope to gain. Each entry might look something like this:

Contact Name	Address	Phone #	Purpose
Mr. Tim Keefe	Wrigley Bldg.		
Dir. of Mines	Suite 72	555-8906	Resume screen

Once you have created this initial list, it will be helpful to keep more detailed information as you begin to actually make the contacts. Using the Network Contact Record form in Exhibit 4.1, keep good information on all your network contacts. They'll appreciate your recall of details of your meetings and conversations, and the information will help you to focus your networking efforts.

Create Your Self-Promotion Tools

There are two types of promotional tools that are used in the networking process. The first is a resume and cover letter, and the second is a one-minute "infomercial," which may be given over the telephone or in person.

Exhibit 4.1

Network Contact Record

Name: Be certain your spelling is absolutely correct.

Title: Pick up a business card to be certain of the correct title.

Employing organization: Note any parent company or subsidiaries.

Business mailing address: This is often different from the street address.

Business telephone number: Include area code/alternative numbers/fax/E-mail.

Source for this contact: Who referred you, and what is their relationship?

Date of call or letter: Use plenty of space here to record multiple phone calls or visits, other employees you may have met, names of secretaries/receptionists, etc.

Content of discussion: Keep enough notes here to remind you of the substance of your visits and telephone conversations in case some time elapses between contacts.

Follow-up necessary to continue working with this contact: Your contact may request that you send him or her some materials or direct you to contact an associate. Note any such instructions or assignments in this space.

Name of additional networker: Here you would record the
Address: names and phone numbers of
Phone: additional contacts met at this
Name of additional networker: employer's site. Often you will
Address: be introduced to many people,
Phone: some of whom may indicate
Name of additional networker: a willingness to help in your
Address: job search.
Phone:

Date thank-you note written: May help to plan your next contact.

Follow-up action taken: Phone calls, visits, additional notes.

continued

---

continued

Other miscellaneous notes: Record any other additional
interaction you think may be
important to remember in working
with this networking client. You will
want this form in front of you when
telephoning or just before and after
a visit.

Techniques for writing an effective resume and cover letter are covered in Chapter 2. Once you have reviewed that material and prepared these important documents, you will have created one of your self-promotion tools.

The one-minute infomercial will demand that you begin tying your interests, abilities, and skills to the people or organizations you want to network with. Think about your goal for making the contact to help you understand what you should say about yourself. You should be able to express yourself easily and convincingly. If, for example, you are contacting an alumnus of your institution to obtain the names of possible employment sites in a distant city, be prepared to discuss why you are interested in moving to that location, the types of jobs you are interested in, and the skills and abilities you possess that will make you a qualified candidate.

To create a meaningful one-minute infomercial, write it out, practice it if it will be a spoken presentation, rewrite it, and practice it again if necessary until expressing yourself comes easily and is convincing.

Here's a simplified example of an infomercial for use over the telephone:

Hello, Mr. Goodman? My name is Anna Middleton. I am a recent graduate of State College, and I wish to begin a career in zoology. I was a biology major and feel confident I have many of the skills I understand are valued in zoology, such as researching skills, computer skills, an ability to think analytically, and good observation skills. What's more, I work well on my own or in a team. I have read that can be a real advantage in this profession!

Mr. Goodman, I'm calling you because I still need more information about the field of zoology. I'm hoping you'll have the time to sit down with me for about half an hour and discuss your perspective on this career. There are so many possible options, and I am seeking some advice on which of those might be the best bet for my particular combination of skills and experience.

Would you be willing to do that for me? I would greatly appreciate it. I am available most mornings, if that's convenient for you.

....

Other effective self-promotion tools include portfolios for those in the arts, writing professions, or teaching. Portfolios show examples of work, photographs of projects or classroom activities, or certificates and credentials that are job related. There may not be an opportunity to use the portfolio during an interview, and it is not something that should be left with the organization. It is designed to be explained and displayed by the creator. However, during some networking meetings, there may be an opportunity to illustrate a point or strengthen a qualification by exhibiting the portfolio.

BEGINNING THE NETWORKING PROCESS

Set the Tone for Your Contacts

It can be useful to establish "tone words" for any communications you embark upon. Before making your first telephone call or writing your first letter, decide what you want your contact to think of you. If you are networking to try to obtain a job, your tone words might include words like *genuine, informed,* and *self-knowledgeable.* When trying to acquire information, your tone words may have a slightly different focus, such as *courteous, organized, focused,* and *well-spoken.* Use the tone words you establish for your contacts to guide you through the networking process.

Honestly Express Your Intentions

When contacting individuals, it is important to be honest about your reasons for making the contact. Establish your purpose in your own mind and be able and ready to articulate it concisely. Determine an initial agenda, whether it be informational questioning or self-promotion, present it to your contact, and be ready to respond immediately. If you don't adequately prepare before initiating your contacts, you may find yourself at a disadvantage if you're asked to immediately begin your informational interview or self-promotion during the first phone conversation or visit.

Start Networking Within Your Circle of Confidence

Once you have organized your approach—by utilizing specific researching methods, creating a system for keeping track of the people you will contact, and developing effective self-promotion tools—you are ready to begin networking. The best place to begin networking is by talking with a group of people you trust and feel comfortable with. This group is usually made up of your family, friends, and career counselors. No matter who is in this inner circle, they will have a special interest in seeing you succeed in your job search. In addition, because they will be easy to talk to, you should try taking some risks in terms of practicing your information-seeking approach. Gain confidence in talking about the strengths you bring to an organization and the underdeveloped skills you feel hinder your candidacy. Be sure to review the section on self-assessment for tips on approaching each of these areas. Ask for critical but constructive feedback from the people in your circle of confidence on the letters you write and the one-minute infomercial you have developed. Evaluate whether you want to make the changes they suggest, then practice the changes on others within this circle.

Stretch the Boundaries of Your Networking Circle of Confidence

Once you have refined the promotional tools you will use to accomplish your networking goals, you will want to make additional contacts. Because you will not know most of these people, it will be a less comfortable activity to undertake. The practice that you gained with your inner circle of trusted friends should have prepared you to now move outside of that comfort zone.

It is said that any information a person needs is only two phone calls away, but the information cannot be gained until you (1) make a reasonable guess about who might have the information you need, and (2) pick up the telephone to make the call. Using your network list that includes alumni, instructors, supervisors, employers, and associations, you can begin preparing your list of questions that will allow you to get the information you need. Review the question list shown below and then develop a list of your own.

Questions You Might Want to Ask

1. In the position you now hold, what do you do on a typical day?

2. What are the most interesting aspects of your job?

3. What part of your work do you consider dull or repetitious?

4. What were the jobs you had that led to your present position?

5. How long does it usually take to move from one step to the next in this career path?

6. What is the top position to which you can aspire in this career path?

7. What is the next step in *your* career path?

8. Are there positions in this field that are similar to your position?

9. What are the required qualifications and training for entry-level positions in this field?

10. Are there specific courses a student should take to be qualified to work in this field?

11. What are the entry-level jobs in this field?

12. What types of training are provided to persons entering this field?

13. What are the salary ranges your organization typically offers to entry-level candidates for positions in this field?

14. What special advice would you give a person entering this field?

15. Do you see this field as a growing one?

16. How do you see the content of the entry-level jobs in this field changing over the next two years?

17. What can I do to prepare myself for these changes?

18. What is the best way to obtain a position that will start me on a career in this field?

19. Do you have any information on job specifications and descriptions that I may have?

20. What related occupational fields would you suggest I explore?

21. How could I improve my resume for a career in this field?

22. Who else would you suggest I talk to, both in your organization and in other organizations?

Questions You Might Have to Answer

In order to communicate effectively, you must anticipate questions that will be asked of you by the networkers you contact. Review the list below and see if you can easily answer each of these questions. If you cannot, it may be time to revisit the self-assessment process.

1. Where did you get my name, or how did you find out about this organization?

2. What are your career goals?

3. What kind of job are you interested in?

4. What do you know about this organization and this industry?

5. How do you know you're prepared to undertake an entry-level position in this industry?

6. What course work have you taken that is related to your career interests?

7. What are your short-term career goals?

8. What are your long-term career goals?

9. Do you plan to obtain additional formal education?

10. What contributions have you made to previous employers?

11. Which of your previous jobs have you enjoyed the most, and why?

12. What are you particularly good at doing?

13. What shortcomings have you had to face in previous employment?

14. What are your three greatest strengths?

15. Describe how comfortable you feel with your communication style.

General Networking Tips

Make Every Contact Count. Setting the tone for each interaction is critical. Approaches that will help you communicate in an effective way include politeness, being appreciative of time provided to you, and being prepared and thorough. Remember, *everyone* within an organization has a circle of influence, so be prepared to interact effectively with each person you encounter in the networking process, including secretarial and support staff. Many information or job seekers have thwarted their own efforts by being rude to some individuals they encountered as they networked because they made the incorrect assumption that certain persons were unimportant.

Sometimes your contacts may be surprised at their ability to help you. After meeting and talking with you, they might think they have not offered much in the way of help. A day or two later, however, they may make a contact that would be useful to you and refer you to it.

With Each Contact, Widen Your Circle of Networkers. Always leave an informational interview with the names of at least two more people who can help you get the information or job that you are seeking. Don't be shy about asking for additional contacts; networking is all about increasing the number of people you can interact with to achieve your goals.

Make Your Own Decisions. As you talk with different people and get answers to the questions you pose, you may hear conflicting information or get conflicting suggestions. Your job is to listen to these "experts" and decide what information and which suggestions will help you achieve *your* goals. Implement only those suggestions that you believe will work for you.

SHUTTING DOWN YOUR NETWORK

As you achieve the goals that motivated your networking activity—getting the information you need or the job you want—the time will come to deactivate all or parts of your network. As you do so, be sure to tell your primary supporters about your change in status. Call or write to each one of them and give them as many details about your new status as you feel is necessary to maintain a positive relationship.

Because a network takes on a life of its own, activity undertaken on your behalf will continue even after you cease your efforts. As you get calls or are contacted in some fashion, be sure to inform these networkers about your change in status, and thank them for assistance they have provided.

Information on the latest employment trends indicates that workers will change jobs or careers several times in their lifetime. If you carefully and thoughtfully conduct your networking activities now, you will have solid experience when you need to network again.

CHAPTER FIVE

INTERVIEWING

*C*ertainly, there can be no one part of the job search process more fraught with anxiety and worry than the interview. Yet seasoned job seekers welcome the interview and will often say "Just get me an interview and I'm on my way!" They understand that the interview is crucial to the hiring process and equally crucial for them, as job candidates, to have the opportunity of a personal dialogue to add to what the employer may already have learned from a resume, cover letter, and telephone conversations.

Believe it or not, the interview is to be welcomed, and even enjoyed! It is a perfect opportunity for you, the candidate, to sit down with an employer and express yourself and display who you are and what you want. Of course, it takes thought and planning and a little strategy; after all, it *is* a job interview! But it can be a positive, if not pleasant, experience and one you can look back on and feel confident about your performance and effort.

For many new job seekers, a job, any job, seems a wonderful thing. But seasoned interview veterans know that the job interview is an important step for both sides—the employer and the candidate—to see what each has to offer and whether there is going to be a "fit" of personalities, work styles, and attitudes. And it is this concept of balance in the interview, that both sides have important parts to play, that holds the key to success in mastering this aspect of the job search strategy.

Try to think of the interview as a conversation between two interested and equal partners. You both have important, even vital, information to deliver and to learn. Of course, there's no denying the employer has some leverage, especially in the initial interview for recruitment or any interview scheduled by the candidate and not the recruiter. That should not prevent the interviewee from seeking to play an equal part in what should be a fair exchange of information. Too often the untutored candidate allows the interview to become one-sided. The employer asks all the questions and the candidate simply responds. The ideal would be for two mutually interested parties to sit down and discuss possibilities for each. For this is a *conversation of significance,* and it requires pre-interview preparation, thought about the tone of the interview, and planning of the nature and details of the information to be exchanged.

PREPARING FOR THE INTERVIEW

Most initial interviews are about thirty minutes long. Given the brevity, the information that is exchanged ought to be important. The candidate should be delivering material that the employer cannot discover on the resume and, in turn, the candidate should be learning things about the employer that he or she could not otherwise find out. After all, if you have only thirty minutes, why waste time on information that is already in print? The information exchanged is more than just factual, and both sides will learn much from what they see of each other as well. How the candidate looks, speaks, and acts is important to the employer. The employer's attention to the interview and awareness of the candidate's resume, the setting, and the quality of information presented are important to the candidate.

Just as the employer has every right to be disappointed when a prospect is late for the interview, looks unkempt, and seems ill-prepared to answer fairly standard questions, the candidate may be disappointed with an interviewer who isn't ready for the meeting, hasn't learned the basic resume facts, and is constantly interrupted for telephone calls. In either situation there's good reason to feel let down.

There are many elements to a successful interview, and some of them are not easy to describe or prepare for. Sometimes there is just a chemistry between interviewer and interviewee that brings out the best in both, and a good exchange takes place. But there is much the candidate can do to pave the way for success in terms of his or her resume, personal appearance, goals, and interview strategy—each of which we will discuss. However, none of this preparation is as important as the time and thought the candidate gives to personal self-assessment.

Self-Assessment

Neither a stunning resume nor an expensive, well-tailored suit can compensate for candidates who do not know what they want, where they are going, or why they are interviewing with a particular employer. Self-assessment, the process by which we begin to know and acknowledge our own particular blend of education, experiences, needs, and goals, is not something that can be sorted out the weekend before a major interview. Of all the elements of interview preparation, this one requires the longest lead time and cannot be faked.

Because the time allotted for most interviews is brief, it is all the more important for job candidates to understand and express succinctly why they are there and what they have to offer. This is not a time for undue modesty (or for braggadocio either); but it is a time for a compelling, reasoned statement of why you feel that you and this employer might make a good match. It means you have to have thought about your skills, interests, and attributes; related those to your life experiences and your own history of challenges and opportunities; and determined what that indicates about your strengths, preferences, values, and areas needing further development.

A common complaint of employers is that many candidates didn't take advantage of the interview time—didn't seem to know why they were there or what they wanted. When candidates are asked to talk about themselves and their work-related skills and attributes, employers don't want to be faced with shyness or embarrassed laughter; they need to know about you so they can make a fair determination of you and your competition. If you lose the opportunity to make a case for your employability, you can be certain the person ahead of you has or the person after you will, and it will be on the strength of those impressions that the employer will hire.

If you need some assistance with self-assessment issues, refer to Chapter 1. Included are suggested exercises that can be done as needed, such as making up an experiential diary and extracting obvious strengths and weaknesses from past experiences. These simple, pen-and-paper assignments will help you look at past activities as collections of tasks with accompanying skills and responsibilities. Don't overlook your high school or college career office. Many offer personal counseling on self-assessment issues and may provide testing instruments such as the Myers-Briggs Type Indicator (MBTI),® the Harrington-O'Shea Career Decision Making® System (CDM), the Strong Interest Inventory (SII),® or any of a wide selection of assessment tools that can help you clarify some of these issues prior to the interview stage of your job search.

The Resume

Resume preparation has been discussed in detail, and some basic examples of various types were provided. In this section we want to concentrate on how best to use your resume in the interview. In most cases the employer will have seen the resume prior to the interview, and, in fact, it may well have been the quality of that resume that secured the interview opportunity.

An interview is a conversation, however, and not an exercise in reading. So, if the employer hasn't seen your resume and you have brought it along to the interview, wait until asked or until the end of the interview to offer it.

Otherwise, you may find yourself staring at the back of your resume and simply answering "yes" and "no" to a series of questions drawn from that document.

Sometimes an interviewer is not prepared and does not know or recall the contents of the resume and may use the resume to a greater or lesser degree as a "prompt" during the interview. It is for you to judge what that may indicate about the individual doing the interview or the employer. If your interviewer seems surprised by the scheduled meeting, relies on the resume to an inordinate degree, and seems otherwise unfamiliar with your background, this lack of preparation for the hiring process could well be a symptom of general management disorganization or may simply be the result of poor planning on the part of one individual. It is your responsibility as a potential employee to be aware of these signals and make your decisions accordingly.

....

In any event, it is perfectly acceptable for you to get the conversation back to a more interpersonal style by saying something like, "Mr. Smith, you might be interested in some recent research experience I gained in a zoology internship that is not detailed on my resume. May I tell you about it?" This can return the interview to two people talking to each other, not one reading and the other responding.

....

By all means, bring at least one copy of your resume to the interview. Occasionally, at the close of an interview, an interviewer will express an interest in circulating a resume to several departments, and you could then offer to provide those. Sometimes an interview appointment provides an opportunity to meet others in the organization who may express an interest in you and your background, and it may be helpful to follow that up with a copy of your resume. Our best advice, however, is to keep it out of sight until needed or requested.

Appearance

Although many of the absolute rules that once dominated the advice offered to job candidates about appearance have now been moderated significantly, conservative is still the watchword unless you are interviewing in a fashion-related industry. For men, conservative translates into a well-cut dark suit with appropriate tie, hosiery, and dress shirt. A wise strategy for the male job seeker looking for a good but not expensive suit would be to try the men's department of a major department store. They usually carry a good range of sizes, fabrics, and prices; offer professional sales help; provide free tailoring; and have associated departments for putting together a professional look.

For women, there is more latitude. Business suits are still popular, but they have become more feminine in color and styling with a variety of jacket and skirt lengths. In addition to suits, better-quality dresses are now worn in many environments and, with the correct accessories, can be most appropriate. Company literature, professional magazines, the business sections of major newspapers, and television interviews can all give clues about what is being worn in different employer environments.

Both men and women need to pay attention to issues such as hair, jewelry, and makeup; these are often what separates the candidate in appearance from the professional work force. It seems particularly difficult for the young job seeker to give up certain hair styles, eyeglass fashions, and jewelry habits, yet those can be important to the employer, who is concerned with your ability to successfully make the transition into the organization. Candidates often find the best strategy is to dress conservatively until they find employment. Once employed and familiar with the norms within your organization, you can begin to determine a look that you enjoy, works for you, and fits your organization.

Choose clothes that suit your body type, fit well, and flatter you. Feel good about the way you look! The interview day is not the best for a new hairdo, a new pair of shoes, or any other change that will distract you or cause you to be self-conscious. Arrive a bit early to avoid being rushed, and ask the receptionist to direct you to a restroom for any last-minute adjustments of hair and clothes.

Employer Information

Whether your interview is for graduate school admission, a corporate position, or a civil service position with a local or national government organization, it is important to know something about the employer or the organization. Keeping in mind that the interview is relatively brief and that you will hopefully have other interviews with other organizations, it is important to keep your research in proportion. If secondary interviews are called for, you will have additional time to do further research. For the first interview, it is helpful to know the organization's mission, goals, size, scope of operations, etc. Your research may uncover recent areas of challenge or particular successes that may help to fuel the interview. Use the "Where Are These Jobs, Anyway?" section of Chapter 3, your library, and your career or guidance office to help you locate this information in the most efficient way possible. Don't be shy in asking advice of these counseling and guidance professionals on how best to spend your preparation time. With some practice, you'll soon learn how much information is enough and which kinds of information are most useful to you.

INTERVIEW CONTENT

We've already discussed how it can help to think of the interview as an important conversation—one that, as with any conversation, you want to find pleasant and interesting and to leave you with a good feeling. But because this conversation is especially important, the information that's exchanged is critical to its success. What do you want them to know about you? What do you need to know about them? What interview technique do you need to particularly pay attention to? How do you want to manage the close of the interview? What steps will follow in the hiring process?

Except for the professional interviewer, most of us find interviewing stressful and anxiety-provoking. Developing a strategy before you begin interviewing will help you relieve some stress and anxiety. One particular strategy that has worked for many and may work for you is interviewing by objective. Before you interview, write down three to five goals you would like to achieve for that interview. They may be technique goals: smile a little more, have a firmer handshake, be sure to ask about the next stage in the interview process before leaving, etc. They may be content-oriented goals: find out about the company's current challenges and opportunities, be sure to speak of your recent research writing experiences or foreign travel, etc. Whatever your goals, jot down a few of them as goals for this interview.

Most people find that, in trying to achieve these few goals, their interviewing technique becomes more organized and focused. After the interview, the most common question friends and family ask is "How did it go?" With this technique, you have an indication of whether you met *your* goals for the meeting, not just some vague idea of how it went. Chances are, if you accomplished what you wanted to, it informed the quality of the entire interview. As you continue to interview, you will want to revise your goals to continue improving your interview skills.

Now, add to the concept of the significant conversation the idea of a beginning, a middle, and a closing and you will have two thoughts that will give your interview a distinctive character. Be sure to make your introduction warm and cordial. Say your full name (and if it's a difficult-to-pronounce name, help the interviewer to pronounce it) and make certain you know your interviewer's name and how to pronounce it. Most interviews begin with some "soft talk" about the weather, chat about the candidate's trip to the interview site, national events, etc. This is done as a courtesy to relax both you and the interviewer, to get you talking, and to generally try to defuse the atmosphere of excessive tension. Try to be yourself, engage in the conversation, and don't try to second-guess the interviewer. This is simply what it appears to be—casual conversation.

Once you and the interviewer move on to exchange more serious information in the middle part of the interview, the two most important concerns become your ability to handle challenging questions and your success at asking meaningful ones. Interviewer questions will probably fall into one of three categories: personal assessment and career direction, academic background, and knowledge of the employer. The following are some examples of questions in each category:

Personal Assessment and Career Direction

1. How would you describe yourself?

2. What motivates you to put forth your greatest effort?

3. In what kind of work environment are you most comfortable?

4. What do you consider to be your greatest strengths and weaknesses?

5. How well do you work under pressure?

6. What qualifications do you have that make you think you will be successful in this career?

7. Will you relocate? What do you feel would be the most difficult aspect of relocating?

8. Are you willing to travel?

9. Why should I hire you?

Academic Assessment

1. Why did you select your college or university?

2. What changes would you make at your alma mater?

3. What led you to choose your major?

4. What subjects did you like best and least? Why?

5. If you could, how would you plan your academic study differently? Why?

6. Describe your most rewarding college experience.

7. How has your college experience prepared you for this career?

8. Do you think that your grades are a good indication of your ability to succeed with this organization?

9. Do you have plans for continued study?

Knowledge of the Employer

1. If you were hiring a graduate of your school for this position, what qualities would you look for?

2. What do you think it takes to be successful in an organization like ours?

3. In what ways do you think you can make a contribution to our organization?

4. Why did you choose to seek a position with this organization?

The interviewer wants a response to each question but is also gauging your enthusiasm, preparedness, and willingness to communicate. In each response you should provide some information about yourself that can be related to the employer's needs. A common mistake is to give too much information. Answer each question completely, but be careful not to run on too long with extensive details or examples.

Questions About Underdeveloped Skills

Most employers interview people who have met some minimum criteria of education and experience. They interview candidates to see who they are, to learn what kind of personality they exhibit, and to get some sense of how this person might fit into the existing organization. It may be that you are asked about skills the employer hopes to find and that you have not documented. Maybe it's grant-writing experience, knowledge of the European political system, or a knowledge of the film world.

To questions about skills and experiences you don't have, answer honestly and forthrightly and try to offer some additional information about skills you do have. For example, perhaps the employer is disappointed that you have no grant-writing experience. An honest answer may be as follows:

> No, unfortunately, I was never in a position to acquire those skills. I do understand something of the complexities of the grant-writing process and feel confident that my attention to detail, careful reading skills, and strong writing would make grants a wonderful challenge in a new job. I think I could get up on the learning curve quickly.

The employer hears an honest admission of lack of experience but is reassured by some specific skill details that do relate to grant writing and a confident manner that suggests enthusiasm and interest in a challenge.

For many students, questions about their possible contributions to an employer's organization can prove challenging. Because your education has probably not included specific training for a job, you need to review your academic record and select capabilities you have developed in your major that an employer can appreciate. For example, perhaps you read well and can analyze and condense what you've read into smaller, more focused pieces. That could be valuable. Or maybe you did some serious research and you know you have valuable investigative skills. Your public speaking might be highly developed and you might use visual aids appropriately and effectively. Or maybe your skill at correspondence, memos, and messages is effective. Whatever it is, you must take it out of the academic context and put it into a new, employer-friendly context so your interviewer can best judge how you could help the organization.

Exhibiting knowledge of the organization will, without a doubt, show the interviewer that you are interested enough in the available position to have done some legwork in preparation for the interview. Remember, it is not necessary to know every detail of the organization's history, but rather to have a general knowledge about why it is in business and how the industry is faring.

Sometime during the interview, generally after the midway point, you'll be asked if you have any questions for the interviewer. Your questions will tell the employer much about your attitude and your desire to understand the organization's expectations so you can compare it to your own strengths. The following are some selected questions you might want to ask:

1. What are the main responsibilities of the position?

2. What are the opportunities and challenges associated with this position?

3. Could you outline some possible career paths beginning with this position?

4. How regularly do performance evaluations occur?

5. What is the communication style of the organization? (meetings, memos, etc.)

6. Describe a typical day for me in this position.

7. What kinds of opportunities might exist for me to improve my professional skills within the organization?

8. What have been some of the interesting challenges and opportunities your organization has recently faced?

Most interviews draw to a natural closing point, so be careful not to prolong the discussion. At a signal from the interviewer, wind up your presentation, express your appreciation for the opportunity, and be sure to ask what the next stage in the process will be. When can you expect to hear from them? Will they be conducting second-tier interviews? If you're interested and haven't heard, would they mind a phone call? Be sure to collect a business card with the name and phone number of your interviewer. On your way out, you might have an opportunity to pick up organizational literature you haven't seen before.

With the right preparation—a thorough self-assessment, professional clothing, and employer information—you'll be able to set and achieve the goals you have established for the interview process.

CHAPTER SIX

NETWORKING OR INTERVIEWING FOLLOW-UP

Quite often there is a considerable time lag between interviewing for a position and being hired, or, in the case of the networker, between your phone call or letter to a possible contact and the opportunity of a meeting. This can be frustrating. "Why aren't they contacting me?" "I thought I'd get another interview, but no one has telephoned." "Am I out of the running?" You don't know what is happening.

CONSIDER THE DIFFERING PERSPECTIVES

Of course, there is another perspective—that of the networker or hiring organization. Organizations are complex with multiple tasks that need to be accomplished each day. Hiring is but one discrete activity that does not occur as frequently as other job assignments. The hiring process might have to take second place to other, more immediate organizational needs. Although it may be very important to you and it is certainly ultimately significant to the employer, other issues such as fiscal management, planning and product development, employer vacation periods, or financial constraints, may prevent an organization or individual within that organization from acting on your employment or your request for information as quickly as you or they would prefer.

USE YOUR COMMUNICATION SKILLS

Good communication is essential here to resolve any anxieties, and the responsibility is on you, the job or information seeker. Too many job seekers and networkers offer as an excuse that they don't want to "bother" the organization by writing letters or calling. Let us assure you here and now, once and for all, that if you are troubling an organization by over-communicating, someone will indicate that situation to you quite clearly. If not, you can only assume you are a worthwhile prospect and the employer appreciates being reminded of your availability and interest. Let's look at follow-up practices in both the job interview process and the networking situation separately.

FOLLOWING UP ON THE EMPLOYMENT INTERVIEW

A brief thank-you note following an interview is an excellent and polite way to begin a series of follow-up communications with a potential employer with whom you have interviewed and want to remain in touch. It should be just that—a thank you for a good meeting. If you failed to mention some fact or experience during your interview that you think might add to your candidacy, you may use this note to do that. However, this should be essentially a note whose overall tone is appreciative and, if appropriate, indicative of a continuing interest in pursuing any opportunity that may exist with that organization. It is one of the few pieces of business correspondence that may be handwritten, but always use plain, good quality, monarch-size paper.

If, however, at this point you are no longer interested in the employer, the thank-you note is an appropriate time to indicate that. You are under no obligation to identify any reason for not continuing to pursue employment with that organization, but if you are so inclined to indicate your professional reasons (pursuing other employers more akin to your interests, looking for greater income production than this employer can provide, a different geographic location than is available, etc.), you certainly may. It should not be written with an eye to negotiation for it will not be interpreted as such.

As part of your interview closing, you should have taken the initiative to establish lines of communication for continuing information about your candidacy. If you asked permission to telephone, wait a week following your thank-you note, then telephone your contact simply to inquire how things are progressing on your employment status. The feedback you receive here should be taken at face value. If your interviewer simply has no information, he or she will tell you so and indicate whether you should call again and when. Don't be discouraged if this should continue over some period of time.

If during this time something occurs that you think improves or changes your candidacy (some new qualification or experience you may have had), including any offers from other organizations, by all means telephone or write to inform the employer about this. In the case of an offer from a competing but less desirable or equally desirable organization, telephone your contact, explain what has happened, express your real interest in the organization, and inquire whether some determination on your employment might be made before you must respond to this other offer. If the organization is truly interested in you, they may be moved to make a decision about your candidacy. Equally possible is the scenario in which they are not yet ready to make a decision and so advise you to take the offer that has been presented. Again, you have no ethical alternative but to deal with the information presented in a straightforward manner.

When accepting other employment, be sure to contact any employers still actively considering you and inform them of your new job. Thank them graciously for their consideration. There are many other job seekers out there just like you who will benefit from having their candidacy improved when others bow out of the race. Who knows, you might at some future time have occasion to interact professionally with one of the organizations with whom you sought employment. How embarrassing to have someone remember you as the candidate who failed to notify them of taking a job elsewhere!

In all of your follow-up communications, keep good notes of who you spoke with, when you called, and any instructions that were given about return communications. This will prevent any misunderstandings and provide you with good records of what has transpired.

FOLLOWING UP ON THE NETWORK CONTACT

Far more common than the forgotten follow-up after an interview is the situation where a good network contact is allowed to lapse. Good communications are the essence of a network, and follow-up is not so much a matter of courtesy here as it is a necessity. In networking for job information and contacts, you are the active network link. Without you, and without continual contact from you, there is no network. You and your need for employment are often the only shared elements between members of the network. Because network contacts were made regardless of the availability of any particular employment, it is incumbent upon the job seeker, if not simple common sense, that unless you stay in regular communication with the network, you will not be available for consideration should some job become available in the future.

This brings up the issue of responsibility, which is likewise very clear. The job seeker initiates network contacts and is responsible for maintaining those contacts; therefore, the entire responsibility for the network belongs with him or her. This becomes patently obvious if the network is left unattended. It very shortly falls out of existence because it cannot survive without careful attention by the networker.

A variety of ways are available to you to keep the lines of communication open and to attempt to interest the network in you as a possible employee. You are limited only by your own enthusiasm for members of the network and your creativity. However, you as a networker are well advised to keep good records of whom you have met and spoken with in each organization. Be sure to send thank-you notes to anyone who has spent any time with you, be it a quick tour of a department or a sit-down informational interview. All of these communications should, in addition to their ostensible reason, add some information about you and your particular combination of strengths and attributes.

You can contact your network at any time to convey continued interest, to comment on some recent article you came across concerning an organization, to add information about your training or changes in your qualifications, to ask advice or seek guidance in your job search, or to request referrals to other possible network opportunities. Sometimes just a simple note to network members reminding them of your job search, indicating that you have been using their advice, and noting that you are still actively pursuing leads and hope to continue to interact with them is enough to keep communications alive.

Because networks have been abused in the past, it's important that your conduct be above reproach. Networks are exploratory options, they are not back-door access to employers. The network works best for someone who is exploring a new industry or making a transition into a new area of employment and who needs to find information or to alert people to his or her search activity. Always be candid and direct with contacts in expressing the purpose of your call or letter and your interest in their help or information about their organization. In follow-up contacts keep the tone professional and direct. Your honesty will be appreciated, and people will respond as best they can if your qualifications appear to meet their forthcoming needs. The network does not owe you anything, and that tone should be clear to each person you meet.

FEEDBACK FROM FOLLOW-UPS

A network contact may prove to be miscalculated. Perhaps you were referred to someone and it became clear that your goals and his or her particular needs did not make a good match. Or the network contact may simply not be in a position to provide you with the information you are seeking. Or in some unfortunate situations, the contact may become annoyed by being contacted for this purpose. In such a situation, many job seekers simply say "Thank you" and move on.

If the contact is simply not the right contact, but the individual you are speaking with is not annoyed by the call, it might be a better tactic to express regret that the contact was misplaced and then explain to the contact what you are seeking and ask for his or her advice or possible suggestions as to a next step. The more people who are aware you are seeking employment, the better your chances of connecting, and that is the purpose of a network. Most people in a profession have excellent knowledge of their field and varying amounts of expertise on areas near to or tangent to their own. Use their expertise and seek some guidance before you dissolve the contact. You may be pleasantly surprised.

Occasionally, networkers will express the feeling that they have done as much as they can or provided all the information that is available to them. This may be a cue that they would like to be released from your network. Be alert to such attempts to terminate, graciously thank the individual by letter, and move on in your network development. A network is always changing, adding and losing members, and you want the network to be composed only of those who are actively interested in supporting your interests.

A FINAL POINT ON NETWORKING FOR BIOLOGY MAJORS

In any of the fields a biology major might consider as a potential career path, it's important to remember that networkers and interviewers will be critically evaluating all of your written and oral communications. This should serve to emphasize the importance of the quality of your interactions with people in a position to help you in your job search.

In your telephone communications, interview presentation, follow-up correspondence, and ability to deal with negative feedback, your warmth, style, and personality, as evidenced in your spoken and written use of English, will be part of the portfolio of impressions you create in those you meet along the way.

CHAPTER SEVEN

JOB OFFER CONSIDERATIONS

for many recent college graduates, the thrill of their first job and, for some, the most substantial regular income they have ever earned seems an excess of good fortune coming at once. To question that first income or be critical in any way of the conditions of employment at the time of the initial offer seems like looking a gift horse in the mouth. It doesn't seem to occur to many new hires even to attempt to negotiate any aspect of their first job. And, as many employers who deal with entry-level jobs for recent college graduates will readily confirm, the reality is that there simply isn't much movement in salary available to these new college recruits. The entry-level hire generally does not have an employment track record on a professional level to provide any leverage for negotiation. Real negotiations on salary, benefits, retirement provisions, etc., come to those with significant employment records at higher income levels.

Of course, the job offer is more than just money. It can be comprised of geographic assignment, duties and responsibilities, training, benefits, health and medical insurance, educational assistance, car allowance or company vehicle, and a host of other items. All of this is generally detailed in the formal letter that presents the final job offer. In most cases this is a follow-up to a personal phone call from the employer representative who has been principally responsible for your hiring process.

That initial telephone offer is certainly binding as a verbal agreement, but most firms follow up with a detailed letter outlining the most significant parts of your employment contract. You may certainly choose to respond immediately at the time of the telephone offer (which would be considered a binding oral contract), but you will also be required to formally answer the letter of offer with a letter of acceptance, restating the salient elements of the employer's description of your position, salary, and benefits. This ensures that both parties are clear on the terms and conditions of employment and remuneration and any other outstanding aspects of the job offer.

IS THIS THE JOB YOU WANT?

Most new employees will write this letter of acceptance, glad to be in the position to accept employment. If you've worked hard to get the offer and the job market is tight, other offers may not be in sight, so you will say "Yes, I accept!" What is important here is that the job offer you accept be one that does fit your particular needs, values, and interests as you've outlined them in your self-assessment process. Moreover, it should be a job that will not only use your skills and education, but also challenge you to develop new skills and talents.

Jobs are sometimes accepted too hastily, for the wrong reasons, and without proper scrutiny by the applicant. For example, an individual might readily accept a sales job only to find the continual rejection by potential clients unendurable. An office worker might realize within weeks the constraints of a desk job and yearn for more activity. Employment is an important part of our lives. It is, for most of our adult lives, our most continuous productive activity. We want to make good choices based on the right criteria.

If you have a low tolerance for risk, a job based on commission will certainly be very anxiety provoking. If being near your family is important, issues of relocation could present a decision crisis for you. If you're an adventurous person, a job with frequent travel would provide needed excitement and be very desirable. The importance of income, the need to continue your education, your personal health situation—all of these have an impact on whether the job you are considering will ultimately meet your needs. Unless you've spent some time understanding and thinking about these issues, it will be difficult to evaluate offers you do receive.

More importantly, if you make a decision that you cannot tolerate and feel you must leave that job, you will then have both unemployment and self-esteem issues to contend with. These will combine to make the next job search tough going, indeed. So make your acceptance a carefully considered decision.

NEGOTIATING YOUR OFFER

It may be that there is some aspect of your job offer that is not particularly attractive to you. Perhaps there is no relocation allotment to help you move your possessions, and this presents some financial hardship for you. It may be that the medical and health insurance is less than you had hoped. Your initial assignment may be different than you expected, either in its location or in the duties and responsibilities that comprise it. Or it may simply be that the salary is less than you anticipated. Other considerations may be your official starting date of employment, vacation time, evening hours, dates of training programs or schools, etc.

If you are considering not accepting the job because of some item or items in the job offer "package" that do not meet your needs, you should know that most employers emphatically wish that you would bring that issue to their attention. It may be that the employer can alter it to make the offer more agreeable for you. In some cases it cannot be changed. In any event the employer would generally like to have the opportunity to try to remedy a difficulty rather than risk losing a good potential employee over an issue that might have been resolved. After all, they have spent time and funds in securing your services, and they certainly deserve an opportunity to resolve any possible differences.

Honesty is the best approach in discussing any objections or uneasiness you might have over the employer's offer. Having received your formal offer in writing, contact your employer representative and indicate your particular dissatisfaction in a straightforward manner. For example, you might explain that, while very interested in being employed by this organization, the salary (or any other benefit) is less than you have determined you require. State the terms you do need, and listen to the response. You may be asked to put this in writing, or you may be asked to hold off until the firm can decide on a response. If you are dealing with a senior representative of the organization, one who has been involved in hiring for some time, you may get an immediate response or a solid indication of possible outcomes.

Perhaps the issue is one of relocation. Your initial assignment is in the Midwest, and because you had indicated a strong West Coast preference, you are surprised at the actual assignment. You might simply indicate that, while you understand the need for the company to assign you based on its needs, you are disappointed and had hoped to be placed on the West Coast. You could inquire if that were still possible and, if not, would it be reasonable to expect a West Coast relocation in the future.

If your request is presented in a reasonable way, most employers will not see this as jeopardizing your offer. If they can agree to your proposal, they will. If not, they will simply tell you so, and you may choose to continue your candidacy with them or remove yourself from consideration as a possible employee. The choice will be up to you.

Some firms will adjust benefits within their parameters to meet the candidate's need if at all possible. If a candidate requires a relocation cost allowance, he or she may be asked to forego tuition benefits for the first year to accomplish this adjustment. An increase in life insurance may be adjusted by some other benefit trade-off; perhaps a family dental plan is not needed. In these decisions you are called upon, sometimes under time pressure, to know how you value these issues and how important each is to you.

Many employers find they are more comfortable negotiating for candidates who have unique qualifications or who bring especially needed expertise to the organization. Employers hiring large numbers of entry-level college graduates may be far more reluctant to accommodate any changes in offer conditions. They are well supplied with candidates with similar education and experience, so that if rejected by one candidate, they can draw new candidates from an ample labor pool.

COMPARING OFFERS

With only about 40 percent of recent college graduates employed three months after graduation, many graduates do not get to enjoy the experience of entertaining more than one offer at a time. The conditions of the economy, the job seekers' particular geographic job market, and their own needs and demands for certain employment conditions may not provide more than one offer at a time. Some job seekers may feel that no reasonable offer should go unaccepted for the simple fear there won't be another.

In a tough job market, or if the job you seek is not widely available, or when your job search goes on too long and becomes difficult to sustain financially and emotionally, it may be necessary to accept an offer. The alternative is continued unemployment. Even here, when you feel you don't have a choice, you can at least understand that in accepting this particular offer, there may be limitations and conditions you don't appreciate. At the time of acceptance, there were no other alternatives, but the new employee can begin to use that position to gain the experience and talent to move toward a more attractive position.

Sometimes, however, more than one offer is received at one time, and the candidate has the luxury of choice. If the job seeker knows what he or she wants and has done the necessary self-assessment honestly and thoroughly, it may be clear that one of the offers conforms more closely to those expressed wants and needs.

However, if, as so often happens, the offers are similar in terms of conditions and salary, the question then becomes which organization might provide the necessary climate, opportunities, and advantages for your professional development and growth. This is the time when solid employer research and astute questioning during the interviews really pay off. How much did you learn about the employer through your own research and skillful questioning?

When the interviewer asked during the interview "Do you have any questions?" did you ask the kinds of questions that would help resolve a choice between one organization and another? Just as an employer must decide among numerous applicants, so must the applicant learn to assess the potential employer. Both are partners in the job search.

RENEGING ON AN OFFER

An especially disturbing occurrence for employers and career counseling professionals is when a job seeker formally (either orally or by written contract) accepts employment with one organization and later reneges on the agreement and goes with another employer.

There are all kinds of rationalizations offered for this unethical behavior. None of them satisfies. The sad irony is that what job seekers are willing to do to the employer—make a promise and then break it—they would be outraged to have done to them—have the job offer pulled. It is a very bad way to begin a career. It suggests the individual has not taken the time to do the necessary self-assessment and self-awareness exercises to think and judge critically. The new offer taken may, in fact, be no better or worse than the one refused. Job candidates should be aware that there have been incidents of legal action following job candidates reneging on an offer. This adds a very sour note to what should be a harmonious beginning of a lifelong adventure.

CHAPTER EIGHT

THE GRADUATE SCHOOL CHOICE

The reasons for continuing one's education in graduate school can be as varied and unique as the individuals electing this course of action. Many continue their studies at an advanced level because they simply find it difficult to end the educational process. They love what they are learning and want to learn more and continue their academic exploration.

Continuing to work with a specific subject in great depth, such as how particular cells react to certain drugs or physical stimulation, and studying, researching, and writing critically on what you and others have discovered can provide excitement, challenge, and serious work. Some biology majors have loved this aspect of their academic work and want to continue that activity.

Others go on to graduate school for purely practical reasons; they have examined employment prospects in their field of study, and all indications are that a graduate degree is requisite. If you have earned a B.A. in biology as a stepping stone to a career as a research microbiologist, for example, going on for further training becomes mandatory. As a B.A. level biology major, you realize you cannot move above the assistant or technician level without a master's degree or even a Ph.D. A review of jobs in different areas will suggest that at least a master's degree is important to be competitive. Alumni who are working in the fields you are considering can be a good source of what degree level the fields are hiring. Ask your college career office for some alumni names and give them a telephone call. Prepare some questions on specific job prospects in their field at each degree level. A thorough examination of the marketplace and talking to employers and professors will give you a sense of the scope of employment for a bachelor's degree, master's degree, or doctorate. College teaching will require an advanced degree.

The more senior positions in the career paths outlined in this book will require advanced education and perhaps some particular specialization in a subject area (psychology, chemistry, computer science, etc.). Employers may well put a premium on the advanced degree because the market is oversupplied in some areas and the employer can afford to make this demand or, in other areas, because the advanced training and research are necessary requirements to function in the job.

CONSIDER YOUR MOTIVES

The answer to the question of "Why graduate school?" is a personal one for each applicant. Nevertheless, it is important to consider your motives carefully. Graduate school involves additional time out of the employment market, a high degree of critical evaluation, significant autonomy as you pursue your studies, and considerable financial expenditure. For some students in doctoral programs, there may be additional life choice issues, such as relationships, marriage, and parenthood, that may present real challenges while in a program of study. You would be well-advised to consider the following questions as you think about your decision to continue your studies.

Are You Postponing Some Tough Decisions by Going to School?

Graduate school is not a place to go to avoid life's problems. There is intense competition for graduate school slots and for the fellowships, scholarships, and financial aid available. This competition means extensive interviewing, resume submission, and essay writing that rival corporate recruitment. Likewise, the graduate school process is a mentored one in which faculty stay aware of and involved in the academic progress of their students and continually challenge the quality of their work. Many graduate students are called upon to participate in teaching and professional writing and research as well.

In other words, this is no place to hide from the spotlight. Graduate students work very hard and much is demanded of them individually. If you elect to go to graduate school to avoid the stresses and strains of the "real world," you will find no safe place in higher academics. Vivid accounts, both fiction and nonfiction, have depicted quite accurately the personal and professional demands of graduate school work.

The selection of graduate studies as a career option should be a positive choice—something you *want* to do. It shouldn't be selected as an escape from other, less attractive or more challenging options, nor should it be selected as the option of last resort (i.e., "I can't do anything else; I'd better just stay in school."). If you're in some doubt about the strength of your reasoning about continuing in school, discuss the issues with a career counselor. Together you can clarify your reasoning, and you'll get some sound feedback on what you're about to undertake.

On the other hand, staying on in graduate school because of a particularly poor employment market and a lack of jobs at entry-level positions has proven to be an effective "stalling" strategy. If you can afford it, pursuing a graduate degree immediately after your undergraduate education gives you a year or two to "wait out" a difficult economic climate while at the same time acquiring a potentially valuable credential.

Have You Done Some "Hands-On" Reality Testing?

There are experiential options available to give some reality to your decision-making process about graduate school. Internships or work in the field can give you a good idea about employment demands, conditions, and atmosphere.

••

Perhaps, as a biology major, you're considering a doctoral program in a specialized area with an eye to university teaching. Begin with your own college professors and ask them to talk to you about their own educational and career paths to their current teaching posts. They can also talk to you about the time they spend outside the classroom, in research activities or in departmental meetings dealing with faculty and budget concerns.

Even hearing the experience of only one professor, you have a stronger concept of the pace of the job, interaction with colleagues, subject matter, and pressure to do research and publish results. Talking to people and asking questions are invaluable as an exercise to help you better understand the objective of your graduate study.

For biology majors especially, the opportunity to do this kind of reality testing is invaluable. It demonstrates far more authoritatively than any other method what your real-world skills are, how they can be put to use, and what aspect of your academic preparation you rely on. It has been well documented that biology majors do well in occupations once they identify their real skills. Internships and co-op experiences speed that process up and prevent the frustrating and expensive process of investigation many graduates begin only after graduation.

••

Do You Need an Advanced Degree to Work in Your Field?

Certainly there are fields such as law, psychiatry, medicine, and college teaching that demand advanced degrees. Is the field of employment you're considering one that also puts a premium on an advanced degree? You may be surprised. Read the want ads in a number of major Sunday newspapers for positions you would enjoy. How many of those require an advanced degree?

Retailing, for example, has always put a premium on what people can do, rather than how much education they have had. Successful people in retailing come from all academic preparations. A Ph.D. in Biology may bring only prestige to the individual employed as a lab technician. It may not bring a more senior position or better pay. In fact, it may disqualify you for some jobs because an employer might believe you will be unhappy to be overqualified for a particular position. Or your motives in applying for the work may be misconstrued, and the employer might think you will only be working at this level until something better comes along. None of this may be true for you, but it comes about because you are working outside of the usual territory for that degree level.

When economic times are especially difficult, we tend to see stories featured about individuals with advanced degrees doing what is considered unsuitable work, such as the Ph.D. in English driving a cab or the Ph.D. in chemistry waiting tables. Actually, this is not particularly surprising when you consider that as your degree level advances, the job market narrows appreciably. At any one time, regardless of economic circumstances, there are only so many jobs for your particular level of expertise. If you cannot find employment for your advanced degree level, chances are you will be considered suspect for many other kinds of employment and may be forced into temporary work far removed from your original intention.

Before making an important decision such as graduate study, learn your options and carefully consider what you want to do with your advanced degree. Ask yourself whether it is reasonable to think you can achieve your goals. Will there be jobs when you graduate? Where will they be? What will they pay? How competitive will the market be at that time, based on current predictions?

If you're uncertain about the degree requirements for the fields you're interested in, you should check a publication such as the U.S. Department of Labor's *Occupational Outlook Handbook.* Each entry has a section on training and other qualifications that will indicate clearly what the minimum educational requirement is for employment, what degree is the standard, and what employment may be possible without the required credential.

For example, for physicists and astronomers, a doctoral degree in physics or a closely related field is essential. Certainly this is the degree of choice in academic institutions. However, the *Occupational Outlook Handbook* also indicates what kinds of employment may be available to individuals holding a master's or even a bachelor's degree in physics.

Have You Compared Your Expectations of What Graduate School Will Do for You with What It Has Done for Alumni of the Program You're Considering?

Most colleges and universities perform some kind of postgraduate survey of their students to ascertain where they are employed, what additional education they have received, and what levels of salary they are enjoying. Ask to see this information either from the university you are considering applying to or from your own alma mater, especially if it has a similar graduate program. Such surveys often reveal surprises about occupational decisions, salaries, and work satisfaction. This information may affect your decision.

The value of self-assessment (the process of examining and making decisions about your own hierarchy of values and goals) is especially important in this process of analyzing the desirability of possible career paths involving graduate education. Sometimes a job requiring advanced education seems to hold real promise but is disappointing in salary potential or number of opportunities available. Certainly it is better to research this information before embarking on a program of graduate studies. It may not change your mind about your decision, but by becoming better informed about your choice, you become better prepared for your future.

Have You Talked with People in Your Field to Explore What You Might Be Doing After Graduate School?

In pursuing your undergraduate degree, you will have come into contact with many individuals trained in the field you are considering. You might also have the opportunity to attend professional conferences, workshops, seminars, and job fairs where you can expand your network of contacts. Talk to them all! Find out about their individual career paths, discuss your own plans and hopes, get their feedback on the reality of your expectations, and heed their advice about your prospects. Each will have a unique tale to tell, and each will bring a different perspective on the current marketplace for the credentials you are seeking. Talking to enough people will make you an expert on what's out there.

Are You Excited by the Idea of Studying the Particular Field You Have in Mind?

This question may be the most important one of all. If you are going to spend several years in advanced study, perhaps engendering some debt or postponing some lifestyle decisions for an advanced degree, you simply ought to enjoy what you're doing. Examine your work in the discipline so far. Has it been fun? Have you found yourself exploring various paths of thought? Do you read in your area for fun? Do you enjoy talking about it, thinking about it, and sharing it with others? Advanced degrees often are the beginning of a lifetime's involvement with a particular subject. Choose carefully a field that will hold your interest and your enthusiasm.

It is fairly obvious by now that we think you should give some careful thought to your decision and take some action. If nothing else, do the following:

❑ Talk and question (remember to listen!)

❑ Reality-test

❑ Soul-search by yourself or with a person you trust

FINDING THE RIGHT PROGRAM FOR YOU: SOME CONSIDERATIONS

There are several important factors in coming to a sound decision about the right graduate program for you. You'll want to begin by locating institutions that offer appropriate programs, examining each of these programs and their requirements, undertaking the application process by obtaining catalogs and application materials, visiting campuses if possible, arranging for letters of recommendation, writing your application statement, and finally following up on your applications.

Locate Institutions with Appropriate Programs

Once you decide on a particular advanced degree, it's important to develop a list of schools offering such a degree program. Perhaps the best sources of graduate program information are Peterson's *Guides to Graduate Study*. Use these guides to build your list. In addition, you may want to consult the College Board's *Index of Majors and Graduate Degrees,* which will help you find graduate programs offering the degree you seek. It is indexed by academic major and then categorized by state.

Now, this may be a considerable list. You may want to narrow the choices down further by a number of criteria: tuition, availability of financial aid, public versus private institutions, U.S. versus international institutions, size of student body, size of faculty, application fee (this varies by school; most fall within the $10 to $75 range), and geographic location. This is only a partial list; you will have your own important considerations. Perhaps you are an avid scuba diver and you find it unrealistic to think you could pursue graduate study for a number of years without being able to ocean dive from time to time. Good! That's a decision and it's honest. Now, how far from the ocean is too far, and what schools meet your other needs? In any case, and according to your own criteria, begin to build a reasonable list of graduate schools that you are willing to spend the time investigating.

Examine the Degree Programs and Their Requirements

Once you've determined the criteria by which you want to develop a list of graduate schools, you can begin to examine the degree program requirements, faculty composition, and institutional research orientation. Again, using resources such as Peterson's *Guides to Graduate Study* can reveal an amazingly rich level of material by which to judge your possible selections.

In addition to degree programs and degree requirements, entries will include information about application fees, entrance test requirements, tuition, percentage of applicants accepted, numbers of applicants receiving financial aid, gender breakdown of students, numbers of full- and part-time faculty, and often gender breakdown of faculty as well. Numbers graduating in each program and research orientations of departments are also included in some entries. There is information on graduate housing, student services, and library, research, and computer facilities. A contact person, phone number, and address are also standard pieces of information in these listings. In addition to the standard entries, some schools pay an additional fee to place full-page, more detailed program descriptions. The location of such a display ad, if present, would be indicated at the end of the standard entry.

It can be helpful to draw up a chart and enter relevant information about each school you are considering in order to have a ready reference on points of information that are important to you.

Undertake the Application Process

The Catalog. Once you've decided on a selection of schools, send for catalogs and applications. It is important to note here that these materials might take many weeks to arrive. Consequently, if you need the materials quickly, it might be best to telephone and explain your situation to see whether the process can be speeded up for you. Also, check a local college or university library, which might have current and complete college catalogs in a microfiche collection. These microfiche copies can provide you with helpful information while you wait for your own copy of the graduate school catalog or bulletin to arrive.

When you receive your catalogs, give them a careful reading and make notes of issues you might want to discuss on the telephone or in a personal interview, if that's possible. Does the course selection have the depth you had hoped for?

What is the ratio of faculty to the required number of courses for your degree? How often will you encounter the same faculty member as an instructor?

・・・・・・・・・・・・・・・・・・・・・・・・・・・・・・・・・

If you are interested in graduate work in animal behavior, for example, in addition to classic courses in experimental psychology and physiology, consider the availability of directed research opportunities and hands-on training programs.

・・・・・・・・・・・・・・・・・・・・・・・・・・・・・・・・・

If, for example, your program offers a practicum or off-campus experience, who arranges this? Does the graduate school select a site and place you there, or is it your responsibility? What are the professional affiliations of the faculty? Does the program merit any outside professional endorsement or accreditation?

Critically evaluate the catalogs of each of the programs you are considering. List any questions you have and ask current or former teachers and colleagues for their impressions as well.

The Application. Preview each application thoroughly to determine what you need to provide in the way of letters of recommendation, transcripts from undergraduate schools or any previous graduate work, and personal essays that may be required. Make a notation for each application of what you need to complete that document.

Additionally, you'll want to determine entrance testing requirements for each institution and immediately arrange to complete your test registration. For example, the Graduate Record Exam (GRE) and the Medical College Admission Test (MCAT) each have several weeks between the last registration date and the test date. Your local college career office should be able to provide you with test registration booklets, sample test materials, information on test sites and dates, and independent test review materials that might be available commercially.

Visit the Campus If Possible

If time and finances allow, a visit, interview, and tour can help make your decision easier. You can develop a sense of the student body, meet some of the faculty, and hear up-to-date information on resources and the curriculum. You will have a brief opportunity to "try out" the surroundings to see if they fit your needs. After all, it will be home for a while. If a visit is not possible but you have questions, don't hesitate to call and speak with the dean of the graduate school. Most are more than happy to talk to candidates and want them to have the answers they seek. Graduate school admission is a very personal and individual process.

Arrange for Letters of Recommendation

This is also the time to begin to assemble a group of individuals who will support your candidacy as a graduate student by writing letters of recommendation or completing recommendation forms. Some schools will ask you to provide letters of recommendation to be included with your application or sent directly to the school by the recommender. Other graduate programs will provide a recommendation form that must be completed by the recommender. These graduate school forms vary greatly in the amount of space provided for a written recommendation. So that you can use letters as you need to, ask your recommenders to address their letters "To Whom It May Concern," unless one of your recommenders has a particular connection to one of your graduate schools or knows an official at the school.

Choose recommenders who can speak authoritatively about the criteria important to selection officials at your graduate school. In other words, choose recommenders who can write about your grasp of the literature in your field of study, your ability to write and speak effectively, your class performance, and your demonstrated interest in the field outside of class. Other characteristics that graduate schools are interested in assessing include your emotional maturity, leadership ability, breadth of general knowledge, intellectual ability, motivation, perseverance, and ability to engage in independent inquiry.

When requesting recommendations, it's especially helpful to put the request in writing. Explain your graduate school intentions and express some of your thoughts about graduate school and your appreciation for their support. Don't be shy about "prompting" your recommenders with some suggestions of what you would appreciate being included in their comments. Most recommenders will find this direction helpful and will want to produce a statement of support that you can both stand behind. Consequently, if your interaction with one recommender was especially focused on research projects, he or she might be best able to speak of those skills and your critical thinking ability. Another recommender may have good comments to make about your public presentation skills.

Give your recommenders plenty of lead time in which to complete your recommendation, and set a date by which they should respond. If they fail to meet your deadline, be prepared to make a polite call or visit to inquire if they need more information or if there is anything you can do to move the process along.

Whether or not you are providing a graduate school form or asking for an original letter to be mailed, be sure to provide an envelope and postage if the recommender must mail the form or letter directly to the graduate school.

Each recommendation you request should provide a different piece of information about you for the selection committee. It might be pleasant for letters of recommendation to say that you are a fine, upstanding individual, but a selection committee for graduate school will require specific information. Each recommender has had a unique relationship with you, and their letters should reflect that. Think of each letter as helping to build a more complete portrait of you as a potential graduate student.

Write Your Application Statement

....

> For you as a biology major, the application and personal
> essay should be a welcome opportunity to express your
> deep interest in pursuing graduate study. Your under-
> standing of the challenges ahead, your commitment to
> the work involved, and your expressed self-awareness
> will weigh heavily in the decision process of the gradu-
> ate school admissions committee.

....

An excellent source to help in thinking about writing this essay is *How to Write a Winning Personal Statement for Graduate and Professional School* by Richard J. Stelzer. It has been written from the perspective of what graduate school selection committees are looking for when they read these essays. It provides helpful tips to keep your essay targeted on the kinds of issues and criteria that are important to selection committees and that provide them with the kind of information they can best utilize in making their decision.

Follow Up on Your Applications

After you have finished each application and mailed it along with your tran-script requests and letters of recommendation, be sure to follow up on the progress of your file. For example, call the graduate school administrative staff to see whether your transcripts have arrived. If the school required your recommenders to fill out a specific recommendation form that had to be mailed directly to the school, you will want to ensure that they have all arrived in good time for the processing of your application. It is your responsibility to make certain that all required information is received by the institution.

RESEARCHING FINANCIAL AID SOURCES, SCHOLARSHIPS, AND FELLOWSHIPS

Financial aid information is available from each school, so be sure to request it when you call for a catalog and application materials. There will be sev-eral lengthy forms to complete, and these will vary by school, type of school (public versus private), and state. Be sure to note the deadline dates for these important forms.

There are many excellent resources available to help you explore all of your financial aid options. Visit your college career office or local public library to find out about the range of materials available. Two excellent resources include Peterson's *Grants for Graduate Students* and the Foundation Center's *Foundation Grants to Individuals*. These types of resources generally contain information that can be accessed by indexes including field of study, specific eligibility requirements, administering agency, and geographic focus.

EVALUATING ACCEPTANCES

If you apply to and are accepted at more than one school, it is time to return to your initial research and self-assessment to evaluate your options and select the program that will best help you achieve the goals you set for pursuing graduate study. You'll want to choose a program that will allow you to complete your studies in a timely and cost-effective way. This may be a good time to get additional feedback from professors and career professionals who are familiar with your interests and plans. Ultimately, the decision is yours, so be sure you get answers to all the questions you can think of.

SOME NOTES ABOUT REJECTION

Each graduate school is searching for applicants who appear to have the qualifications necessary to succeed in its program. Applications are evaluated on a combination of undergraduate grade point average, strength of letters of recommendation, standardized test scores, and personal statements written for the application.

A carelessly completed application is one reason many applicants are denied admission to a graduate program. To avoid this type of needless rejection, be sure to carefully and completely answer all appropriate questions on the application form, focus your personal statement given the instructions provided, and submit your materials well in advance of the deadline. Remember that your test scores and recommendations are considered a part of your application, so they must also be received by the deadline.

If you are rejected by a school that especially interests you, you may want to contact the dean of graduate studies to discuss the strengths and weaknesses of your application. Information provided by the dean will be useful in reapplying to the program or applying to other, similar programs.

PART TWO

THE CAREER PATHS

CHAPTER NINE

INTRODUCTION TO BIOLOGY CAREER PATHS

With so much diversity in the field of biology, choosing the right career path can sometimes present quite a dilemma. The level of education you possess, the area of interest that consumes you, the amount of time you are willing to devote to study, and the setting in which you choose to work, will all contribute toward determining the right career path for you to take.

But before you commit yourself to a path, explore it first. And if possible, begin that exploration early, with the diverse educational programs offered around the country.

CHOOSING THE RIGHT BIOLOGY PROGRAM

There are almost as many different names and focuses for biology programs as there are job possibilities. Universities often divide their departments into particular areas of concentration and it's important for the incoming student to know the department's focus before applying. The University of Colorado at Boulder, for example, has two programs: one is called EPO (environmental, populations, organisms) and the other is MCDB (molecular, cellular, developmental biology). This division is made clear so students who want to study microbes won't end up accidentally in a "Birds of North America" course, and the future zoologist won't be trying to learn how to conduct gel electrophoresis.

Other universities offer integrated programs. For example, at the University of California at Berkeley the following related but separate fields are offered in one department: botany, evolutionary biology, ecology, marine biology, paleontology, and zoology. UC Berkeley interestingly places cellular and molecular biology into two separate departments, while other universities might combine them under one major discipline.

Many colleges and universities divide their programs into two basic categories based on what kind of system is studied: organismic biology and cellular biology. The main difference between these two categories is their primary level of focus. The whole organism is the center of interest with organismic biology, and cellular biology focuses more on what is happening at the cellular and molecular level within an organism.

How a university houses or groups its biology specialties, however, is not as important as the specialties it offers. To make sure you end up in the right program, do your research ahead of time. You can study college catalogs and make phone calls to department heads or advisors. Investigate the university's offerings and how those particular subject areas apply to the career path you are considering.

If you are not sure what area of biology you want to pursue as a career upon graduation, look for a university that offers a good general program, or one that has interdisciplinary studies that would allow you to cross over between subfields. Sometimes taking one particular course in an area, or being influenced by one dynamic professor, can help make the choice more evident to you. A program that allows you to experience a number of areas to help in your decision making would be the best bet.

In actuality, with a general degree in biology, you could pursue most of the career paths covered in this book and specialization isn't required until the graduate level. But it is important to keep in mind that the career you might want to pursue could possibly require a master's or even a doctorate degree. The level of education you are willing to pursue will affect your career choice and as a result, the undergraduate program you decide to attend.

Most major colleges and universities can provide a good basic biology preparation and for those who want to go on to graduate school, a general background is what is most sought after. Make sure to add math by way of calculus, some statistics, and some computer science to your curriculum. Your English, reading, and writing skills should be top notch, too.

Selecting the right graduate school is more directed to specialization. You should not plan to study marine mammals at a school where no professors are involved in that specialty. You need to determine where the people are located who are involved in the area of concentration that interests you the most. By the time you have reached your last year of undergraduate study and you have done all the necessary groundwork, you should have a good idea of what you want to accomplish with graduate study.

THE CAREER PATHS

What college student doesn't hope to find a great job upon graduation? With four years of study and careful planning throughout your college program, and for some fields, a stint of graduate study, there is no reason why, as a biology major, you shouldn't walk into the plum job of your choosing.

There are a lot of choices, however, and the aim of this book is to help you narrow them down and find the career path that best suits your education, interests, and skills.

For the purpose of this book, five main paths have been identified and explored, but they are in no way exhaustive. As you have already probably gleaned from reading the introduction to this book, the list of main tracks numbers close to two dozen. Within those tracks are thousands of different job titles. Many are explored throughout the following five chapters, as primary paths or secondary and related paths; some are provided for you later in this chapter, under Other Biology Career Paths and New Fields in Biology.

The five paths are as outlined here:

Path 1: Botanists

Path 2: Zoologists

Path 3: Aquatic Scientists

Path 4: Medical Scientists, Technologists, and Technicians

Path 5: Biology Educators

As mentioned earlier, this list is by no means comprehensive. Many university programs allow for a great deal of latitude in designing majors and courses of study. It is now common practice to pursue interdisciplinary degrees. With a little bit of guidance and creativity, you should be able to make a case for your biology degree in any area you wish to enter.

OTHER BIOLOGY CAREER PATHS

Agriculture

The world of agriculture, animal husbandry, food, and nutrition is a wide open path for biology majors. It covers agronomy, which works to improve the quality and production of field crops; animal science, which is an area that conducts research in selecting, breeding, feeding, managing, and marketing of domesticated animals; food science, which involves the study of the chemical, physical, and biological nature of food to learn how to safely produce, preserve, package, distribute, and store it; and nutrition, which is concerned with counseling individuals or groups on sound nutritional practices to maintain and improve health.

Within this career path you will find job titles such as:

Agricultural economist	Food and drug inspector
Agronomist	Food scientist
Arborculturist	Grower
Brewmaster	Livestock scientist
Dairy manager/Owner	Nutritionist
Farmer	Pest control specialist

Environmental Biology

In some universities environmental biology and ecology programs stand on their own; in others this discipline is considered a subfield of zoology.

Within this career path you will find job titles such as:

Animal ecologist	Evolutionary ecologist
Community ecologist	Evolutionary biologist
Conservation biologist	Fisheries biologist
Ecological physiologist	Forest economist
Ecologist	Forester
Ecosystem ecologist	Microbial ecologist
Ecotoxicologist	Naturalist
Environmental education specialist	Natural resources manager
Environmental health officer	Nature center curator
Environmental impact analyst	Paleoecologist
Environmental planner	Paleontologist
Environmental policy manager	Park ranger
Environmental scientist	Plant ecologist

Pollution control technician

Population ecologist

Resource policy analyst

Recreation manager

Soil toxicologist

Water engineer

Waste water engineer

Watershed manager

Wildlife ecologist/Manager (see a first-hand account for this job title in Chapter 11)

Information Systems

Categorizing and maintaining information and making it available to scholars, researchers, and the general public is an important aspect of biology work. There are thousands of public, private, university, and hospital libraries that need professional librarians with a strong science background. Strong computer skills are also crucial.

Within this career path you will find job titles such as:

Information systems specialist

Library assistant

Medical librarian

Science librarian

Science Writing, Illustration, and Photography

Science writers write about scientific and technical issues and often cover new discoveries or trends for newspapers, magazines, books, television, and radio. Some specialize in a particular topic, such as medicine or environmental issues, while others generalize and will write about any topic they know there's a market for. An important part of science writing is making technical information clear and understandable to the general public.

The work of scientific illustrators and photographers is used in medical textbooks and other publications, for research purposes, and in lectures and other presentations.

Within this career path you will find job titles such as:

Biological illustrator

Biological photographer

Media specialist

Medical illustrator

Science writer

Forensic Science

Forensic science is a catch-all phrase that includes any of the sciences as they are applied to litigation or adjudication, including chemistry, molecular biology, entomology, and toxicology.

Areas of study—and employment—include:

Arson

Chemistry

Computer investigation

DNA

Drugs

Engineering

Fingerprints

Firearms

Hair and fibers

Handwriting

Image processing

Linguistics and voice analysis

Medicine

Photography

Shoe prints

Tire tracks

Toxicology

Traffic accident investigation

NEW FIELDS IN BIOLOGY

Two new fields in biology that are growing rapidly are biophysics and computer theoretical biology or computational biology, as it is also known.

Biophysics tends to have strong medical applications in x-rays, petscans, and MRI scans. Computer theoretical biology is, in part, an attempt to move away from using animals in research. Instead, computer models are used to explore evolution, development, and how a drug acts in a given cell system.

FOR MORE INFORMATION

Researching the right career path to follow takes more than reading just one book. The more informed you are, the happier you will be with your career choice. At the end of each of the chapters that follow and in the appendix you will find scores of publications to investigate and professional associations to contact. Each will have something to offer you.

In addition, throughout this book you will read first-hand accounts from people actually working in the various fields. They tell what each job really entails, what the duties are, what the lifestyle is like, what the upsides and downsides are. All of the professionals reveal what drew them to the field and how they got started. And so that you can make the best career decisions for yourself, each professional offers you some expert advice based on years of personal experience.

But don't stop with these accounts. Find your own professionals to talk to and follow around for a day or so. You can make contacts through your university's biology department or through the career guidance center. Nothing is more valuable than getting to see for yourself what a job is really like.

CHAPTER TEN

PATH 1: BOTANISTS

Botany is the study of plants. Plants have fascinated people for thousands of years. Without plants, we would not be able to breathe. Plants absorb carbon dioxide from the air and release life-sustaining oxygen. Without plants, we would not be able to eat. Our food—vegetables, fruit, meat, grains—is all derived, directly or indirectly, from plants.

Plants provide aesthetic beauty, enriching our homes and the environment. Our clothing, shelter, fuel, the medicines that keep us healthy, the paper upon which these words are printed, in fact every aspect that allows our existence to be are all dependent upon plants and their contributions.

To most people, the word "plant" means a range of living organisms from the smallest bacteria to the giant redwood and sequoia trees. With this definition in mind, plants include: algae, fungi, lichens, mosses, ferns, conifers, and flowering plants.

Modern scientists today place bacteria, algae, and fungi into their own distinct kingdoms, but most general botany courses in most college and university botany departments still teach about these groups.

Botanists study plants and their environment. Some study all aspects of plant life; others specialize in areas such as identification and classification of plants, the structure and function of plant parts, the biochemistry of plant processes, the causes and cures of plant diseases, and the geological records of plants.

DEFINITION OF THE CAREER PATH

With such a broad field, there are many kinds of botanists and many different career paths available.

Some botanists are called field botanists or field biologists and, with their strong interest in ecology, study the interactions of plants with other organisms and the environment.

Some botanists working in the field study the structure of plants. They concentrate on the pattern of the whole plant. Other field botanists look for new species or conduct research and do experiments to discover how plants grow under different conditions.

There are botanists who conduct research and those who use the results to increase and improve our supply of food, medicines, fibers, building materials, and other plant products.

Someone concerned about the world food supply can study plant pathology or plant breeding.

Conservationists with botanical knowledge and qualifications manage parks, forests, range lands, and wilderness areas.

Public health and environmental protection professionals use their botanical knowledge and understanding of plant science to help solve pollution problems.

Some botanists work in labs and use microscopes to study the detailed structure of individual cells. They perform experiments to discover how plants convert simple chemical compounds into more complex chemicals. They might study how genetic information in DNA controls plant development. Botanists also study the time scales of processes, ranging from fractions of a second in individual cells to those that take eons of time.

People with a mathematical background to couple with their knowledge of botany might pursue the fields of biophysics, developmental botany, genetics, modeling, or systems ecology.

Those with an interest in chemistry can become plant physiologists, plant biochemists, molecular biologists (discussed in Chapter 13), or chemotaxonomists. Those intrigued by microscopic organisms can choose microbiology (examined in Chapter 13), phycology, or mycology.

Those who prefer to work with plants on an aesthetic level can enter into the fields of ornamental horticulture and landscape design.

Botanists who enjoy working with people have a wide range of opportunities in teaching and public service, fields that are covered in more depth in Chapter 14.

As you can see, there are many specializations for biology majors and more specifically for those who wish to pursue botany. How the different paths are categorized varies from institution to institution and scientist to scientist but, in general, how universities combine or separate their departments often provides the easiest way to look at the different areas.

What follows are definitions of the different subdisciplines of botany:

BOTANY AREAS OF SPECIALIZATION

Plant Biology

Anatomy studies microscopic plant structure—cells and tissues.

Biochemistry covers the chemical aspects of plant life processes and includes the chemical products of plants (phytochemistry).

Biophysics is the application of physics to plant life processes.

Chemotaxonomy uses the chemicals produced by plants to aid in their identification.

Cytology is the study of the structure, function, and life history of plant cells.

Ecology studies the relationships between plants and their environments, both individually and in communities.

Genetics investigates plant heredity and variation. Plant geneticists study genes and gene function in plants.

Molecular Biology studies the structure and function of biological macromolecules, including the biochemical and molecular aspects of genetics.

Morphology studies macroscopic plant forms. It is also the study of evolution and development of leaves, roots, and stems.

Paleobotany studies the biology and evolution of fossil plants.

Physiology investigates the functions and vital processes of plants (and animals) under normal and abnormal conditions. Two examples of subjects studied by plant physiologists are photosynthesis and mineral nutrition.

Systematics studies evolutionary history and relationships among plants.

Systems Ecology uses mathematical models to demonstrate concepts such as nutrient cycling.

Taxonomy covers the identifying, naming, and classifying of plants.

Applied Plant Sciences

Agronomy studies crop and soil sciences. Agronomists make practical use of plant and soil sciences to increase field crop yields.

Biotechnology uses biological organisms in a number of ways: to produce useful products, improve crops, develop new drugs, or harness microbes to recycle wastes, to name just a few. Today many scientists narrow the definition even further and consider biotechnology to be the genetic modification of living organisms to produce useful products.

Breeding involves the development of better types of plants, including selecting and crossing plants with desirable traits such as disease resistance.

Economic Botany covers plants with commercial importance. Economic botany also includes the study of harmful and beneficial plants and plant products.

Food Science and Technology involves the development of food from various plant products.

Forestry is managing forests for the production of timber and conservation.

Horticulture covers the production of ornamental plants and fruit and vegetable crops. Landscape design is also an important subdiscipline in horticulture.

Natural Resource Management is the responsible use and protection of our natural resources for the benefit of all.

Plant Pathology studies plant diseases, both the biological aspects of disease and disease management or control.

Organismal Specialties

Bryology is the study of mosses and similar plants, covering all aspects of these plants, including their identification, classification, and ecology.

Lichenology is the study of lichens, dual organisms that are composed of both a fungus and an alga.

Mycology is the study of fungi. Fungi have a tremendous impact on our world and are important in the biosphere because they help recycle dead organic material. Some fungi are important producers of biological products such as vitamins and antibiotics.

Microbiology is the study of microorganisms. Microbiologists may be grouped by the organism they study, such as bacteria, or by the branch of biology, such as microbial ecology.

Pteridology is the study of ferns and similar plants.

Phycology is the study of algae, the base of the food chain in aquatic environments. Phycologists who study algae in oceans are sometimes called marine biologists, covered in Chapter 12.

Botany Education

Botany Educators provide knowledge and insight about plants, plant biology, and the ecological roles of plants. This specialty includes teaching in schools, museums, and botanical gardens, development of educational materials, and science writing.

POSSIBLE JOB TITLES

For every "ology" there's an "ist," an "er"—and more. Here is an alphabetical listing of possible job titles for botanists:

Agronomist	Ecologist
Algologist	Economic botanist
Arborist	Florist
Biochemist	Food scientist
Biophysicist	Food technologist
Biotechnician	Forest economist
Biotechnologist	Forester
Botany educator	Gardener
Breeder	Garden photographer
Bryologist	Garden writer
Chemotaxonomist	Geneticist
Curator	Golf course manager
Cytologist	Groundskeeper

Grower	Nursery worker
Herbalist	Paleobotanist
Historic landscape preservationist	Physiologist
Horticultural therapist	Plant breeder
Horticulturist	Plant pathologist
Interiorscaper	Plant physiologist
Landscape architect	Pteridologist
Landscape designer	Science writer
Lichenologist	Soil scientist
Mapper and labeler	System ecologist
Microbiologist	Taxonomist
Molecular biologist	Topiary trainer
Morphologist	Tree surgeon
Natural resources manager	Wood technologist

POSSIBLE EMPLOYERS

The major employers of plant biologists are educational institutions, federal and state agencies, industries, and on a smaller scale, botanical gardens.

Educational institutions, which employ the majority of botanists, range from high schools and community colleges to universities. Although high schools and community colleges have relatively few openings for those wanting to teach specialized courses—and there is little time or equipment for research activity—botanists who enjoy working with people and sharing their knowledge can find these positions satisfying.

Most positions for professional plant scientists are in colleges and universities. Almost all colleges and universities offer courses in the various disciplines of botany and plant science and botanists with different specialities can be successful at finding faculty positions. Educational institutions also employ botanists as researchers and as administrators.

Government agencies on both the federal and state level employ botanists in many different fields. Plant biologists work in various branches of the U.S. Department of Agriculture, including the Medical Plant Resources Laboratory, the Germplasm Resources Laboratory, the Animal and Plant Health Inspection Service, the National Arboretum, and the U.S. Forest Service.

The U.S. Department of the Interior—which includes the National Park Service, the Bureau of Land Management, and the U.S. Geological Survey—also employs botanists.

Plant scientists also work in several other federal agencies, including the Public Health Service, State Department, National Aeronautics and Space Administration, Smithsonian Institution, and the Environmental Protection Agency.

Each of the 50 state governments also employs plant scientists in agencies parallel to those of the federal government. Environmental organizations, such as the Nature Conservancy, also hire botanists.

Industry is the third largest employer of botanists. The oil and chemical industries, drug companies, lumber and paper companies, seed and nursery companies, fruit growers, food companies, fermentation industries (including breweries), biological supply houses, and biotechnology firms all hire trained botanists.

Botanical gardens and arboreta (the plural of arboretum) also provide a place for botanists. Botanical gardens and arboreta are parks open to the general public, students, and research scientists. Plants, flowers, trees, and shrubs are collected from all over the world and exhibited in arrangements by family, country of origin, or with regard to aesthetics.

Typical visitors to botanical gardens and arboreta generally fall into six categories: dedicated professional scientists and horticulturalists who utilize the gardens' collections for research purposes or to identify specific plants; professional and amateur gardeners who participate in adult education classes and training programs; horticultural students enrolled in internship programs through their universities; local residents who come to enjoy a peaceful sanctuary; schoolchildren and their teachers; and international travelers and scientists interested in the collections and history of the gardens.

Public botanical gardens and arboreta play an important role in horticultural education. Through the design, interpretation, and management of a variety of collections of plants, trees, and shrubs, botanical gardens and arboreta perform the following functions:

Public Programs

Botanical gardens and arboreta generally offer public programs such as classes in gardening, question and answer hotlines to help with gardening problems, tours of the grounds, and lectures on the various collections. These programs help to teach people how to care for their plants, add to their knowledge of unusual or new plants, and help foster an understanding of and appreciation for landscape design.

Research

Most botanical gardens and arboreta are involved with ongoing research issues. Curators and other horticulturists go on collection trips to add to the types of plants in their gardens and to study the plant life in other geographic regions. Living plants are added to the grounds and pressed and dried plants are stored in herbaria and are shared with researchers all over the world. Through these activities, garden professionals are able to save rare and endangered plants by studying their requirements and offering a protected environment while reintroducing them to the wild.

Introduction of New Plants

Public gardens play a role in introducing new plants to the nursery and home landscaping markets through plant collecting, selection, and breeding.

Beautification

Public gardens provide a tranquil setting in the midst of busy cities for walkers and nature lovers.

Preservation

Historic gardens are preserved and interpreted to the public through the use of slides, films, lectures, brochures, and labels.

Conservation Education

Public gardens help both children and adults to develop an appreciation for gardening and a concern about protecting the natural environment.

Community Improvement

Public gardens participate in city beautification projects through education, plant breeding, and selection.

Plant biologists and biology majors with an interest in botany or training in related disciplines also find work in nurseries and floral shops, landscape architecture and design firms, and for the Cooperative Extension Service, which tries to bring university research into the community.

Botany offers a range of interesting and worthwhile career opportunities. The work is frequently varied and the surroundings usually pleasant. Because of the diversity in the plant sciences, people with many different educational backgrounds, skills, and interests can find a satisfying career in botany.

CAREER OUTLOOK

Plant science is becoming a very popular field as more and more people realize how important plants are to the many different aspects of society. Because of this, some areas are more competitive than others. For example, in recent years the number of ecology graduates has outnumbered the job openings. Other areas are more promising. For example, positions are open in agronomy and biotechnology.

But, much of research and development is funded by the federal government. Anticipated budget tightening should lead to smaller increases in research and development expenditures, further limiting the dollar amount of each grant and slowing the growth of the number of grants awarded to researchers. If, at the same time, the number of newly trained scientists continues to increase at a rate similar to that of the 1980s, both new and established scientists will experience greater difficulty winning and renewing research grants.

On a more positive note, new positions in botany are expected to increase at an above-average rate through the turn of the century. Growing world population continues to increase the need for better food supplies. Environmental concerns, such as air, water, and soil pollution, will create more openings for ecologists in government and industry. The search for new drugs and medicines and useful genes for improving crop plants will continue to create a need for botanical explorers.

A degree in botany provides a solid scientific foundation to make graduates more employable in many of the different botany fields.

CLOSE-UPS

With a degree as far-reaching as biology and a specialty of botany encompassing so many fields, it's impossible to give a full look at each one in the scope of just one book. However, to give you a taste of what a few selected careers are like that would appeal to some botany majors, read the following first-hand accounts. You'll find other first-hand accounts from people in related fields in the chapters to come. What better way to learn about a career than from a person working in the field?

RICK DARKE, CURATOR OF PLANTS
AT LONGWOOD GARDENS

Longwood Gardens is located in Kennett Square, Pennsylvania, a suburb of Philadelphia. Curator of plants, Rick Darke, explains its function:

"We're not really a botanic garden; we're a display garden, a pleasure garden. We have quite a few plants that could be called collections, but they exist for the sake of the landscape texture. That's how we differ from a traditional botanical garden. We have a lot more emphasis on the art of the landscape, the pleasure derived by people being in that landscape, than we have people coming to study these plants as objects.

"A botanical garden is usually a garden whose primary emphasis is collecting plants, keeping data on them for the purpose of display and study.

"Pierre Dupont, the founder of Longwood Gardens, was interested in creating a mood and a sense of place that would allow people to interact within a garden setting. Even though he had a lot of unusual and great specimens, his main emphasis was on the art of horticulture and the setting he was creating. At a botanical garden they worry secondly how well the spaces work for art or entertainment.

"We do have a research division at Longwood within our horticultural division, but our research is not at the micro level. In other words, we're not doing research on projects useful only in laboratory settings or that would not have much practical applicability. What we're trying to do is bring science to bear on display horticulture. We do have true Ph.D. scientists in our division but they're here to use their knowledge of science to help us be efficient, imaginative, and responsible to the environment in our fabricating of plant displays.

"It's a historic garden in some sense. There was an arboretum here started by a Quaker family who got the land from a grant from William Penn, whom Pennsylvania is named for. They planted trees in the 1780s that still exist today. It was that core arboretum that was the compelling factor in Pierre Dupont's decision to buy the property. The trees were due to be logged and Dupont bought the land to save them. He fell in love with the place and over the years developed Longwood Gardens around it.

"Pierre Dupont was an engineer who had a love of water in the garden, so he built fountain gardens which were inspired by his visits to Europe. These are major attractions. We also have a theater garden with live performances. The curtain is a curtain of water jets.

"There's also a topiary garden of abstract shapes and lots of wonderful old trees, grand vistas, and monumental architecture at the conservatories, with bronze windows and mica-shaded lamps inside.

"We intend it to be gorgeous and I think we succeed. We wow people in a very classy way."

Duties of a Curator of Plants

Longwood Gardens has a little over 1,000 acres; of that there are about 250 acres accessible to the public, and of that about 80 acres are actually display gardens.

Rick Darke has been at Longwood Gardens for close to 18 years. He talks about his job:

"I'm a plantsman for Longwood, someone who is knowledgeable about the diversity of plants that exists in the world because we grow plants from the world over. First and foremost, if there is any one thing that has to get done here, we keep everything at Longwood identified and labeled and that's the most important thing. I organize and oversee the identification, mapping, and labeling that is done by the curatorial assistants I supervise.

"I also have a very steady role in making recommendations and working in team settings to make and refine and restore the gardens at Longwood. To that end, I participate regularly on landscape and advisory committees. My role is to suggest plants we could use in place of what we're using now, or sometimes it overlaps into related areas. I'm often making comments on architectural details or labeling and other interpretive materials.

"I also get to travel a lot looking for new plants for Longwood. I've traveled to Australia, New Zealand, Japan, South Africa, Brazil, England, and Germany. I bring back beautiful

continued

continued

plants from all kinds of climates. We have four acres under glass here so we can grow things that are hardy. We can also create specialized environments that provide the essentials of the environment the plants are from.

"I do quite a bit of teaching, it's a considerable part of the job. We have many different student programs here and I regularly teach a botany course for our PG (Professional Gardener) students, and other classes for our graduate student program. I teach courses for our continuing education program, which includes evening lectures and field trips. I lead tours to native areas and other gardens.

"I also write. I contribute to our inhouse publication, which is essentially a record of the employees and happenings around the garden, and I also write articles for magazines on what Longwood is doing. For example, when I went to Brazil I worked with a landscape architect there and brought him back to Longwood. He made a garden for us and I wrote an article on that. I worked with our photographer to get that published. It's a celebration of the gardens at Longwood."

Rick is a member of the Garden Writers Association of America and is the author of *For Your Garden: Ornamental Grasses* (Little Brown).

The eclectic mix of his job and the interaction he gets to have with students is what Rick likes most about his work. "We usually have an intern in our office and I'm constantly teaching people as they move through the organization. Over the years you can imagine the wonderful network you make of friends and professional colleagues around the country and around the world.

"In my job I get to do something that's fun. It's not just going to work at eight and ending at five. It's much more than that. It really is something that teaches you. In these past 18 years I have become someone who loves his garden at home. I'm out there digging and planting and designing and it's gotten to the point that features of the garden are publishable, and it provides a source of photography. All of that has become a wonderful enrichment that comes from my job. Because it's so close to what I would do if I just had the time to play, it blurs the line between vocation and avocation.

The Skills You'll Need

Rick Darke suggests that the following skills, in addition to a love of plants, are necessary for success in his profession:

"You need good writing skills and verbal communication. I could not do what I do, and I would not have had the opportunities if I hadn't worked on being able to articulate my notions."

Rick Darke's Background

Rick has a bachelor's degree in plant sciences from the University of Delaware. "I took a circuitous route. I spent seven years as an undergraduate and went through art and anthropology on the way to plant science. Longwood was my first job. I started as an intern there, then moved into an assistant taxonomist position. I did go back and take some graduate courses in plant systematics and taxonomy. However, instead of going back and completing a graduate degree, it worked to my advantage to stay here. I ended up taking over a Ph.D. position in taxonomy that was rewritten as a curator of plants. The man I was working for was due to retire in two years and it was a question of would I learn more by staying on the job and developing the skills I'd need to take over, or would I learn more by getting into a graduate program. My choice to stay worked out."

SUSAN KELLEY, CURATORIAL ASSOCIATE

Susan Kelley is a curatorial associate for the living collections at Arnold Arboretum, located in Jamaica Plain, Massachusetts, a section of Boston. The arboretum is affiliated with Harvard University and its mission is the biology, cultivation, and conservation of temperate woody plants. Her job involves mapping the living specimens on the grounds and labeling each plant.

continued

continued

Getting Started

Susan started out as a violinist and earned both a bachelor's and master's degree in music before she decided to switch careers.

"I was freelancing in New York and it was a difficult life. I had plenty of work but everyone was so unhappy living there. Plants had always been an interest of mine growing up in Tennessee and I loved gardening.

"I went back to school to City University of New York and got my M.A. in plant population ecology.

"I worked at the Harvard University Herbaria in Cambridge for a while as a partial employee of Arnold Arboretum. So naturally I met people from the Arnold Arboretum; they would come to Cambridge, and I would go to Jamaica Plain. When my current position became available I applied. I prefer being outdoors as opposed to working indoors all day.

"Because of the relationship of Harvard and the Arboretum we are all technically employees of Harvard—and we get all the benefits of a Harvard employee. We can take courses for forty dollars, there are excellent health benefits, life insurance, and a free pass to all the museums in Boston and the surrounding area."

On the Job

"We're more than a horticultural garden. Our collections are used scientifically. We have a lot of visitors from all over the world who use our collections for study. Maps showing where each individual plant is on the grounds have been kept since the 1930s.

"Right now we're in the process of switching over from a series of about 100 hand-drawn maps to a computerized mapping system using a computer-aided design system. We're honing down to about 65 maps plus insets. My job is not only to transcribe the hand-drawn maps to the computerized ones, but also to maintain current hand-drawn maps in the interim. We have two major plantings a year, in the spring and in the fall, and probably 1,000 new plants go out every year onto the grounds. My job is to put the new plantings on the maps.

"I also field check each individual specimen for condition. If it's damaged I let the propagator know it might need to be repropagated. I recommend to the horticultural taxonomist or the superintendent of the grounds if something needs to be removed. The plant could be dying, diseased, or suffering damage from the weather or vandalism.

"I'm also responsible for making sure that every plant is labeled. The labels are hung directly on the plant. Each plant is supposed to have two labels that give an accession number, the name of the plant, the family, where it came from, and the map location.

"When a plant goes from the nursery to the grounds I take over and maintain the records on each plant. We have about 15,000 on the grounds now. My boss is the horticultural taxonomist and we work very closely together. He decides what goes out on the grounds every spring and fall, assessing what's in the nursery and what will be planted. He puts together the planting bulletins that are then handed to me. I use those to map the new plantings.

"And I'm supposed to be able to identify everything. Labels do get lost sometimes, or switched by the public. If there are any problems and I can't figure out what a plant is, for example, I ask him. There are specific plant families he's interested in and people from all over the world send him things to identify.

"The labels I'm responsible for are the size of a credit card and are made out of anodized aluminum. We gather the information on the plant from our computer's database and lay it out with the correct number of lines and spaces. We have an embossing machine that actually prints out the labels.

"Seventy percent of my time is spent outdoors, even in the winter. I have a lot of mapping and record keeping to do then. It's a great time to field check the conifer collection, the pines, the firs, the spruce, etc. You can also find labels more easily when there aren't any leaves on the trees, because they're hung above the ground level. With shrubs, though, it's a disaster to find the labels when there's snow on the ground."

continued

continued

The Pluses and Minuses

"What I love most is being outdoors in this great collection of plants. It's one of the best collections in the world. There are very old specimens and then we have all these new plants coming in. I also like that I have some indoor work. The computer work I do is challenging mentally. The mix is ideal.

"The only stress I have is that we're understaffed and my job is extensive enough that three people should really be doing it. I do have volunteers I coordinate and I have two interns in the summertime who help. But managing people can also add to the stress. You have to take the time to train them and it's extra work. We get applicants from all over the world for the internship program here and we don't interview in person. It's always tricky to interview someone over the phone and try to get an idea of how they would work out.

"But whenever I need to regroup I can just go outside. I have a beautiful place in which to do it."

The Career Ladder for Mappers and Labelers

Susan discusses the options:

"This is a great job; I could feasibly stay here for a long time. There's so much more to learn. For example, there's another mapping system I'm interested in—GIS, Geographic Information System.

"With more experience, more study and research and publications, one could move up into a curatorial position. I'd want to become more proficient with taxonomic work and go on collecting trips. We have a research program in Indonesia and I'd love to go there one day and do mapping at their botanical gardens."

EARNINGS

According to the National Association of Colleges and Employers, beginning salary offers in private industry in 1997 averaged $25,400 a year for bachelor's degree recipients in biological science; about $36,900 for master's degree recipients; and about $52,400 for doctoral degree recipients.

Median annual earnings for biological and life scientists were about $36,300 in 1996; the middle 50 percent earned between $28,400 and $50,900. Ten percent earned less than $22,000, and 10 percent earned more than $66,000.

In the federal government in 1997, general biological scientists in non-supervisory, supervisory, and managerial positions earned an average salary of $52,100; microbiologists averaged $58,700; ecologists, $52,700; physiologists, $65,900; and geneticists, $62,700.

The sense of accomplishment and satisfaction that comes from doing interesting and worthwhile work is one of the rewards of a career in plant science. In addition, many positions in botany provide other benefits such as individual freedom, varied work, pleasant surroundings, stimulating associates, and the opportunity to travel.

Salaries always depend on experience and education. In addition, the geographical location of the employer also makes a difference. In general, salaries vary with the cost of living in any particular region.

TRAINING AND QUALIFICATIONS

A bachelor's degree is the usual minimum requirement for most careers in botany. With a bachelor's degree, graduates can find positions as laboratory technicians or technical assistants in education, industry, government, museums, parks, and botanical gardens.

As is true in many other fields, the more education you have, the wider the range of positions that are open to you. Many positions require a master's or doctorate.

The Ph.D. is required for most teaching and research positions in colleges and universities.

The courses you select in your undergraduate program will vary depending on the curriculum of the college you attend and your own interests. To be best prepared for the job market, you should get a broad general education in language, arts, humanities, and the social sciences in addition to specializing in plant biology. Most positions require good oral and written skills and computer abilities, too.

Most botany programs require courses in math and statistics, as well as chemistry and physics. For those hoping to work abroad, foreign language expertise is also desirable.

Many colleges and universities require a core program in biology before you can enroll in specialized botany courses. At other institutions you are allowed to take botany courses right away.

STRATEGIES FOR FINDING THE JOBS

In any type of career pursuit, coupling hands-on training with your theoretical program is highly desirable. If possible, arrange to do field work or an undergraduate research project under one of your professors. The project might include helping the professor with his or her research or pursuing your own interests. The experience will help you decide the area or areas of botany you like best—or might want to avoid. Research experience will also be very helpful should you decide to pursue graduate work.

In addition, internships, work study, cooperative education, or summer jobs can provide important additional experience. Students who establish themselves during one of these programs often find they have a foot firmly planted in the door once graduation comes and they are looking for full-time employment.

These positions occur in government agencies, college and university research laboratories, botanical gardens and arboreta, agricultural experiment stations, freshwater and marine biological stations, and within private industries.

The more experience you can add to your resume while you're still studying, the more employable you'll be.

Don't forget your faculty members and advisors as a great source of leads and contacts. Networking really does work.

Contact the following professional associations for more information about careers in botany. Many publish books, pamphlets, and brochures with career information, as well as newsletters and journals that list job openings.

PROFESSIONAL ASSOCIATIONS

American Institute of Biological Sciences
730 11th Street NW
Washington, DC 20001-4584

American Physiological Association
1200 17th Street NW
Washington, DC 20036

American Phytopathological Society
3340 Pilot Knob Road
St. Paul, MN 55121

American Society for Horticultural Science
600 Cameron St.
Alexandria, VA 22314

American Society of Agronomy
677 S. Segoe Road
Madison, WI 53711

American Society of Plant Physiologists
15501-A Monona Drive
Rockville, MD 20955-2768

American Society of Plant Taxonomists
Department of Botany
University of Wyoming
Laramie, WY 82071-3165

Botanical Society of America
Business Office
1725 Neil Avenue
Columbus, OH 43210-1293

Ecological Society of America
2010 Massachusetts Avenue NW
Suite 400
Washington, DC 20036

**Mycological Society of America
and Phycological Society of America**
P.O. Box 1897
Lawrence, KS 66044-8897

The Mycological Society of America
Department of Botany
University of Toronto, Erindale Campus
Mississuaga, Ontario
Canada L5L IC6

Palentology Research Institute
1259 Trumansberg Road
Ithaca, NY 14850

Society of American Foresters
5400 Grosvenor Lane
Bethesda, MD 20814
(forestry career packet)

CHAPTER ELEVEN

PATH 2: ZOOLOGISTS

f or some the term *zoology* conjures up images of bespectacled gentlemen peering through microscopes or gutsy women out in the wild communing with chimpanzees or gorillas. The reality is that zoology is a broad field that defies stereotypes and offers many career choices.

A counterpart to botany, zoology is the discipline of biology that studies animals. Zoologists include in the definition of animals: birds, insects, reptiles, fish, invertebrates, mammals, and microscopic organisms. Zoology covers physiology on a microscopic level, development throughout an animal's lifespan, the interaction of animals with their environments, and how things have changed over long periods of time. Zoologists study both land and marine animal life at all levels of organization: ecosystem, community, population, whole organism, cellular, and molecular.

Just as with botany, which was covered in the previous chapter, knowledge of biological principles related to zoology is central to the well-being of mankind, particularly at a time when increasing populations and the accompanying strain are hurting our planet's ecosystems. There is also a new awareness of the need to solve health and social problems. Many zoologists are also addressing humane and ethical issues.

DEFINITION OF THE CAREER PATH

Zoology is a discipline that offers a broad choice of career paths. Your degree can serve you well in a number of settings, from industry to health care. In short, you can find zoologists employed in the obvious as well as most unexpected places.

Zoology can be viewed as a basic science or an applied one. As a basic science, the zoologist satisfies his or her curiosity about living things but does not consider whether the information gained is immediately useful.

Applied or field scientists use their knowledge for the betterment of mankind and animal life.

Zoology can be broadly grouped into the following categories:

Applied zoology includes wildlife management, environmental protection, agriculture, fisheries, aquaculture, and public education programs such as those found in zoos and aquariums.

Behavior experts study animal behavior for a number of purposes including handling, training, and research.

Ecology studies the interactions of animals with other organisms and the environment.

Evolution and systematics study evolutionary history and relationships among animals.

Molecular biology (as related to zoology) and genetics study the structure and function of biological macromolecules, including the biochemical and molecular aspects of genetics.

Morphology studies macroscopic animal forms.

Paleontology studies the fossil remains of animals (and plants). Scientists trace the evolution and development of past life and use fossils to reconstruct prehistoric environments and geography. They also make models of animals that have become extinct, such as dinosaurs.

Physiology investigates the functions and vital processes of animals.

Systematics or Taxonomy is the identification and study of the kinds of organisms of the past and living today, and of the relationships among these organisms.

POSSIBLE JOB SETTINGS

Education

This sector is probably the largest employer of graduates with a degree in biology. Opportunities in schools, colleges, and universities are discussed in Chapter 14.

Health Care

A degree in biology and specifically in zoology can be the stepping stone for work as a medical clinician, scientist, or technician. Opportunities in the medical field are covered in depth in Chapter 13.

Government

Although many positions in government involve policymaking and regulation, other government scientists are engaged in basic and applied research. The Bureau of Land Management, Bureau of Indian Affairs, Bureau of Reclamation, U.S. Forestry Service, the U.S. Fish and Wildlife Service, U.S. Army Corps of Engineers, the U.S. Department of Agriculture, Department of Defense, the U.S. Food and Drug Administration, the Department of Environmental Protection and Energy, the National Park Service, and the Department of the Interior are just a few of the federal agencies that employ zoologists.

Industry

Most zoologists with positions in industry are likely to be involved in research and product development. However, many jobs in industry and commerce do not necessarily involve the direct application of knowledge gained from a zoology degree. Employers prefer applicants with university degrees and utilize their talents in sales and management positions.

Information and Arts

There is a wide spectrum of jobs in publishing, broadcasting, and filmmaking for zoology majors. With the general public's increased interest in current science and technology issues, particularly those related to the environment, conservation, and health, there is a large market for nature-related programs, books, and articles.

Newspapers and magazines run regular features and need writers with scientific backgrounds to translate their knowledge into language that is easily understood by the general public.

Publishers of professional journals also need biologists for inhouse editing and publishers of textbooks might require biological illustrators.

Many industries require skilled writers to produce technical documents describing their products and their proper use. A bachelor's degree is usually adequate for these types of positions but additional training in communications, journalism, or broadcasting, as well as demonstrated writing skill, is often required.

Museums, Zoos, and Aquariums

For many field zoologists, museums, zoos, and aquariums are the natural choice for a career setting and offer many different kinds of positions for those with a zoology degree. Positions involve research, working directly with the animals, administration, and public education.

Although aquatic science is an area of zoology, it is such a large—and popular—field, it can be considered a separate career path and, thus, has been given the attention it deserves in its own chapter, Chapter 12.

POSSIBLE JOB TITLES

Because of the varied job settings, the job titles a biology major can hold are as equally varied. There is often overlap, too, between the different job settings. You can find a curator, for example, working in a natural history museum or in a zoo or marine park.

Here is an alphabetical listing of many of the most common job titles. Your own research will probably allow you to add to the list:

Agricultural scientist	Environmental lawyer
Agricultural zoologist	Environmental physiologist
Animal attendant	Ethologist
Animal behavior consultant	Fisheries biologist
Animal behaviorist	Food and drug officer
Animal nutritionist	Forester
Animal physiologist	Game manager
Apiarist	Herpitologist
Aquarist	Ichthyologist
Aquarium/Zoo director	Life sciences technician
Conservation officer	Mammalogist
Curator	Marine biologist
Developmental biologist/Embryologist	Microbiologist
Entomologist	Molecular biologist
Environmental impact analyst	Museum technician

Naturalist

Natural resources manager

Nature center director

Oceanographer

Ornithologist

Parasitologist

Program manager

Research officer

Systematic biologist

Taxidermist

Trainer

Wildlife biologist

Zookeeper

Zoologist

CAREER OUTLOOK

Present demographic data indicate there will be a shortage of trained scientists, including zoologists, into the 21st century. But predictions are never 100 percent reliable and it is best to be prepared for the tough competition the field always enjoys.

With zoology careers, just like in any other profession, the best trained and most experienced applicants will get the best jobs.

GETTING AHEAD

From the beginning of your degree program you should be aware that your academic record will follow you wherever you go. You will be competing with other new graduates, and in addition to personal references and hands-on training earned through internships or work-study positions, your grade point average will be another criterion used to judge you.

Getting ahead in your chosen career can also be closely linked to your academic performance. For example, a scholarship might be necessary to pursue a master's or doctorate degree or you may need to take an expensive course that has a fee-wavier for students with the strongest needs and the best records.

In addition to your academic record, you will need to acquire practical experience as soon as possible during your undergraduate years. Most university departments and many government agencies and private industries provide summer job opportunities or academic year internships, co-op jobs, or work-study programs for research assistants or other entry-level positions.

These positions will not only provide you with the training you need, they will also help you make valuable contacts that will be useful for permanent career positions after your formal education has been completed.

Communication skills are also crucial to getting ahead in this field. Concise writing and the ability to make oral presentations are part of most jobs.

Computer literacy is also a fundamental skill most employers require of their new hirees.

When choosing your training program, remember also that those with combined degrees will fare best in certain fields. For example, a B.S.-level zoologist who goes on to earn a law degree can work in environmental law, or a zoologist with a communications minor can work as a scientific writer or illustrator.

CLOSE-UPS

LEON FAGER, THREATENED AND ENDANGERED SPECIES PROGRAM MANAGER (Retired)

Leon Fager worked for the U.S. Forest Service for 31 years and was posted in a variety of places such as Arizona (Soil Conservation Service); Las Vegas (Nevada Game and Fish Department); Custer, South Dakota, in Black Hills National Forest; Michigan State University (Forest Service Long-Term Training); Lakewood, Colorado (Rocky Mountain Regional Office); and Albuquerque, New Mexico (Southwestern Region Regional Office).

He earned his B.S. in wildlife management from the University of Arizona in Tucson in 1965 and his M.S. in forestry from Michigan State University in East Lansing in 1983.

His Attraction to the Field

"I chose the biology profession because of my interest in wildlife and wildlands. I used to hunt and in those days I couldn't think of a better job than working with the animals I hunted. I don't hunt now. Instead, I enjoy doing work with nonhunting, environmental groups such as the Audubon Society.

"When I was in high school I knew a few people that were working in the wildlife field and I became very interested in their work and decided to commit myself to the profession. I lived near three National Wildlife Refuges and became

continued

continued

familiar with the management of habitat for waterfowl and desert bighorn sheep in these areas. It was always a special experience for me to be out in these areas where the influence of man was minimal.

"The work appealed to me because with most wildlife and fish habitat improvement projects you can see immediate results, the wildlife or fish benefiting from my work. I enjoyed being part of a national effort to improve conditions for wildlife on our public lands."

What the Job's Really Like

"The entry-level biologist in a federal or state agency spends time learning how the agency functions and how to implement its mission. When I first started, I worked with foresters, range conservationists, soil scientists, engineers, and others to get a feel of how the different jobs fit together. I spent a lot of time helping foresters design timber sites to provide food and cover for wildlife such as elk and turkey. This is done by planning areas where the harvest of timber can create openings but leave dense timber areas for cover. We also developed water for wildlife in these areas.

"The Endangered Species Act requires that the Forest Service protect habitat for all federally listed species. The biologist must survey large areas for the presence of rare species such as the goshawk and spotted owl. The reason we did this was to ensure that Forest Service management activities such as harvesting timber do not destroy nesting and cover areas for these species.

"Once the survey is done, the biologist prepares a report on the possible impact of the proposed project on listed species. The report is then sent to the U.S. Fish and Wildlife Service for their review and concurrence.

"Today most of the biologists' time is spent reviewing land management projects and preparing reports.

"As I progressed in the Forest Service I spent less time in the field and a lot of time doing administrative activities such as formulating the budget and planning.

"The Forest Service is the object of many lawsuits and I found myself preparing litigation reports on lawsuits involving alleged violations of the Endangered Species Act.

"I was responsible for coordination with other federal and state agencies such as the U.S. Fish and Wildlife Service and state wildlife agencies. The states are involved because they manage the wildlife, whereas the Forest Service manages the habitat.

"I also worked closely with conservation organizations such as Ducks Unlimited. These organizations provided money to the Forest Service for habitat improvement projects. I would design the project, oversee the construction, and provide a completion report to the organization. Examples are wildlife water development, wetland development, and stream improvement."

The Upsides and Downsides

"In my early years in the Forest Service I enjoyed the work because I spent most of my time outdoors, working on various projects. I received a great deal of satisfaction, seeing one of my projects completed and having wildlife use it. The people I worked with were great and the Forest Service was like a big family.

"In my later years, prior to my retirement, I spent most of my time working in the office. Most of the work involved litigation reports in relation to the Endangered Species Act and other environmental laws. I didn't enjoy this as I felt that biologists were being used to defend livestock grazing and timber harvesting, practices that most of us felt were damaging to wildlife habitat.

"Working for a federal agency is a very structured experience. I was required to be at work at a given time, keep a time sheet, and follow regulations. Performance is measured more by the ability to follow the rules and being loyal to the Forest Service than creativity and production."

Salary Structures

"The salaries are structured by a schedule from the Civil Service Commission. Each job is classified by the complexity and skills needed to do the job. They're scaled as GS ratings and most entry-level biologists come in at either a GS-5 or GS-7. The GS-7 is for those with advanced degrees. I began

continued

continued

my career as a GS-5 and retired as a GS-13 at $65,000 per year. A GS-5 now earns around $20,000 per year.

Advice from Leon Fager

"In college I think it would be very valuable to take as many political science, communications, and social science courses as possible. Students like to take the biology courses because that's what they're interested in, but when you get into the job you soon find that politics and your ability to effectively communicate is just, and maybe more, important than the biology.

"After graduation, my advice is to find work either with a state wildlife agency or a private contractor. I think that the Forest Service is going to continue to be the whipping boy for interest groups and will be a very stressful place to work. Biologists are becoming discouraged that they are not able to be proactive in improving wildlife habitat, but rather are faced with the task of defending timber sales and livestock grazing on National Forests.

"State agencies work with animals and are generally less structured than the Forest Service. The opportunity to be in the field is much greater. There is an increasing number of private contractors who do surveys, reports, and projects for the Forest Service. I suggest that this would be a good place to work without having to conform to the rules and regulations of the Forest Service."

ELIZABETH JOHNSON, SENIOR ZOOKEEPER

Elizabeth Johnson is a senior zookeeper at the Detroit Zoological Institute in Royal Oak, Michigan. She earned her B.S. in biology in 1988 from Saginaw Valley State University in Saginaw, Michigan, and her Master's of Science, also in biology, in 1995 from Wayne State University Graduate School in Detroit. Elizabeth has been working in the field since 1988.

Getting Started

"Actually zookeeping never occurred to me as a career. I was going to school for a career in research involving animals. After graduating from Saginaw Valley State University in May 1988, I was hired by the Belle Isle Nature Center. I was responsible for performing naturalist duties, such as caring for the animals in their shelter, giving talks, and doing rehabilitation work with injured wildlife.

"In March of 1989, while still employed with the nature center, I was picking up an application for another job when I found out that the city had just opened the position for zookeeper and was accepting applications. I decided to turn in an application, and was hired by the Detroit Zoo three months later."

What the Job Is Like

"I have been employed at the Detroit Zoological Institute for almost eight years now. Zookeeping is a very interesting career. It seems as though there are never two days alike. You learn something new everyday. When I first started, I could not believe I was actually getting paid for doing what I was doing.

"I have been taking care of elephants and rhinos for seven and a half years now. Recently, our elephant unit has picked up the care of the giraffe, too. There are five keepers in the elephant unit. We have three female Asian elephants (ages 32, 39, and 46), one Black Rhino (age 45), and three giraffe (two males ages 15 and 5, and one female age 11). A typical day for me begins with all the keepers meeting in the administration basement so that the head keepers can pass out daily duties or advise us on any changes that have taken place. The keepers then all go to the exhibit they are assigned for that day. For me, I start either at the elephant house or the giraffe house (taking turns among the keepers in our unit).

"First order of business is to check all the animals under your care that day to make sure all are well. Then the fun part begins—all the cleaning of the exhibits. The cleaning usually takes a couple of hours. Then every day at 10:30 we

continued

continued

bathe our elephants for the public to see. The bath usually lasts for about an hour. During the bath we hose them off, scrub their skin for any stains, and perform footcare on them. Since elephants in captivity are restricted to the area in their exhibit, footcare is very important. We file and sand their nails to prevent them from growing too long. If their nails are too long, they can become cracked and lead to further problems. We also trim their cuticles regularly and most important, we trim the bottoms of their feet. The bottom of an elephant's foot is like a hard callus that can get many cracks and grooves. If these cracks and grooves are not cleaned out and trimmed, they can lead to infections. We do a little footcare on each one daily. We keep the sessions short and pleasant. The elephants don't seem to mind at all; they are used to their routine footcare. During the bath we scrub their skin so as not to get a build-up of dead skin. After the bath, if it is during the summer, we will lead them into their pool in their yard. After coming out of their pool they will head directly to their sandbox and start dusting themselves, protecting their skin from the sun and insects. If it is too cold, they will get sawdust for dusting.

"Usually by this time it is lunch time. After lunch at 1:00 we perform a demonstration with the elephants for the public. We will tail them up and walk them around the pool, then work them individually, picking up logs, pushing logs, and lying down. After their demonstration, we give them each a treat bucket of hay and then answer any questions from the public.

"During the winter we take the elephants for laps inside for exercise. After this we usually go "browse hunting" for our animals. We venture out for grapevine, mulberry, elm, maple, sorghum, and bamboo. Of course, browse is limited in the winter here in Michigan, but the elephants still eat trees with no leaves. Occasionally, they will also get palm that has been trimmed back from the birdhouse.

"The few hours we have left in the day are spent on providing behavioral enrichment for our animals and doing extra cleaning of our exhibits and extra duty handed out from the head keepers. This can include unloading hay truck pallets, moving other animals to different exhibits, cutting grass, weed-whacking, cleaning exhibit pools, performing overall maintenance of our buildings (painting, dusting), and helping out other keepers on their exhibits doing jobs too labor intensive for one person.

"By this time of the day we start setting up the exhibits for closing, the animals' food is put down, they are brought inside, and secured for the evening. A little more cleaning and the day is over.

"The job can be both busy or relaxed. It just depends on the day. Overall, I feel by keeping busy during the day, I go home feeling as if I have accomplished quite a bit. I feel more rewarded."

The Upsides and Downsides

"Working with elephants can be very rewarding. In a sense you are more than just a handler, you are actually part of their herd, your little family away from home. They are very intelligent and affectionate animals and a pleasure to work with. I have learned a lot. You have respect for them and they respect you. It's a mutual relationship. Knowing that you are responsible for the daily care of these animals and doing it correctly and efficiently leaves you with a great feeling. Observing your animals can also be fun, watching them eat the trees you just cut down for them, or watching the elephants splash and play in the big sprinkler you hooked up for them over their sandbox, just knowing that you are doing your best to make sure that these animals have the best possible care that you can give them.

"You can also be rewarded in other ways. I have been sent to three elephant managers' conferences. At one I presented a paper written with one of my co-workers.

"It's never boring, but you can get cabin fever in the winter, the animals too. I really do not dislike that much about the job other than some of the politics that can get in the way, such as disagreeing with your boss."

Advice from Elizabeth Johnson

"You should realize that taking care of animals is a great responsibility and just do the best you can possibly do. Being

continued

continued
a zookeeper can be a very rewarding and educational career."

MARY LEE NITSCHKE, ANIMAL BEHAVIORIST

Mary Lee Nitschke has a Ph.D. in comparative developmental psychobiology from Michigan State University and more than 30 years' experience in this exciting field. In addition to the many hats she wears, Dr. Nitschke is also a consultant to the Metro Washington Park Zoo in Portland, Oregon. Dr. Nitschke explains: "The Washington Park Zoo employs a full-time animal behaviorist. I work on a consulting basis with her, doing training seminars for zookeepers on how to interact with and handle animals.

"I also give talks on wolf-dog crosses because the zoo gets questions about them all the time. The zoo has wolves so people come to us with their concerns about their own pets and they want answers to their questions. The Northwest is a hotbed for people owning wolves as pets. It's pretty hard on everyone, though it doesn't keep people from doing it. From a wolf-dog cross, the biggest problem I see professionally is the quality of life for that animal. If it's high percentage wolf, it's likely to be terrified of people. The second problem is unpredictability. We have no way of knowing when the wolf part is going to be operative and when the dog part is. These wolf-dog crosses have a rap very similar to pit bulls and rottweilers. It's not the same problem at all, but it looks like the same problem because they maul children frequently.

"I also do training with the zookeepers, teaching them how to manage animals in the zoo environment and how to understand and use operant behavior and clicker training. The animal is trained to click a bar that will deliver food to it as a reward. One of my colleagues was working with a chimp that was diabetic and needed to have a blood sample drawn every day. Through clicker training, she taught the chimp to put its arm in a sleeve outside the cage and grasp a bar so that the blood sample could be taken quickly and efficiently without anybody being endangered. The reward was food and the animal was fine about it.

"Another one she did was to teach an elephant to present its feet for cleaning through the fence. This was an aggressive male elephant and nobody could go in and do this. Through operant conditioning, it was taught to hold its feet up to a little panel and then they could be cleaned that way.

"I also worked with one of their birds of prey that wouldn't allow keepers in so we did some work with that. Basically, when they have a problem they call me."

Becoming an Animal Behaviorist

"For someone who wants to become an animal behaviorist, first of all, you have to have hands-on experience. And the more time you spend observing animals and learning how to interact with them, the better off you're going to be. The second thing is that you have to get educated to learn to understand, evaluate, and think like a scientist.

"Hands-on experience is very important. I don't think this is a profession that can be done totally by theory. On the other hand, the hands-on experience can't come totally from trial and error methods.

"I think the best route is to take a lot of experimental courses—psychology or in other fields. Some anthropology courses do a good job of preparing people. There are disciplines of animal behavior both within psychology and zoology. I think that a good psychology background is important, not just for experimental psych, but if you take a major in psychology in almost any school in the country, you will have to take experimental psychology and statistics."

The Different Hats an Animal Behaviorist Wears

In addition to her zoo consulting work, Dr. Nitschke is a full-time tenured, full professor in the psychology department at Linfield College in Portland, Oregon. There she teaches a variety of courses from Applied Animal Behavior and Human-Animal Relationships to People-Pet Partnerships in Health Care.

continued

continued

She is also owner of Animal School Incorporated (in Beaverton, Oregon), and through private consultations and classes, provides clients with help in solving pet behavior problems.

Here is an example of the kind of problems she sees. "Recently, a fellow came in with a six-year-old bull dog mix. It looked an awful lot like a pit bull: big dog, 90 pounds, and he had bitten about seven people. I reviewed each bite. Some of these bites are almost to be expected because they resulted from inappropriate behavior on the part of the owner. In one instance the owner sent a plumber carrying a pipe into the dog's territory without announcing him. Well, he already knew the dog was territorial and didn't usually admit strangers. I don't count that bite. That was to be expected. In another instance, a teenage boy had been playing with the dog, then turned very abruptly and jumped on his bike and the dog went for him. Given this particular dog, the probability of that happening is pretty high, and when you add all those bites up, the probability that the dog is going to bite again is also very high. Putting the dog to sleep is one of the major options I counseled him about, but you can't make that decision for the client. My job in that situation is to say, here are the likely scenarios—what will happen if you do nothing or if you do this, that, or the other.

"What he wanted from me was to give him a training program that would guarantee that the dog wouldn't bite anyone again. But there is no such program. Most of the time you're working with the person, not the animal, and that's why you must have some grounding in counseling to do this work."

In addition, Dr. Nitschke does a lot of public speaking and is also a consultant for the invisible fencing industry. "Those are the major things," Dr. Nitschke explains, "but other things come up. I do training for the animal control people sometimes. I train them on how to handle animals, how to approach an animal when they have to go onto a property—because that's one of the most dangerous jobs in the world, going onto an animal's property and trying to pick it up."

How Mary Lee Nitschke Got Started

"I grew up on the range in Texas and my major entertainment and stimulation came from observing animals. One of my earliest memories is lying in the grass watching bobwhite quails coming to drink water in the summer. My young life was devoted to animals.

"I had spent a lot of time with animals, horses especially, both showing them and training them and when I got to college I was attracted to both engineering psychology—because I was in love with machines—and animal behavior.

"What I thought was so interesting and has fueled me throughout life in some ways, was that the theoretical stuff I was learning in college, psychology and learning theory, seemed to me to be wasted if it wasn't applied. Yet my professors knew nothing about training and here we were discussing learning theory.

"And by the same token, trainers knew nothing about learning theory. I couldn't imagine that both of these areas couldn't be enriched by the other so I kept bouncing back and forth between what was going on in the training world and what was going on in learning theory in the academic world. And then when I got to grad school and discovered I could actually study this as an academic subject, too, I was just fascinated with putting that together.

"Most of my research in graduate school was aimed at the 'interspecies communication of distress.' In my dissertation I did research with bobwhite quail, jack rabbits, coyotes, blue jays, and human babies. What I was looking for was whether there was some universality of understanding of the distress call between species.

"After I graduated I taught at Michigan State University. I taught operant behavior among other things, then I taught pet communication patterns in the veterinary school there and I taught developmental psychobiology with a specialization in toxicology—again looking across species—what the common elements are in how toxins affect behavior in various species.

continued

continued

"Before I even went to college I trained horses. What I later realized is that I trained every animal I came into contact with—I just didn't realize that's what it was called.

"While I was an undergraduate, one of the things that fueled my interest in applied psychology was that I started out working in a kennel that bred and trained collies. It was really one of the golden fortunes of my life that the couple I worked for had incredible integrity and ethics about breeding. They bred for the love of the dog and could not be bought by local fashions and current fads. They knew exactly what they were breeding for—solid temperaments. I learned an incredible amount from them. I started there just cleaning dog runs and by the time I left I was handling their line of collies professionally."

Animal Assisted Therapy

Another arena in which people work is animal assisted therapy. Dr. Nitschke explains: "Animal assisted therapy is where the animal becomes part of the therapeutic process with people. They can be used with a wide range of problems, anything from a social dog for a child who may have emotional/social problems, up through people who need a dog as a prosthesis as a seeing eye, hearing ear, or seizure alert dog, for example. Animal behaviorists train animals for these roles."

Dr. Nitschke is also involved teaching others about hippotherapy and how to work with horses to help humans with neuromuscular difficulties. "I hope I'm carving out a path that will become more common as the years go by—teaching people to use animals therapeutically. One of these programs is called People-Pet Partnerships in Health Care.

"Hippotherapy is horseback riding directed by a physical therapist or a kinesiologist. The movement of the horse is used as a way of stimulating neuromuscular interaction patterns with the person. My mission with this course is to teach people in the medical field some of the wonderful possibilities that are available therapeutically with animals.

"Another application is showcased by the work of Dr. Mary Birch. She works with crack babies who have no inhibitory control and scream most of the time. Those babies are very hard for the nurses to take care of. It is also very hard to impact them in any way.

"What Dr. Birch did was use a concept called entrainment. You take the rhythm that's occurring in the patient and you match something to it that will correspond to that rhythm and then you start bringing it down. She started with little, active, very flighty finches in a cage right next to the baby. The babies eventually entrained on those finches. Then, what she did was substitute the finches with other birds that moved more slowly, to the point where she could finally put a chinchilla in with that baby and it would soothe the baby. It's a combination of biofeedback, animal behavior, and circadian rhythm. There are all sorts of ways that, if you understand what is happening with the animal and its behavior, you can use it therapeutically."

Training Trainers

Teaching other people how to train animals is a viable career path for animal behaviorists. Although the notion of training animals for circuses or television or film work might be abhorrent to some (there are many people who believe that animals should be left in the wild and not used for any purposes related to mankind's needs), as mentioned earlier, animals can be humanely trained to interact with humans in a therapeutic setting. (See more on training animals for medical behaviors in Chapter 12.)

"There are a lot of folks out there who still believe that punishment is the most effective and most efficient way to train. If you get a trainer who believes that and also does not have good anger management, then the potential for abuse arises very quickly. I spend a lot of time trying to educate people about what it means to be a humane trainer. What we teach is essentially the same thing that is taught in positive parenting classes—rewarding good behavior, ignoring the bad. That's traditional behavior modification."

Income for Animal Behaviorists

Salaries will vary widely depending upon the specific work you do and the area of the country in which you live. Those

continued

continued

working for a university would expect to be on the same pay scale as any other faculty member of the same rank and experience.

As a consultant and trainer, Dr. Mary Lee Nitschke says, "I charge everyone $90 an hour, no matter what I'm doing for them. All my consulting is $90 an hour. I set that fee based on the average fee that psychologists charge in my area. And it's about to go up. I'll probably go up to $100 or a little over that. Right now, we have about 20 different classes and the cost is about $85 to $90 per student for a set of six classes."

LION COUNTRY SAFARI

Lion Country Safari, a private zoological park in West Palm Beach, Florida, offers visitors the chance to drive through 500 acres of natural wildlife preserve. More than 1,000 wild animals from all over the world roam freely, including lions, giraffes, chimpanzees, bison, ostrich, antelope, elephants, rhinos, and many more. On the grounds there is also a petting zoo, a newborn nursery, paddleboats, and a campground.

Lion Country Safari's philosophy is to educate and entertain as well as provide a safe habitat where many endangered species may live and breed.

The Curator's Role at Lion Country Safari

There are two curators at Lion Country Safari, each responsible for different areas of the park as well as for the people who take care of those areas.

The Curator of the Preserve is responsible for the drive-through area of the park. He manages the care of all the large antelope, lions, elephants, chimps, and others. He organizes the keepers and schedules them and makes sure that everything that is supposed to be accomplished in a day gets done. He also works closely with the director (see the first-hand account of Lion Country Safari's wildlife director next), suggesting breeding plans and programs.

The Curator of the Nursery manages this area in the walk-through area of the park. The curator is responsible for the nursery itself and also for the bird and primate exhibits, the reptile park, the petting zoo, and the hospital.

TERRY WOLF, WILDLIFE DIRECTOR, LION COUNTRY SAFARI

Terry Wolf is the wildlife director at Lion Country Safari. He is responsible for all animal-oriented operations in the park including husbandry, diet, construction of exhibits, breeding programs, personnel training, and acquisitions of materials and feed. He supervises 25 keepers, two curators, and an animal manager.

Terry Wolf's Background

"I have always had a love for animals. When I was a kid I worked in poodle shops and pet shops. One of the first jobs I had was bathing dogs and taking care of them. I guess I could blame my mother for this. She got me involved in a lot of this when I was younger, especially working with dogs.

"I had a break in college and needed to find work so I applied at Lion Country Safari and got a job in the maintenance department. That was in 1970. I worked my way up the ranks through the entertainment end of it, taking care of the boat ride and other rides. But I always wanted to be a keeper and, when an opening came about, I applied and was hired. I worked up through the ranks on that side and I was transferred to another park in Texas, owned by the same people, where I was made a manager. I stayed there for several years, but they went bankrupt in the seventies so I went back to school and got my master's degree.

"I then came back to Lion Country Safari in the early eighties and because there were no upper-level jobs open at the time, I took a temporary position working the elephant ride. Within six months, I was promoted to the Wildlife Director position."

continued

continued

Working at Lion Country Safari

"I enjoy working with the animals the most, but now a lot of my job involves people and management and safety concerns. I still have to work hard to keep in touch with the animals and work with them. Most of us prefer to work with the animals and we just put up with the other stuff.

"Right now, in addition to my other duties, I am directly responsible for the training of elephant keepers and chimp keepers. I am the only experienced person here in those two fields. I enjoy the chimps and the elephants the most. I work closely with them and find them to be some of the most intelligent animals on earth. The elephants have real personalities—they are real characters. And they live for such a long time, so I get to develop a prolonged relationship with them.

"We are working on a new lion exhibit, too. The lions are kept in a building at night; it's the state law. They stay out during the day. A keeper stays in the vicinity—we have zebra-striped trucks for them to ride around in—to keep an eye on them, but mostly to watch out for the people to make sure they don't get out of their cars. The lions appear to be tame, but they are not. They behave here just as they do in the wild, letting cars come up close to them. If you were to get out of the car, though, they would feel intimidated and might attack.

"We work with the animals every day. Besides the lions, the elephants are moved into a barn at night and the giraffes and antelopes go into holding pens. We have conditioned them to respond when we call them, to round them up so we can get a head count and check on them. We try to make them as comfortable as possible as we work with them.

"Anytime you deal with life, you deal with death and that's the downside to my work. Sometimes we lose an animal that we've known for a long time. You get pretty close to them and it's hard. Just recently we had to euthanize an old chimp I'd known since I started working in the park in 1970. He was about 55 years old and had severe arthritis in his spine. The pain was just tearing him down. It's tough to deal with."

Advice from Terry Wolf

"You need to stay in school. Education is becoming more and more important. The market is limited and there are only a certain number of keeper jobs available and there is a lot of competition. All around the country the educational standards are being raised every year. Within ten years from now a master's degree will be needed to get anywhere. And to get into management now, it's almost mandatory that you have a master's degree.

"Experience is always helpful, but it's harder now to get the experience without the education. There are places you can volunteer, such as wildlife conservation organizations, or you can get experience in other settings such as farms and ranches or veterinarian clinics. Those things all help toward building your resume and at least getting an interview. Whenever we have an opening—and Lion Country Safari, compared to a lot of other places, is pretty small budget-wise—we still get 30 to 40 applications from around the country for an entry-level position."

CARIN PETERSON, ANIMAL CURATOR, AUSTIN ZOO, AUSTIN, TEXAS

Carin Peterson earned her B.A. in zoology in 1991 and is currently working on a master's degree in wildlife biology. She has attended seminars and has participated in veterinary technician training. She started working in the field in 1992.

Getting Started

"I have always been interested in research science and nature and especially animals, and thought this would be a good way to combine all my interests. Basically, I saw an ad in the local newspaper looking for an animal caretaker. I came to the zoo for an interview and was hired on the spot. I started out as a zookeeper and worked my way up to animal department supervisor. We are a small zoo, so the

continued

continued

chances for advancement probably happen quicker than at a larger institution."

On the Job

"My job duties vary from day to day, although there are some things that always have to be done. My basic job description includes the following: maintaining the animal records, coordinating veterinary care and visits, advising on diets and husbandry, providing input on acquisitions and departures (sometimes coordinating them), and supervising and training the keeper staff.

"I also do the following: answer our e-mail, maintain our web page, work with some basic animal training, and fill in for keeper staff when someone is absent.

"The animal training can be as complicated as teaching an animal an extensive series of behaviors ("tricks") or as simple as getting an animal to accept human presence without stress. In reality, however, this may not be that simple and may take as long to teach as training another animal to do a complicated behavior. We mostly train animals to be used in educational programs. This means getting them acclimated to a leash or harness or accepting human contact such as being handled and picked up without stress.

"The method of training we use is called operant conditioning (also known as bridge-target training), which uses positive reinforcement to shape desired behaviors. There are many people who have extensive experience with this type of training—both in the domestic and exotic animal worlds. We had seminars presented inhouse taught by specialists. The American Zoo and Aquarium Association (AZA) and the American Association of Zookeepers (AAZK) can provide more information."

The Upsides and Downsides

"Usually my day is pretty relaxed, but that can change in an instant. There can be a lot of stress involved, especially if there is a complicated veterinary procedure to be done or an animal is sick or very pregnant, if the weather is bad, or if there are deadlines to be met—just like anywhere else.

"This job is almost always interesting, though, and there's almost always something else to find out about an individual animal or group of animals. I usually work full time (40 hours) but often stay late or come in early or on my days off to help out. The work atmosphere for the most part is pretty relaxed. Most everyone here really enjoys what they are doing and are self-motivated, so we have a pretty good team.

"What I like most is observing and learning about animals, discovering what their likes and dislikes are and what makes them thrive. I also enjoy helping to provide the public with an enjoyable and informative setting that lends to their appreciation and respect for animals. I would have to say that the hardest aspect of this job is losing an animal. We are a small zoo and we know our animals pretty well, so it's never easy. Also, we are in Texas so the summers can be extremely hot and dry and not at all pleasant. I also do not like it when certain members of the public feel the need to torment our animals."

Advice from Carin Peterson

"Education and experience are both important. Most zoos today want at least two years of college focusing on classes in the natural sciences. If you can't get paid experience, volunteer or intern if possible. Working anywhere with animals is helpful, but exotics have special needs so experience with them is a plus. Be well-rounded. Zoo employees need skills such as working with and talking to the public, computer literacy, time management, and handling basic tools—not just animal experience.

"Also, join professional organizations such as the American Association of Zookeepers or the American Zoo and Aquarium Association to know what is happening in the field."

LA GAURDAR WILDLIFE REHABILITATION AND EDUCATION CENTER

Permitted by the U.S. Fish and Wildlife Service and the Florida Game and Fresh Water Fish Commission, La

continued

continued

Guardar Inc. seeks a positive and cooperative relationship with all efforts to conserve our natural environment and resources.

Wildlife entering the Center are examined and treated by the volunteer staff in cooperation with local veterinarians. They enter the rehabilitation program after being monitored and considered ready. Injured and orphaned wildlife are cared for until they can be released back in the wild in the vicinity where they were found or to a suitable habitat where they naturally occur.

Wildlife that recover but are permanently impaired are housed and used for public educational programs, or they are given to acceptable zoological parks. Those that do not survive are donated to public educational or scientific institutions.

La Guardar Inc. in Webster, Florida, is publicly funded by memberships, donations, grants, bequests, and fundraisers. It receives no governmental support and has no paid employees or officers.

SHELBY RODNEY CARTER, ASSISTANT CURATOR, VICE PRESIDENT, CO-FOUNDER OF LA GUARDAR INC. WILDLIFE REHABILITATION AND EDUCATION CENTER

Shelby Carter (Rod) is the founder of La Guardar. This is the account of how he got started:

"In the late spring of 1986, a gentleman entered our real estate and construction office. He inquired of my wife if she knew of anyone that could help an injured Barred Owl. On his way to work he had hit the owl with his car. The owl was in shock and had an injured wing.

"The upset gentleman was late for work but he waited while my wife called the Florida Game and Fresh Water Fish Commission. A representative informed my wife of a wildlife rehabilitation center located in St. Petersburg, Florida. She also informed her that the possession of even the feather of bird of prey carried a stiff penalty, unless there was a federal and state permit involved.

"My wife and I owned a small cattle ranch at the time and were experienced in caring for animals. She knew that the owl would not survive the two-hour journey to the wildlife center. She informed the Florida Game and Fresh Water Fish representative that she intended to care for the owl and asked her to send her the necessary permit application. The representative agreed and gave my wife the address to apply for a federal permit.

"Relieved of his burden of the injured owl, the gentleman left a donation along with the injured owl and departed.

"Thus began the adventure of caring for injured and orphaned wildlife. My plans on retiring the following year to sail around the world ended.

"Word got around that my wife cared for wildlife and a year later we were knee deep in injured and orphaned wildlife. Lack of space and funding were becoming a problem.

"On five acres near our ranch, I had begun construction in early 1985 on what was to be our retirement home. It was a 1,200-square-foot building, with a kitchen, bedroom, bath, storage, and double carport. Our plan was to duplicate the building on an acre we owned in the mountains of western North Carolina. We planned to spend the seasons, when we were not sailing, at the two small homes.

"I enclosed the double carport and the building became a wildlife rehabilitation center. We sold the ranch and moved into the building along with the animals. A year later, I had completed a 1,500-square-foot home tied to the wildlife center by a foyer. During that year I built numerous habitats to house recuperating wildlife.

"Beginning in early 1987, I set up La Guardar Inc., a nonprofit, tax-exempt, Florida corporation. The corporation is structured to provide immediate and continuing care for injured and orphaned Florida native wildlife. It is governed by a board elected by the active membership. Officers are appointed by the board.

"La Guardar is Spanish for 'The Keep,' which is the center of a castle where things of value are gathered in times

continued

continued

of peril. We believe that all wildlife is vital to the ecosystem, which is the very heart of all life."

The Upsides and Downsides

"A career in wildlife rehabilitation, while it may not be very rewarding monetarily, is so in many other ways. The primary reward is the joy of seeing an animal released back into the wild after recovering from injuries. You also get to meet a special class of people who volunteer their time to care for wildlife. Knowing that you are giving something of value back is very rewarding. Wildlife, while they cannot speak to thank us, honor us with their spirit, antics, tenacity, and beauty.

"The downside is, without a doubt, euthanasia. But taking the life of an injured animal, while difficult, is sometimes the kindest thing we can do.

"Other downsides: we never get to travel. Wildlife require constant attention. The hours are sometimes hard to manage. Rescuing an animal late on a cold rainy night has its drawbacks."

The Day to Day

"As assistant curator, I am involved in rescue and release, accounting, fundraising, grant writing, habitat construction, and maintenance. I also edit a quarterly newsletter. The hours are long, normally twelve to fourteen daily. But the work is not stressful and never boring. Spring is our busy time of the year because of all the orphaned wildlife.

"We house a variety of permanently impaired wildlife, including eagles, hawks, kestrels, owls, songbirds, bobcats, opossum, raccoons, skunks, and reptiles. They require feeding morning and evening. During the day, habitats have to be repaired and cleaned, and water must be provided. This is not always a pleasant chore.

"I have learned that animals are not just species, but individuals. They have personalities much like homo sapiens. For instance, Big Bob, a bobcat that we rescued, was used to train dogs to hunt. He had been wired through his hind legs so he could not escape. However, he managed to escape his tormentors and was found on the front porch of a home.

"Big Bob was found with numerous bites on his hind quarter, his legs were torn, and his hearing was impaired by mites that had eaten most of his ears. Because of his diet during captivity, he had developed fatty liver disease.

"It was nearly a year before Big Bob recovered from his injuries. He remains on a low fat diet. I have observed him converse with several of our domestic cats through the wire of his habitat. He remains proud and wild. He accepts his fate with dignity and provides me with many hours of pleasure watching him when he is not aware.

"We also have two young American eagles that were blown from their nest during a storm. Their wings were damaged beyond repair. They are being trained to the glove for educational programs.

"The eagles, Stormy and Windy, are a joy to watch. They are like children growing up. They play with pine cones, limbs, and their food. In their pond, they bath and argue with each other. Brother and sister, but she dominates. After four years their white feathers are just coming in. They are proud birds.

"I honestly would pay someone to let me work with wildlife."

Advice from Shelby Rodney Carter

"If you are interested in wildlife rehabilitation, you should volunteer at an established center. After you gain some experience, you may be able to find paid employment with some of the larger centers. Contact your local Game Commission or Wildlife Rehabilitators Association. Also, check out 'Wildlife Rehabilitation' on the Internet."

EARNINGS

Salaries for zoologists differ greatly, depending upon the setting, type of job, and experience. Zoologists do not enter their profession for the love of money. Although wages can be considered small compared to other more high-profile careers, zoologists over time can advance up the payscale and earn a comfortable living.

As discussed earlier in this chapter, government employees are subject to the government payscale. Those working in educational settings earn the same as other educators in different fields. Consultants can charge a flat hourly fee for their work.

Zookeepers often begin at the bottom of the salary scale, usually in the high teens or low twenties. As they move up the ranks to positions of increasing responsibility, their salaries move up too. Curators earn anywhere between $30,000 to $55,000 or $60,000, depending upon the facility's budget and the amount of experience and seniority they have amassed.

Those working in research and development or sales for private industry can expect to earn the highest dollar amounts.

Those who move up the administrative ladder in almost any setting also increase their earnings. But as mentioned earlier, the more administrative the job, the less hands-on work is involved. And hands-on work was often the original attraction to the field.

HELP IN LOCATING EMPLOYERS

Hit the library! There are directories galore that list professional associations, zoos, universities, and corporations by industry. Make friends with your reference librarian and bring plenty of change for the copy machine.

The following publications only begin to scratch the surface.

Publications

Basic Wildlife Rehabilitation 1AB, by Jan White, DVM. (This is the manual that goes along with the Basic Wildlife Rehab. 1AB skills seminar—upon completion of the seminar you are "certified"; medical and diet calculation information.) International Wildlife Rehabilitation Council, 4437 Central Place, Suite B-4, Suisun, CA 94585.

Care and Rehabilitation of Injured Owls, 4th ed., by Katherine McKeever. (An excellent resource book for anyone who deals with raptors of any kind.) W. F. Rannie, P.O. Box 700, Beamsville, Ontario, Canada L0R 1B0.

Careers for Animal Lovers. Interviews by Russell Shorto. Brookfield, CT: The Millbrook Press, 1992.

Caring for Birds of Prey, by Jerry Olsen. Faculty of Education, University of Canberra, P.O. Box 1, Belconnen ACT, Australia 2615.

The Center for Wildlife Law quarterly newsletter. (For a complimentary copy write to: Center for Wildlife Law, 1117 Stanford N.E., Albuquerque, NM 87131.)

Conservation Directory. National Wildlife Federation, 1400 16th Street NW, Washington, DC 20036. (Ask for most recent edition.)

Conservation Resource Guide. Various technical and popular articles, fact sheets, brochures, and directory updates. American Association of Zoological Parks and Aquariums, 7970-D Old Georgetown Road, Bethesda, MD 20114.

The Directory of National Environmental Organizations. U.S. Environmental Directories, P.O. Box 65156, St. Paul, MN 55165.

The Environmental Career Guide, by Nicholas Basta. New York, NY: John Wiley & Sons, 1992.

The Exotic Animal Formulary, by Dr. James W. Carpenter. Veterinary Specialty Products, Inc., P.O. Box 812005, Boca Raton, FL 33481.

Housing Avian Insectivores During Rehabilitation, by Paul D. and Georgean Z. Kyle. Driftwood Wildlife Association, P.O. Box 39, Driftwood, TX 78619.

Living with Wildlife, a Sierra Club book by the California Center for Wildlife with Diana Landau and Shelley Stump. (A good book for the general public; stresses who is qualified to care for injured and orphaned animals and also gives info on rehab, permits, etc; available at most bookstores.)

The New Complete Guide to Environmental Careers. Island Press, 1993. CEIP Fund, 68 Harrison Avenue, Fifth Floor, Boston, MA 02111-1907.

Primer of Wildlife Care & Rehabilitation, by Patti L. Raley. (Contains extensive diet information, lab techniques, veterinary info, zoonoses, charts with species information, etc.). Brukner Nature Center, 5995 Horseshoe Bend Road, Troy, OH 45373.

Raptor Rehabilitation —A Manual of Guidelines, by Mathias Engelmann and Pat Marcum. Carolina Raptor Center, P.O. Box 16443, Charlotte, NC 28297-6443.

The Songbird Diet Index, by Marcy Rule. Coconut Creek Publishing Co., 2201 N.W. Terrace, Coconut Creek, FL 33066-2032.

Species Survival Plans: Strategies for Wildlife Conservation, AZA Annual Report on Conservation and Science. American Association of

Zoological Parks and Aquariums, 7970-D Old Georgetown Road, Bethesda, MD 20114.

State Wildlife Laws Handbook, by Ruth S. Musgrave and Maryann Stein. The University of New Mexico Center for Wildlife Law, 4 Research Place, Suite 200, Rockville, MD 20850.

They Work with Wildlife: Jobs for People Who Want to Work with Animals, by E. R. Rucciuti. New York, NY: Harper & Row Publishers, Inc., 1983.

Training Opportunities for Rehabilitators, NWRA. (A listing of all the locations available in the United States for internship opportunities in wildlife rehabilitation.) NWRA Publications, 14 N. 7th Avenue, St. Cloud, MN 56303.

Wild Animal Care and Rehabilitation Manual, 4th ed., by the Kalamazoo Nature Center. Kalamazoo Nature Center, 7000 N. Westnedge Avenue, Kalamazoo, MI 49007.

Wild Ones. (They sell a variety of books on wildlife rehabilitation and other topics, and can order anything you request.) P.O. Box 947, Springville, CA 93265-0947.

Wildlife Feeding and Nutrition, 2nd ed., by Charles T. Robbins. San Diego, CA: Academic Press, 1994.

Wildlife Rehabilitation and Care Manual, by Wildlife Welfare, Inc., c/o Jan Eisenhower Jackson, 4216 Mountainbrook Road, Apex, NC 27502.

Wildlife Rehabilitation Minimum Standards & Accreditation Program, by IWRC and NWRA (recommended for all wildlife rehabilitators). IWRC, 4437 Central Place, Suite B-4, Suisun, CA 94585.

Wildlife Rehabilitation Today. (Published quarterly.) Coconut Creek Publishing Company, 2201 N.W. 40th Terrace, Coconut Creek, FL 33066-2032.

Willowbrook Wildlife Haven Volunteer Handbook, by Willowbrook Wildlife Haven. (An excellent volunteer manual. Good for general information as well as a model for volunteer manuals. Good species care and natural history information.) Willowbrook Wildlife Haven, P.O. Box 2339, Glen Ellyn, IL 60138.

PROFESSIONAL ASSOCIATIONS

The following list of associations can be used as a valuable resource guide in locating additional information about specific careers. Many of the organizations publish newsletters listing job and internship opportunities, and still others offer an employment service to members. A quick look at the organizations' names will give you an idea of how large the scope is.

General information about education and careers in science in the United States may be obtained from:

National Science Foundation
1800 G Street NW
Washington, DC 20550

The Society for Integrative and Comparative Biology
401 N. Michigan Avenue
Chicago, IL 60611-4267

ANIMAL BEHAVIOR

American Society of Animal Science
309 W. Clark Street
Champaign, IL 61820

Association for the Study of Animal Behaviour
The Membership Secretary
82A High Street
Sawston, Cambridge
England CB2 4HJ

IMATA (International Marine Animal Trainers Association)
1720 S. Shores Road
San Diego, CA 92109

This organization can provide you with a list of recognized training programs.

Latham Foundation
"Promoting respect for all life through education."
Latham Plaza Building
Clement and Schillers Streets
Alameda, CA 94501

Animal School, Inc.
Dr. Mary Nitschke
Koll Business Center
Building 9
7850 S.W. Nimbus Avenue
Beaverton, OR 97005

EATM (Exotic Animal Training and Management)
7075 Campus Road
Moorpark, CA 93021
(A two-year training program.)

ANIMAL CARETAKING

For information on animal caretaking and the animal shelter and control personnel training program, write to:

Animal Caretakers Information
The Humane Society of the United States
Companion Animals Division
Suite 100
5430 Grosvenor Lane
Bethesda, MD 20814

To obtain a listing of grooming schools or the name of the nearest certified dog groomer in your area, send a stamped, self-addressed envelope to:

National Dog Groomers Association of America
Box 101
Clark, PA 16113

For information on training and certification of kennel staff and owners, contact:

American Boarding Kennel Association
4575 Galley Road
Suite 400-A
Colorado Springs, CO 80915

CONSERVATION, WILDLIFE, AND REHABILITATION

The National Wildlife Rehabilitators Association is an organization for people interested in and concerned about the welfare of wildlife. Structured mainly for active rehabilitators, NWRA membership also includes professional wildlife personnel, conservationists, educators, naturalists, researchers, veterinarians, people from zoos and humane societies, and many others interested in improving knowledge of wild animals and assuring their survival. The NWRA is incorporated solely for the support of the science and profession of wildlife rehabilitation and its practitioners.

For more information and to become a member, contact:

National Wildlife Rehabilitators Association
Central Office
14 N. 7 Avenue
St. Cloud, MN 56303

The International Wildlife Rehabilitation Council (IWRC) is a professional organization for wildlife rehabilitators, founded to develop and disseminate information on the rehabilitation and care of wild animals, with the goal of returning them to their native environment.

For more information and to become a member, contact:

International Wildlife Rehabilitation Council
4437 Central Place
Suite B-4
Suisun City, CA 94585

For information from other sources, contact:

American Institute of Biological Sciences
1401 Wilson Boulevard
Arlington, VA 22209

Department of Environmental Protection and Energy
Division of Fish, Game, and Wildlife
CN 400
Trenton, NJ 08625

National Wildlife Federation
1400 16th Street NW
Washington, DC 20036

Student Conservation Association
Resource Assistant Program
Department EW, Box 550
Charlestown, NH 03603

U.S. Fish and Wildlife Service
Volunteer Program
1011 E. Tudor Road
Anchorage, AK 99503

U.S. Office of Personnel Management
Summer Job Opportunities in the
    Federal Government No. 414 (Free Copies)

1900 E Street NW, Room 1416
Washington, DC 20415

VETERINARY MEDICINE AND VETERINARY TECHNOLOGY ASSOCIATIONS

For information on careers in veterinary medicine and veterinary technology, contact:

American Association of Zoo Veterinarians
Dr. Wilbur Amand, Executive Director
6 N. Pennell Road
Media, PA 19063

American Veterinary Medical Association
1931 N. Meacham Road
Suite 100
Schaumburg, IL 60173-4360

For information on veterinary education, contact:

Association of American Veterinary Medical Colleges
1101 Vermont Avenue NW, Suite 710
Washington, DC 20005

For information on scholarships, grants, and loans, contact the financial aid office at the veterinary schools to which you wish to apply.

ZOO AND AQUARIUM ASSOCIATIONS

Zoo associations have been formed in many different countries. The largest is the American Association of Zoological Parks and Aquariums, founded in 1924. Other zoo federations include those of Great Britain and Ireland, Spain and Spanish America, Japan, Poland, and Germany.

These organizations disseminate information on zoo management, exchange of specimens, and conservation of wildlife.

American Association of Zookeepers
Metro Washington Park Zoo
4001 S.W. Canyon Road
Portland, OR 97221

American Association of Zoological Parks and Aquariums
7970-D Old Georgetown Road
Bethesda, MD 20114

American Zoo and Aquarium Association
Executive Office and Conservation Center
7970-D Old Georgetown Road
Bethesda, MD 20814-2493

American Zoo and Aquarium Association
Office of Membership Services
Oglebay Park
Wheeling, WV 26003-1698

Association of Zoo and Aquarium Docents
9507 Roe Avenue
Overland Park, KS 66207
(For volunteering opportunities.)

Consortium of Aquariums, Universities, and Zoos
Donna Hardy
Department of Psychology
California State University
Northridge, CA 91330

Friends of the National Zoo
c/o Ms. Joan Grumm
National Zoological Park
Washington, DC 20008

CHAPTER TWELVE

PATH 3: AQUATIC SCIENTISTS

o, you want to work with dolphins or whales? In this chapter you'll learn how to go about it. But aquatic science offers much more than just working with marine mammals. Although aquatic science can be categorized as a subfield under botany (for the study of aquatic plant forms) or zoology (for the study of aquatic animals), and because it's a very popular and broad field, it can be looked at as a separate career path and deserves its own chapter.

Even so, aquatic science is still just a general term that encompasses several other fields and career paths. In fact, many universities offer separate programs or departments in the various aspects of aquatic science. Let's take a look at the options.

DEFINITION OF THE CAREER PATH

AQUATIC SCIENCE

Aquatic science is the general term for research conducted in oceans and coastal or inland waters connected to the sea. It is the study of the planet's above-ground waters and includes both salt and freshwater environments.

Aquatic scientists study virtually everything having to do with water. For example, **aquatic chemists** research organic, inorganic, and trace-metal chemistry. **Marine geologists** study how ocean basins were formed and how geothermal and other geological processes interact with seawater. **Freshwater geologists** may study past climates or the organisms found in the sediments.

Aquatic scientists could also study processes that cover time scales ranging from less than a second to millions of years. They may also examine activity in spaces ranging from millimeters to ocean-wide.

Aquatic science is interdisciplinary. While most aquatic scientists generally specialize in just one area, they use information from all fields and often work together with other related scientists in teams or groups. For example, chemists and biologists might work together to understand the ways in which the chemical components of water bodies interact with plants, animals, and microorganisms such as bacteria.

OCEANOGRAPHY

Oceanography is the specific study of the biological, chemical, geological, optical, and physical characteristics of oceans and estuaries. Oceanographer is a term that is usually understood to include ocean scientists, ocean engineers, and ocean technicians.

Ocean scientists investigate how the oceans work. They usually have a graduate degree in oceanography with a bachelor's degree in one of the fundamental science fields such as biology, physics, chemistry, or geology.

Ocean engineers perform the usual tasks of any engineers—such as designing a structure, for example—but they deal with specific issues related to that structure and its environment in the sea. For example, an ocean engineer might design supports for oil well drilling equipment that would stand on the ocean floor. They would have to take into account information about ocean currents and the force the currents would exert on the structure, plus saltwater corrosion, or marine life interference and other similar elements. Ocean engineers also design the equipment oceanographers use to make oceanographic measurements.

Ocean technicians are responsible for equipment calibration and preparation, measurements, sampling at sea, instrument maintenance and repair, and data processing. Ocean technicians usually have a bachelor's degree, although some may be successful at finding work with two-year associate's degrees.

The subfields of oceanography are physical oceanography, chemical oceanography, biological oceanography, and geological and geophysical oceanography.

Physical oceanographers study currents, waves, and motion and the interaction of light, radar, heat, sound, and wind with the sea. They are also interested in the interaction between the ocean and atmosphere and the relationship between the sea, weather, and climate.

Chemical oceanographers study chemical compounds and the many chemical interactions that occur in the ocean and on the ocean floor.

Biological oceanographers are interested in describing the diverse life-forms in the sea, their population densities, and their natural environment. They try to understand how these animals and plants exist in interrelationships with other sea life and substances and also focus on the impact of human intervention on the oceanic environment.

Geological and geophysical oceanographers study the shape and nature and origin of the material of the seafloor.

LIMNOLOGY

Limnology involves the same concerns that oceanography studies but is limited to inland systems such as lakes, rivers, streams, ponds, and wetlands, and includes both fresh and saltwater.

Physical limnologists study water movements.

Optical limnologists study the transmission of light through the water.

MARINE BIOLOGY OR SCIENCE

Marine biology or science refers specifically to the sea—saltwater environments—and covers a surprising variety of disciplines. Examples include planetology, meteorology, physics, chemistry, geology, physical oceanography, paleontology, and biology. Marine science also includes archaeology, anthropology, sociology, engineering, and other studies of human relationships with the sea.

Biologists study living things and their interaction with each other and the environment. Some study single species, others may examine how two or more species interact, and still others seek to understand the workings of an entire ecosystem.

Marine mammal science (yes, the study of dolphins and whales) covers about 100 species of aquatic or marine mammals that depend on fresh water or the ocean for part or all of their lives. The species include pinnipeds, which cover seals, sea lions, fur seals, and walrus; cetaceans, which include baleen and toothed whales, ocean and river dolphins, and porpoises; sirenians, which cover manatees and dugongs; and some carnivores, such as sea otters and polar bears.

Marine mammal scientists work to understand these animals' genetic, systematic, and evolutionary relationships; population structure; community dynamics; anatomy and physiology; behavior and sensory abilities; parasites and diseases; geographic and microhabitat distributions. Marine mammal scientists also study ecology, management, and conservation.

PREPARATION AND REQUIREMENTS FOR AQUATIC SCIENCE

There are a few entry-level positions here and there for people with only high school diplomas, but these positions are rare and opportunities for career advancement would be limited.

Most entry-level jobs require a bachelor's degree in a natural science from an accredited college or university. Because most bachelor degree programs do not usually require research experience, applicants may expect to participate as assistants in research and advance mostly on the basis of on-the-job experience.

A master's degree is required by many employers, especially where research is a large part of the job description. A doctorate is usually necessary for academic positions or in other settings where the employee would manage other scientists and conduct studies of his or her own design.

Job opportunities are varied and exist at all educational levels. As with other fields, the higher-level and better paying jobs require the most education.

Because aquatic science encompasses so many specializations, at the undergraduate level it is advised that future biologists obtain the broadest education possible. There is no guarantee you will gain employment in your area of interest or specialization—at least not right away. Because of this, a general education will provide a foundation for many types of employment.

Aquatic scientists usually acquire a foundation in one or more of the basic sciences such as biology, chemistry, geology, mathematics, or physics before specializing.

Many of the disciplines in aquatic science, such as marine biology, are graduate-level pursuits, so when choosing your undergraduate program, it's a good idea to investigate the strengths and specializations of the biology programs. If you know you want to pursue graduate work in marine science, for example, then taking your undergraduate degree at a university that offers courses in that area will help when it comes time to apply to graduate school. But graduate schools prefer students to major in a core science such as biology, physics, chemistry, or geology rather than a specialized subject such as limnology or oceanography. You can specialize in the areas that interest you the most, but not exclusively. Make sure to add statistics, mathematics, computers, and data management to your curriculum. And as in any profession, good oral and writing skills are crucial.

To increase your employability, involvement in a research project in a science laboratory is also important. This might be pursued through your university as a supervised independent study, working with a particular professor's research project, or through an internship, work-study job, or a stint of volunteering. If your university doesn't offer opportunities in this area, seek out other aquatic scientists, perhaps working at a local aquarium or marine science center and volunteering to help in any way you can.

In addition, many summer research programs are available at universities with graduate-level limnology or oceanography programs. These summer research experiences are usually offered to students after they have completed their sophomore or junior year and offer a good chance to learn more about the discipline as a possible career choice. You can find out about these programs by writing to institutions offering graduate degrees in limnology or oceanography. The programs are open to students from all universities.

To further prepare yourself, you can also attend seminars and join aquatic science organizations such as the American Society of Limnology and Oceanography. (Their address is provided at the end of this chapter.) By doing so you will better understand the field and start making contacts in the community of people with whom you'll eventually work.

Many careers in marine mammal science require additional qualifications such as SCUBA certification and boat-handling experience.

To summarize, make sure you acquire an all-around education and are familiar with what's happening in aquatic science. Get involved, talk to scientists, and participate in any way you can.

FINDING AN AQUATIC SCIENCE PROGRAM

Information on colleges and universities offering programs in aquatic science and all its subfields can be found through various directories such as *Lovejoy's* or *Peterson's,* available at school guidance centers, public libraries, or on the Internet.

You will find the programs listed under various headings such as:

Aquatic science	Marine biology
Biology	Meteorology
Chemistry	Ocean engineering
Earth science	Oceanography
Geology	Physics
Limnology	

CAREER OUTLOOK

In general, opportunities are good for those with bachelor's degrees or higher in science. But some specialty areas present stiff competition to job applicants. For example, there may be 10,000 people who would like a job working with marine mammals, but there are only around 100 jobs in this area nationwide. That is one extreme. In other specializations, there may be only five jobs nationwide but only four qualified applicants.

Generally speaking, there is more interest and therefore more competition for jobs in marine biology than there is in aquatic physics, chemistry, and geology.

Opportunities are best for those with strong training in mathematics or engineering and those who pursued an interdisciplinary program that will allow them to work across disciplines. Funding for graduate students and professional positions is expected to increase in the next ten years in the disciplines of global climate change, environmental research and management, fisheries science, and marine biomedical and pharmaceutical research programs. American students and scientists are also expected to become more involved in international research programs.

Even when the number of available positions in this career path is small, top scientists are always in demand.

It is important to remember that job opportunities and openings in all fields change over time and can change quite quickly. If you follow your interests, work hard, make contacts, and don't give up, you'll find the job of your dreams.

POSSIBLE EMPLOYERS

Aquatic scientists find employment in universities and colleges. They also work for international organizations, federal and state agencies, private companies, nonprofit laboratories, and local governments, or aquariums, zoos, marine parks, and museums. They also may be self-employed.

Government agencies that hire aquatic scientists include:

Army Corps of Engineers

Coast Guard

Department of Commerce

Department of Energy

Department of Interior

Department of Navy

Department of State

Environmental Protection Agency

Marine Mammal Commission

Minerals Management Service

National Aeronautics and Space Administration

National Oceanic and Atmospheric Administration

National Marine Fisheries Service

National Park Service

National Science Foundation

Naval Oceanographic Office

Naval Research Laboratory

Office of Naval Research

Smithsonian Institution

U.S. Fish & Wildlife Service

U.S. National Biological Service

U.S. Navy, Office of Naval Research

Private industry such as oil and gas exploration, production, and transportation as well as commercial fishing hire aquatic scientists when their operations affect marine mammals or produce environmental concerns.

Many environmental, advocacy, and animal welfare organizations as well as legal firms also depend on aquatic scientists and use them for legal/policy development, problem solving, and regulatory and administrative roles.

Aquariums, marine parks, and zoos hire specialists for veterinary care, husbandry, training, research, and education programs. Examples of marine mammal jobs include researcher, field biologist, fishery vessel observer, laboratory technician, animal trainer, animal care specialist, veterinarian, whale-watch guide, naturalist, and educator.

Museums hire specialists for research, educational programs, and curatorial positions.

Magazines, book publishers, television, and radio also provide employment for specialists, but usually on a part-time, freelance, or consulting basis.

WORKING CONDITIONS

Many aquatic science researchers spend time each year engaged in field work, collecting data and samples in natural environments. The data are collected during research cruises on small or large vessels and the amount of time at sea could last from one week to over two months and involve a team of scientists from many disciplines.

Limnological data most often are collected during short, one- to two-day field trips that are usually narrower in scope, or at the other extreme, could involve stays at field stations lasting from days to months.

When not in the field, aquatic research scientists spend most of their time in the laboratory running experiments, or at the computer analyzing data or developing models. They also study papers in scientific journals and relate that research to their own work. Writing their own papers for publication is also part of their routine.

Those working in universities must couple lectures and student conferences with their own research.

In any environment, attending meetings is also part of the job.

Scientists may also spend time writing research proposals to obtain grant money for more research.

For aquatic scientists with administrative jobs, the time is spent in the office or communicating with colleagues and the public. Like any research scientists, they also attend national or international conferences to keep up in their fields.

Hands-on workers, such as those involved with marine mammals or working in aquariums, have jobs that are not as glamorous as our movies or TV programs depict. The work involves hard labor, such as lugging buckets of fish and cleaning tanks.

EARNINGS

Aquatic scientists enter this field for the love of their work—not of the money. The salary you'll earn will depend in part on your educational background, experience, responsibilities, area of specialization, number of years of service, and the size, type, and geographical location of the employing institution. In general, jobs with the government or in industry have the highest pay.

Bachelor's degree holders with no experience may find employment with the federal government at GS-5 to GS-7, a salary range in the teens to the thirties.

Doctorate degree holders generally earn from $30,000 to $80,000 per year, and sometimes more than $100,000 per year for senior scientists or full professors.

But high competition in some areas will most likely keep salaries at a modest level.

Examples of aquatic sciences that presently pay above-average salaries are physical oceanography, marine technology and engineering, and computer modeling.

Some aquatic scientists earn their incomes from more than one source. They teach at universities, for example, then supplement their incomes by obtaining research grants from the federal or state government or private sources, writing for technical publications, and serving as consultants.

CLOSE-UPS

The following three people, who are providing first-hand accounts of their jobs, work in various positions at the New England Aquarium in Boston, Massachusetts.

The New England Aquarium is one of the premiere showcases for the display of marine life and habitats. Its mission is to "present, promote, and protect the world of water." These goals are carried out through exhibits and through education, conservation, and research programs.

Exhibits showcase the diversity, importance, and beauty of aquatic life and habitats, and they also highlight aquatic conservation issues of importance.

The centerpiece for the aquarium is the 187,000-gallon Giant Ocean Tank Caribbean Coral Reef Exhibit, which rises through four stories of the facility. Visitors are afforded a multi-angle view of sea turtles, sharks, moray eels, and the other tropical fish that live inside.

The Ocean Tray, which holds 131,000 gallons of water and surrounds the Great Ocean Tank on the ground floor, is home to a colony of blackfooted and rock hopper penguins.

In a floating pavilion adjacent to the Aquarium, sea lion presentations of natural and learned behaviors are featured every day. Harbor seals reside in the outdoor pool on the Aquarium's plaza. Some of these seals were found as orphaned pups along the New England coast and have been cared for by skilled Aquarium biologists as part of their Rescue and Rehabilitation Program. Through this program, Aquarium staff work with distressed or injured marine animals in the wild such as whales, dolphins, sea turtles, and seals. Their goals are to rescue, rehabilitate, and whenever possible, release the animals back to the wild.

Other research programs include working to preserve the endangered red-bellied turtle species and to help increase the declining population of black-footed penguins.

The New England Aquarium also offers a whale watch program and a "Science at Sea" harbor tour boat.

To maintain such a range of exhibits and programs, the New England Aquarium relies on the skills and experience of a variety of professionals.

STEVEN BAILEY, CURATOR OF FISHES

Steven Bailey has been with the New England Aquarium since 1984. He received his bachelor's degree in zoology from Wilkes University in Wilkes-Barre, Pennsylvania, and completed substantial work toward a master's degree in ichthyology at Northeastern University in Boston. When a full-time job as an aquarist was offered to him at the Aquarium, he jumped at the chance, moving up the ranks to his current position.

Steven Bailey's Background

"When I was in graduate school, I was planning for a job that would allow me to be paid to go diving. It was as simple as that. I definitely had an animal thing going and I had been diving since the sixties. My father, who is a forestry kind of guy, always outdoors, decided that my brother and I should know how to dive at a young age. I grew up in Pennsylvania but spent most of our summers diving at a lake in Maine. The perfect way to start.

"I spent four years in graduate school and they were incredibly busy years, amassing experience to make myself hireable. I volunteered with the National Marine Fishery Service, and on a number of occasions I spent time as a professional collector, gathering specimens that were used for biomedical research. I had a great deal of diving experience and back in the early '80s there weren't a lot of folks around applying for these positions who had that experience. I was working seven days a week and going to school and just generally maximizing every minute. I heard about the job because I was volunteering here while I was going to graduate school. I had a mentor here too who recommended me.

"I started as an aquarist. Over a thirteen-year period I moved up the ranks, or should I say I moved out of the best job in the building to the most aggravating job. I spent ten years as an aquarist, then I got promoted to senior aquarist

continued

continued

and somehow inexplicably bypassed that last supervisor step and went from senior aquarist to my present position as curator of fishes."

Steven Bailey's Responsibilities

"As curator of fishes, I am responsible for everything other than marine mammals—fishes, invertebrates, reptiles, amphibians, birds, and plants. My area involves the Aquarium's two biggest exhibits, the Giant Ocean Tank, which is the centerpiece of the building—it's a 200,000-gallon Caribbean coral reef exhibit—and the penguin colony, which is at the base of the tank.

"I am responsible for 24 people. There are 19 aquarists at different levels and 4 supervisors, the equivalent of assistant curators. I also supervise a curatorial associate who keeps track of everything from how much frozen food we are feeding fishes, to making sure all of our permits are up-to-date. She pitches in wherever she can, whether that's on a collecting trip or helping to haul a 500-pound turtle out of an exhibit for a blood sampling.

"One of my duties is hiring. We can be incredibly selective about that. Every time there is a job opening advertised here we receive at least 200 resumes. We can be particular about the backgrounds that folks have. It must include diving and it is up to them to make sure they have this training. They must also have a degree. Animal biology is preferred but we also have people with environmental science or general biology degrees, too.

"A person's work ethic is also very important. People who work hard to achieve a particular goal are very attractive to us. Sometimes you can see this on a resume. They want to be in contact with animals, so they'll do anything and everything to ensure that that happens, whether it's mucking out stalls, working for a vet, working in pet stores, or running their own grooming businesses. There are a lot of things people can do to be close to animals. Obviously, being interested in fishes is a plus. Maybe someone has been a home hobbyist for years and can go on at length about the animals they've had in that time. Or maybe it is something they've developed more recently in life, as the result of a stimulating course they had in college. Some folks elect to do field experiences that are an epiphany to them. They manage to see something that they never thought of before and become quite enthralled with it.

"Primarily I deal with budget and personnel issues, or that's the way it seems. I am removed from the day-to-day hands-on work. If I had taken accounting courses and abnormal psychology, I would be much more prepared for this particular position than all the biology I studied.

"There are around 80 to 90 exhibits that come around my group's control. Those range in size from the 200,000-gallon Caribbean Reef exhibit to a 50-gallon sea horse and pipe fish exhibit. Those exhibits need an incredible amount of scrutiny, from making sure the animals are nutritionally taken care of to the 3 W's aspect of that—the aesthetics—the windows, the walls, and the water. They all have to be clean and aesthetically appealing so that when folks come to visit us they are immediately assured that professionals are managing the animals. They spend money to visit here and they should get a good return on their dollar. They are seeing the epitome of animal presentation, taking home a lot of good information, and getting a bit of an education while they're here.

"Aquariums and zoos in general have evolved in many ways to where they are stewards of the animals in the wild. The long-term survival of these animals hinges upon the successes of zoos and aquariums in general. What I mean by this is there are many animals that are endangered or threatened or enjoy some sort of status of special concern—and we are breeding facilities, we are restocking facilities for animals that are ready to go back into the wild to reestablish a population. There is no substitute for seeing the real thing. We can get an important message across and this is an admirable and worthwhile job.

"Conservation, research, and animal breeding activities are all a big part of what zoos and aquaria are up to these days. We have an aquarist who spends a great deal of time in the Amazon each year. What he does is run an ecotourism operation where he has people paying to come on trips with

continued

continued

him to assess biodiversity and explore the habitats of a number of the backwaters in the Amazon. The money generated from this is used to support Brazilian researchers who are doing things such as examining the ornamental fish industry. The most popular fish in the world as far as the home aquarist goes is a fish that comes out of the Rio Negro river system, a part of the Amazon River Basin. That animal is called the cardinal tetra. The cardinal tetra is single-handedly—or single-finnedly, I suppose—responsible for the well-being of maybe 40 to 50,000 people who live on that river. They are all in some way a part of that industry because they exact a living from that sustainable fishery and are not in the forest doing slash and burn agriculture, or selling other animal skins or parts. It is one of the most intact areas of the basin.

"I preferred it when I was able to get out in the field instead of being parked in front of a computer screen all day and attending meetings. The positive aspects of this job are much different than what initially attracted me to the field. I don't get out and go collecting that often, but I do manage to get a fair amount of satisfaction and sense of accomplishment from being involved in the design and exhibit construction end of things. We, as a group—the husbandry folks, the design department, education, research—get together to plot our course over the next few years.

"I am also married to someone who works here and is also an animal person. Life couldn't be better."

Advice from Steven Bailey

"It is a career for people who are very serious. There aren't that many opportunities and you have to be really dedicated to this pursuit. Most of the folks here have not been hired right out of college. They spent a good deal of time volunteering at this institution and picking up a lot of other related work experiences, expanding their horizons, and becoming Renaissance-type people. The diversity of experiences that individuals can have are very important as far as making them attractive commodities when the hiring time comes around. There are very few people here who were hired on their first go-round.

"This job requires that you have construction and tool skills. It demands you know your way around the literature or at least be able to find the information to answer a question or solve a problem. It requires an ability to be comfortable with routine and what can often become repetitive work.

"Being an aquatic chambermaid, which almost everyone is, might sound like fun, but when you are cleaning and maintaining an animal's environment day after day, it can get very old for some people. For other people it's a Zen experience. They put it into perspective, they are able to be at peace with the incredible amount of responsibility they have for all of these animals.

"And not all of these animals have the excitement or energy that say a shark has or a killer whale. Those are animals that get a lot of attention from the public, but nevertheless an animal is an animal and whether you are talking about a minnow that is abundant five miles away from this institution or one of those more glamorous animals, such as the California sea otter, the bottom line is still the same. They depend on you and you are responsible for their well-being."

HEATHER URQUHART, SENIOR AQUARIST

Heather Urquhart is a diving aquarist in the Fishes Department at the New England Aquarium in Boston. She is a certified advanced scuba diver and has been working at the Aquarium since 1989.

Heather Urquhart's Background

"I have always known that I wanted to work with animals. Early on I wasn't sure how, whether it would be veterinarian work or zookeeping. The opportunities I was aware of then for working with animals were limited. After I saw Jacques Cousteau, I knew I wanted to work with marine animals. I've always been an ocean buff—I grew up at the ocean. When I was a kid, I was always the one without a suntan. I always had my mask and snorkel on.

continued

continued

"I got a B.S. degree in biology with a concentration in marine biology and a chemistry minor at Salem State College in 1985. Before I got my job here, I thought for sure I'd be going on for a master's, but once you get involved with your work doing something that you love, it's hard to break away to go back to school.

"Growing up in this area, I was always aware of the Aquarium and what was going on. When I started school in Salem, which is very close to the city, I found out through friends at school about the Aquarium's volunteer opportunities. While I was still in college, I volunteered here for six months, two days a week in 1984, coincidentally in the area in which I am now working, with the penguins. Also at the time we had river otters that we took care of. I was able to group all my classes on Mondays, Wednesdays, and Fridays, so I could volunteer Tuesdays and Thursdays.

"Once I graduated in 1985, I had a couple of other jobs—I worked with an environmental consulting firm for six months and did some quality control work with seafood—but was constantly applying whenever a position came open here. I'd scan the newspapers and then send my resume in. It took a little while, but finally they brought me in for an interview and based on the good recommendations I had received as a volunteer and my interview I got hired. That was in 1989 and I've been here ever since. I started as an aquarist-in-training, then to aquarist, then to my current title, senior aquarist. I am in the Fishes Department. Even though I work with the penguins, they are classified under the Fishes Department."

Heather Urquhart's Responsibilities

"I take care of both the Giant Ocean Tank and the penguin colony. I dive into the tank up to five times a day in order to feed, examine, and check on the health of the fish as well as clean and maintain the exhibit. We have five dives going a day, so if we have enough people in, we'll rotate so sometimes we don't have to go in every day.

"The penguin exhibit has a 150,000-gallon tank and we need seven staff people to maintain both exhibits, plus we have volunteers to help us seven days a week. We have 47 penguins right now. We don't have to dive in the penguin exhibit, but we do have to put on a wet suit to get in there. We are in 55-degree water up to our chest. There are days you just don't feel like getting wet but you just grin and bear it. If one of us is ill with a bad cold or the flu, then we try to accommodate each other, but even then I've gone in. There was no choice. The fish have to be fed.

"It's a very physical job and it's not for everyone. Not only because you're in the water, but just the nature of putting on dive equipment and chugging down the hall to get into the tank, then pulling yourself out. Then, there's going up and down four flights of stairs in order to get to the penguin exhibit with 15 pounds of fish in a bucket in each hand. There is an elevator, but it's a big freight elevator and by the time you get yourself in there and down, it's just easier to take the stairs. Besides that, you need a key to open the elevator and when you're in a wet suit in salt water, you don't want to be carrying around metal keys. They corrode.

"Lately, my concentration has been with the penguins. We don't do any training with the penguins; we want people to see them as they would be in the wild. We do have some penguins, though, that have been partially hand-raised and they tend to be more accustomed to human interaction. We can take these penguins out and do what we call an 'animal interview.' They are put in an enclosure outside of the exhibit where visitors, without touching the animal, can still get an up-close and personal look. Some of our staff members will speak about the animal and give a presentation. While they aren't trained per se, these animals don't mind being in the spotlight. It's a joy to work with them.

"I enjoy the animal interactions the most; it's some of the best medicine going. No matter what kind of aggravating day you might be having, when you are working with the animals, it all seems not to matter so much.

"I've been here for quite a while and I've hand-raised a lot of little penguins and that's a wonderful experience to be there from the egg to the adult stage. They imprint on me and they know my voice and will come to me. We have them all banded, but I can recognize who's who. Once the hand-raised penguins mature a little and become interested

continued

continued

in a mate, they tend to ignore us more. We are no longer as interesting to them.

"We keep a genealogy on all our penguins and we keep food records and medical records and records of molting patterns. We also monitor their mating patterns to prevent inbreeding. If we notice a pair that would be a bad pair, we separate them and encourage them to breed with a penguin that would be a better match. In the wild you don't have that problem, but here we have to be careful. And with this particular species we have to be careful because their numbers are so vulnerable in the wild right now.

"In addition to maintaining the exhibit, I've been lucky enough to form a conservation program surrounding our penguins. We house two species of penguins, rock hopper and the African penguin. The African penguins are on the verge of becoming an endangered species in the wild. Through the help of the Aquarium, we've been able to set up a fund and generate monies here through a penny smasher machine. It costs 51 cents—we keep the 50 cents and the penny goes under a barrel that has the imprint of an African penguin on it. The penny gets smooshed with the logo on it and the kids get a souvenir.

In the past two years I've been to South Africa twice and intend to go again soon. We link up with conservation organizations there and join them with their conservation and research work, trying to contribute as much as we can, as well as bringing back the most factual data to the States to educate people about the penguins' plight. We are also educating ourselves. We want to be more than talking heads who have never been in the field. We also contribute to penguin rehabilitation organizations that are helping oiled penguins in South Africa. We have great hopes for the future—we are really moving and shaking with this thing. The past two years have been wonderful, a real windfall for me.

"We do a lot of local travel up and down the east coast for collecting fish and invertebrates for our exhibits. We also run a collecting trip twice a year down to the Bahamas to collect for our Caribbean Reef exhibit. But we don't have to collect that much because we are pretty good at maintaining the exhibit.

"We have sharks in our Caribbean exhibit that we dive with, but they probably are what I worry about least in there. They are docile and they don't pay much attention to us. I think people have a lot of misconceptions about sharks. People aren't on a shark's menu and a lot of times attacks are the result of mistaken identity. In our tank we have some fish that are only about an inch or an inch and a half, yet they are much more aggressive than any shark. Little damsel fish protecting their nests will come right out at you, for example. I've been bitten by damsel fish on numerous occasions. We get our share of bites, not only from the fish, but from the penguins, too. They aren't trying to be mean, but you're down there feeding them and handling them, and they aren't tame animals. Most of the time it's our own mistake. You're feeding a little piece of shrimp to a fish and they miss the shrimp and get your finger. They don't take your finger off, but you get little nips and bites. Nothing serious."

Advice from Heather Urquhart

"Volunteer, volunteer, volunteer. That's the best bet. Not only will the people who work at the institution get to know your work, but you'll get an idea of what you'd be getting into, too.

"The glamorous part is that you get to work with a lot of cute baby animals. The nonglamorous part is all that other stuff—being in a wet suit all day long, cold water, and smelling like fish by the end of the day. Ninety percent of working with animals is cleaning up after them. It's not for everyone.

"But if it is for you, then volunteering is the way to go. The vast majority of the people working here formerly volunteered here. We do pull from within our ranks.

"Also, make sure you go to school, but don't specialize too much early on. For the type of job I have, you'd need to have a biology or zoology degree, one of these general topics. Then if you get to do some volunteer work, you can see more clearly what area to focus on. You might decide you want to work in a lab or in education."

JENNY MONTAGUE,
ASSISTANT CURATOR/ANIMAL TRAINER

Jenny Montague is assistant curator in the Marine Mammals Department at the New England Aquarium. Her position is equivalent to the supervisor job title in the Fishes Department. She has been with the Aquarium since 1988.

Jenny Montague's Background

"I started working at Marine World/Africa USA in Vallejo, California, a marine mammal-zoo combination, as a landscaper while I was still in high school. It was an odd existence for awhile. I was desperately trying to get into marine mammals, so I'd be at Marine World at five in the morning to do landscaping, then I had to go to school, and afterward I'd come back and work until dark.

"I did some community college but I got hired into the marine mammals department at Marine World right out of high school as an assistant trainer. That was 1981. I stayed there for eight years and left there as a senior trainer/show manager. I came to Boston right after that as supervisor of marine mammals. The woman who is curator here had worked briefly at Marine World on a research project so we got to know each other. When the supervisor opening came up, she called me and I said 'yes' pretty quickly. I was ready for a change. As much as I liked Marine World, I felt I had probably gone as far as I could go in the hierarchy. I was interviewed over the phone and our history together clinched the deal."

Jenny Montague's Responsibilities

"I am basically a trainer who has worked her way up through the ranks to an assistant curator position. I do more paperwork than I'd like to, but my basic job right now is to oversee the training and health of the animals. I supervise eight staff people. They range from assistant trainer to senior trainer.

"We work with the colony or resident marine mammals, which include Atlantic harbor seals, California sea lions, and California sea otters. We are responsible for the training, the care, and the presentation to the public of these mammals. We are located next door to the Aquarium on the floating barge, what they call the Barge Discovery. It's an indoor show because of the weather we have in Boston. There are between four and seven shows daily, divided up amongst our staff. Sometimes three or four staff members are involved in the presentation if we're working with more than one animal. I personally do about eight or ten shows a week."

Jenny's Role as Animal Trainer

"We're interested in portraying to the public what the animals' background is, what their natural history is, and also some of the conservation issues that surround them. We do that in what we hope is a fun and educational way. When people can get close to live animals it makes an incredible impression on them. All different levels of trainers participate, from the assistant trainers to assistant curator level. We get out there with the animals and talk to the audience about the different animal behaviors, explaining how they are able to do what they do. We say a little about the physiology and the biology of the animals and also about the training techniques we use. We'll do a demonstration of some of the medical behaviors we have, such as brushing the animal's teeth. They are all trained to sit or lie still and allow a stethoscope to be put on them. They are trained to lie still for x-rays. They open their mouths to let the veterinarians look down their throat. They'll sit still for an eye exam.

"The training is for the medical care of the animals, but it's also for mental stimulation. We find that, like anyone, if they are stimulated mentally and physically they are much happier and healthier animals than if they are just left alone. We feel that training is a very important part of animal management in zoos and aquariums.

"During the presentations, we encourage audience members to participate. We ask them if they can give suggestions as to what we can do as individuals to keep the ocean a safer place for the animals. And anybody that has an interesting idea gets to come down and meet the sea lion. They get to pat him and get a kiss.

continued

continued

"When we are doing training, we keep records of all the advances animals make and what new steps they've accomplished. Each individual animal has a primary trainer. I happen to be primary trainer right now for Ballou, a six-year-old, male California sea lion. There are usually two primary trainers for each animal so every day can be covered. We are basically responsible for getting regular weights on the animals, looking at their diet, and making sure they are getting the proper amount of food. All of the fish we feed them is sent out for analysis so we know exactly how many calories and how many grams of fat are in each kind of fish. We run that through a formula and calculate the right amount based on the animal's age and weight.

"The two primary trainers work as a team and are responsible for deciding what the animal is going to learn, who of the two will train it, and what methods we'll use.

"Each animal has its own personality. Some animals you can work on a particular behavior with for half an hour and do several repeats and then they make a step. We have one sea lion that if we repeat things over and over and lead him slowly through little steps, he'll never forget what you've taught him. Another one, Guthrie, gets bored very easily and he starts to add in his own special flair. We spend more time retraining him than training him, to get rid of all his extraneous stuff. But he's a howl, one of the most fun sea lions to work with.

"How many hours you spend on something depends a lot on the animals and how much they are enjoying it and want to work with you. Tyler, a 13-year-old sea lion, isn't too crazy about having his teeth touched, so we'll only do that once or twice at a time. But he does like the other medical behaviors. He loves to lie around for x-rays, he likes the vets to touch him, but they really have to go slow with his mouth.

"We also do show behaviors, high jumps and hitting a ball, for example. One we're working on now is a gallop, which shows the audience how quickly the sea lions can run on land. We work the sea lions in conjunction with our harbor seals sometimes and there is a major difference in speed between the two. The sea lions are much faster. The seals slug along on their bellies; they're not the most graceful creatures on land. A lot of this might seem circusy but we are actually just trying to demonstrate the natural behavior of the animal. They're taught to do porpoising, for example, which is a natural behavior. We just teach them to do it on command.

"We also train for research behaviors. Recently we started a hearing study and we're at the beginning stages of teaching the animals to allow us to put headphones on them. At the same time they're being taught to respond to a sound cue. We also taught a sea lion to distinguish between the sizes of two objects and choose the larger one."

Animal Training Methods

"We use three different training methods. 'Operant conditioning' is the one most widely used. You break a behavior into small steps and you lead the animal through the steps, providing reinforcement along the way.

"Another method is called 'innovative.' Where operant conditioning is based on repetition, with innovative, we are asking the animals to create something new. After they have a solid operant conditioning understanding, we give them an arbitrary signal, which is crossing our arms across our chest. They have no idea what it means, but they might confuse it with a signal they do know and will offer a behavior. At the beginning we would reward the old behavior, but then we'll only reward every new behavior.

"We use a variety of reinforcers—fish, or some of the animals like to be scratched and rubbed down. You spend a lot of time trying to find what the animals enjoy. Some like particular toys, others like things like ice cubes. So, for example, after the signal, they might give a salute. We'll reward it and then, because they are familiar with operant conditioning, they figure that if they do it again, they'll be rewarded again. But the next time we don't reinforce the salute. You can get a curious look from them at this point. We'll give the signal again and if the salute doesn't work yet again, they'll start to offer something else, whether it's a look in another direction, or moving their whiskers forward in a curious,

continued

continued

questioning look. All of those little subtle movements are rewarded and they start coming up with some pretty wild things. The purpose of this is to stimulate their creativity. It allows them to do things they like to do and it keeps them thinking. It also gives the training staff some ideas. A lot of times they'll come up with things we wouldn't have thought of. Our sea lion Zack used to carry some rings around on his flippers and slap them at the same time. He had all his flippers going and then he'd roll over. It was an amazing little dance.

"The third method is called 'mimicry training.' We ask the animals to focus on us and copy what we do. We got the idea for this because they already did mimic us to some extent. Some of the things they'll mimic is turning around in a circle, hopping up, opening a mouth, or making a sound. It's really fun and it gives them a whole different focus. They have to watch our whole bodies completely, instead of just the usual hand gestures."

The Upsides and Downsides

"One of the nicest things about the job is that you never run out of ideas and you're able to try them out. It's always different every day.

"On the downside, the hours are inconsistent and you can't rely on a 9 to 5 day. Most of our staff works four ten-hour days. We are open seven days a week. Something always comes up, though, which prevents you from having a regular schedule, but then on the other hand, that might be a good thing."

Advice from Jenny Montague

"My advice would be to find any one of the schools that works with animal behavior. The interesting part of this job is that there are different academic subjects that can help you, such as psychology, animal behavior, and zoology. Marine biology, however, is not a direct lead to the training field. It's a misconception a lot of people have. When I was in school it was pretty difficult finding people who were doing animal behavior work. It was happening but it wasn't as accessible as it is today. It wasn't really considered a career path, and if you wanted to work with animal behavior, you did training with pigeons and rats. There are formal training schools now. One is Exotic Animal Training and Management (EATM), in Moorpark, California. There is also a strong program at the University of California in Santa Cruz. International Marine Animal Trainers Association (IMATA) can provide a list of all the training programs.

"I also strongly suggest that people volunteer. A lot of times folks come and see animal shows and they think that's all there is to it. But it isn't. We're up to our elbows in sinks full of dead fish all the time. We're running around in rubber boots all the time and do get damp. There's a lot more to it than the time on the stage. As a volunteer, you'd get a sense of all that.

"It is also important to visit different institutions. Everyone has a different style."

FINDING THAT JOB

Personnel Offices

A good source for job announcements is the personnel department of a specific government agency, private company, educational institution, museum, zoo, marine park, or aquarium.

Publications

The *Chronicle of Higher Education* lists academic positions at junior colleges, colleges, and universities. Its address and information on obtaining academic positions are covered more fully in Chapter 14.

The American Geophysical Union, whose address is listed at the end of this chapter, publishes *Eos,* a weekly newspaper that lists employment opportunities, particularly in government and universities.

Other technical journals carry similar postings.

Many manufacturing companies with significant interest in the oceans advertise in *Sea Technology.*

Other manufacturers, consulting firms, and universities that are potential employers are listed among the corporate sponsors of the Marine Technology Society, and their names are listed in each issue of the society's journal.

The following offer publications and information packets:

Earth Work Career Publications Service. SCA, Attn: Earth Work, P.O. Box 550, Charlestown, NH 03603. (Various publications on environmental careers.)

Ocean Opportunities. Marine Technology Society, 1825 K Street NW, Washington, DC 20006.

A book describing university curricula in oceanography and related fields may be obtained by writing: Marine Technology Society, 1828 L Street NW, Suite 906, Washington, DC 20036-5104.

Careers in Oceanography. American Geophysical Union, 2000 Florida Avenue NW, Washington, DC 20009.

Careers in Oceanography and Marine-Related Fields. The Oceanography Society, 4052 Timber Ridge Drive, Virginia Beach, VA 23455.

The Environmental Sourcebook. Lyons & Burford, 31 W. 21st Street, New York, NY 10010.

Marine Education: A Bibliography of Educational Materials Available from the Nation's Sea Grant College Programs. Sea Grant Marine Education Bibliography, Gulf Coast Research Laboratory, J. L. Scott Marine Education Center and Aquarium, P.O. Box 7000, Ocean Springs, MS 39564-7000. ($2.00/copy)

Marine Science Careers: A Sea Grant Guide to Ocean Opportunities. Sea Grant Communications Office, University of New Hampshire, Kingman Farm, Durham, NH 03824-3512.

Ocean Opportunities—a Guide to What the Oceans Have to Offer. Marine Technology Society, 2000 Florida Avenue NW, Suite 500, Washington, DC 20009. ($3.00/copy)

Opportunities in Marine and Maritime Careers. 2nd ed. With a foreword by Jean-Michel Cousteau. Lincolnwood, IL: VGM Career Horizons, a division of NTC/Contemporary Books. Heitzmann, W. R.

Peterson's Annual Guide to Undergraduate Study, Four-Year Colleges. Department 6608, P.O. Box 2123, 166 Bunn Drive, Princeton, NJ 08543.

Peterson's Guide to Graduate Programs in the Biological and Agricultural Sciences. Department 6608, P.O. Box 2123, 166 Bunn Drive, Princeton, NJ 08543.

Sea Technology Buyer's Guide. Annual Directory, Section F, Educational Institutions, Compass Publications, Inc., Suite 1000, 1117 N. 19th Street, Arlington, VA 22209.

Training and Careers in Marine Science. International Oceanographic Foundation, 3979 Rickenbacker Causeway, Miami, FL 33149. ($1.00/copy)

U.S. Ocean Scientists & Engineers Directory. American Geophysical Union, 2000 Florida Avenue NW, Washington, DC 20009.

University Curricula in Oceanography and Related Fields. Marine Technology Society, 1825 K Street NW, Suite 203, Washington, DC 20006.

Networking

Although what you know is very important, who you know also helps. Many job openings are never announced officially, but are filled by personal recommendations. Volunteers or interns at an organization already have a foot well placed in the door.

A professor might recommend a graduate student he or she is supervising to a colleague.

An informal interview at a scientific conference you attend could result in a job offer.

Internet

More and more organizations post information and job openings on the Web. Fire up any search engine and type in key words such as biology careers or jobs with marine mammals and you'll be surprised at the number of resources you'll find.

PROFESSIONAL ASSOCIATIONS

In addition to information and professional contacts, some professional associations offer grants, scholarships, and training opportunities.

American Cetacean Society
P.O. Box 1391
San Pedro, CA 90733

American Fisheries Society
5410 Grosvenor Lane
Suite 110
Bethesda, MD 20814

American Geophysical Union
2000 Florida Avenue NW
Washington, DC 20009

American Society of Limnology and Oceanography
Great Lakes Research Division
University of Michigan
Ann Arbor, MI 48109

American Society of Mammalogists
Virginia Museum of Natural History
1001 Douglas Avenue
Martinsville, VA 24112
Send self-addressed, stamped envelope with 5.25" or 3.5" IBM-compatible formatted disk to receive a list of grant sources.

American Society of Mammalogists
c/o Dr. Richard S. Ostfeld
Institute of Ecosystem Studies
Box AB
Millbrook, NY 12545
Grants-in-Aid of Research, up to $1,000, open to graduate students and upper-level undergraduates who are members of the American Society of Mammalogists. Annual; application deadline is in March of each year.

American Society of Mammalogists
c/o Dr. Richard S. Ostfeld
Institute of Ecosystem Studies
Box AB
Millbrook, NY 12545
Albert R. and Alma Shadle Fellowship in Mammalogy. Applicants must be United States citizens and enrolled in or accepted for a graduate program in mammalogy in a U.S. college or university.

American Society of Mammalogists
H. Duane Smith, Secretary-Treasurer
501 Widtsoe Building
Brigham Young University
Provo, UT 84602

American Veterinary Medical Association
1931 N. Meacham Road
Suite 1000
Schaumburg, IL 60173

American Zoo and Aquarium Association
Executive Office and Conservation Center
7970-D Old Georgetown Road
Bethesda, MD 20814-2493

American Zoo and Aquarium Association
Office of Membership Services
Oglebay Park
Wheeling, WV 26003-1698

Consortium of Aquariums, Universities and Zoos
Department of Psychology
California State University
Northridge, CA 91330

Environmental Careers Organization
286 Congress Street
Boston, MA 02210

European Association for Aquatic Mammals
Frans J. Engelsma, Secretary/Treasurer
Postbus 58
3910 AB Rhenen
The Netherlands

European Cetacean Society
Dr. Harald Benke
Deutches Museum fur Meereskunde und Fischerei
Katharinenberg 14-20
D-18439 Stralsund
Germany

Gulf Coast Research Laboratory
Scott Marine Education Center
P.O. Box 7000
Ocean Springs, MS 39564

International Association for Aquatic Animal Medicine
c/o Dr. Larisa Ford
Department of Fish & Wildlife Resources
College of Forestry, Wildlife, and Range Sciences
University of Idaho
Moscow, ID 83844

International Marine Animal Trainers Association
1200 S. Lake Shore Drive
Chicago, IL 60605

International Oceanographic Foundation
4600 Rickenbacker Causeway
Miami, FL 33149

Marine Technology Society
1828 L Street NW
Suite 906
Washington, DC 20035

Minority Institutions
Marine Science Association
Biology Department
Box 18540
Jackson State University
Jackson, MS 39217

National Oceanic & Atmospheric Administration
Marine Policy Fellowships
National Sea Grant College Program
1335 East-West Highway
Silver Spring, MD 20910

National Sea Grant Office
1335 East-West Highway
Silver Spring, MD 20910

Oceanic Engineering Society
Institute of Electrical and Electronics Engineers
345 E. 47th Street
New York, NY 10017-2394

The Oceanography Society
1755 Massachusetts Avenue NW
Suite 700
Washington, DC 20036

The Society for Marine Mammalogy
Glenn VanBlaricom
School of Fisheries WH10/U
University of Washington
Seattle, WA 98195

Student Conservation Association
Resource Assistant Program
Earth Work
Department EW
Box 550
Charlestown, NH 03603

Technical Committee on Acoustical Oceanography
Acoustical Society of America
500 Sunnyside Boulevard
Woodbury, NY 11797-2999

Women's Aquatic Network
Box 4993
Washington, DC 20008

SELECTED INTERNSHIPS

Aquarium for Wildlife Conservation
610 Surf Avenue
Brooklyn, NY 11240

Aquarium of Niagara Falls
Intern/Volunteer program
701 Whirlpool Street
Niagara Falls, NY 14301

Atlantic Cetacean Research Center
Intern/Volunteer Program
70 Thurston Point Road
P.O. Box 1413
Gloucester, MA 01930

Belle Isle Zoo & Aquarium
Intern/Volunteer Program
P.O. Box 39
Royal Oak, MI 48068-0039

Center for Coastal Studies
Intern Review Committee
Box 1036
Provincetown, MA 02657

Center for Marine Conservation
Intern/Volunteer Program
1725 DeSales Street NW
Washington, DC 20036

Cetacean Research Unit
Intern/Volunteer Program
P.O. Box 159
Gloucester, MA 01930

Chicago Zoological Park
Brookfield Zoo
Intern/Volunteer Program
3300 Golf Road
Brookfield, IL 60513

Clearwater Marine Aquarium
249 Windward Passage
Clearwater, FL 33767

Dolphins Plus
P.O. Box 2728
Key Largo, FL 33037

Florida Dept. of Environmental Protection
Florida Marine Research Institute
Intern/Volunteer Program
100 8th Avenue, S.E.
St. Petersburg, FL 33701-5095

Friends of the National Zoo
Research Traineeship Program
National Zoological Park
Washington, DC 20008

Kewalo Basin Marine Mammal Laboratory
Intern Coordinator
1129 Ala Moana Boulevard
Honolulu, HI 96814

Marine Mammal Research Group
EPCOT Center, Trailer #251
Attn: Peter Cook
Walt Disney World Company
Lake Buena Vista, FL 32830-1000

Marine Mammal Research Program
Intern/Volunteer Program
Texas A&M University at Galveston
Department of Fisheries and Wildlife
4700 Avenue U
Building 303
Galveston, TX 77551

Mirage Hotel
Intern/Volunteer Program
P.O. Box 7777
Las Vegas, NV 89177-0777

Mote Marine Laboratory
Andrea Davis, Coordinator of Intern/Volunteer Services
1600 Thompson Parkway
Sarasota, FL 34236

Mystic Marinelife Aquarium
Intern/Volunteer Program
55 Coogan Boulevard
Mystic, CT 06355-1997

National Aquarium in Baltimore
Pier 3
501 E. Pratt Street
Baltimore, MD 21202-3194

National Museum of Natural History
Intern Coordinator, Education Office
Room 212, MRC 158
Smithsonian Institution
Washington, DC 20560

New England Aquarium
Intern/Volunteer Program
Central Wharf
Boston, MA 02110-3399

Pacific Whale Foundation
Intern/Volunteer Program
Kealia Beach Plaza
101 N. Kihei Road
Suite 21
Kihei, HI 96753-8833

Pinniped Learning & Behavior Project
Internships
Long Marine Lab
University of California
100 Shaffer Road
Santa Cruz, CA 95060

Tethys Research Institute
Viale G.B. Gadio 2
I-20121 Milan, Italy

The John G. Shedd Aquarium
Internship Coordinator
1200 S. Lake Shore Drive
Chicago, IL 60605

The Oceania Project (humpback whale research)
P.O. Box 646
Byron Bay
248N New South Wales
Australia
E-mail: oceania@nor.com.au

Theater of the Sea
Intern/Volunteer Program
P.O. Box 407
Islamorada, FL 33036

Waikiki Aquarium
Intern/Volunteer Program
2777 Kalakaua Avenue
Honolulu, HI 96815

Whale Museum
Craig Snapp, Volunteer Coordinator
62 First Street North
P.O. Box 945
Friday Harbor, WA 98250

Whale Research Group
Dr. Jon Lien
230 Mount Scio Road
Memorial University of Newfoundland
St. John's, Newfoundland, Canada
A1C 5S7

FIELD PROGRAMS (Pay to Volunteer)

Cetacean Behavior Lab Internships
c/o Dr. R. H. Defran
Department of Psychology
San Diego State University
San Diego, CA 92182

Coastal Ecosystems Research Foundation
2648 Tennis Circle
Vancouver, British Columbia, Canada
V6T 2E1
E-mail: info@cerf.bc.ca

EarthWatch
680 Mount Auburn Street
P.O. Box 403
Watertown, MA 02272-9104

Green Volunteers
1 Greenleaf Woods Drive, #302A
Portsmouth, NH 03810
E-mail: info@greenvol.com
An international list of volunteer opportunities (list costs $16.00 plus $5.00 postage). Lists more than 100 opportunities worldwide. Includes many marine mammal projects. Short- and long-term opportunities available. Some projects require a financial contribution.

Mingan Island Cetacean Study
285 Green Street
St. Lambert, Quebec, Canada
J4P 1T3

Oceanic Society Expeditions
Fort Mason Center—Building E
San Francisco, CA 94123

School for Field Studies
16 Broadway Street
Beverly, MA 01915

University Research Expedition Programs
University of California
Berkeley, CA 94720-6586

CHAPTER THIRTEEN

PATH 4: MEDICAL SCIENTISTS, TECHNOLOGISTS, AND TECHNICIANS

*I*f you always pictured yourself in a white lab coat or are fascinated by the idea of making new discoveries—cures for cancer or AIDS, for example—this may be the career path for you.

But even if you prefer to work with proven methods and have some patient contact, a medical scientist or clinical technician career path could fill the bill.

DEFINITION OF THE CAREER PATH: MEDICAL SCIENTISTS

Biological scientists who do biomedical research are usually called medical scientists. Medical scientists working on basic research into normal biological systems often do so in order to understand the causes of and to discover treatment for disease and other health problems. Medical scientists may try to identify the kinds of changes in a cell, chromosome, or even the gene that signals the development of medical problems, such as different types of cancer. After identifying structures of or changes in organisms that provide clues to health problems, medical scientists may then work on the treatment of problems. For example, a medical scientist involved in cancer research might try to formulate a combination of drugs that will lessen the effects of the disease. Medical scientists who have a medical degree might then administer the drugs to patients in clinical trials, monitor their reactions, and observe the results. (Medical scientists who do not have a medical degree normally collaborate with a medical doctor who deals directly with patients.) The medical scientist might then return to the laboratory to examine the results and, if necessary, adjust the dosage levels to reduce negative side effects or to try to induce even better results.

In addition to using basic research to develop treatments for health problems, medical scientists attempt to discover ways to prevent health problems from developing, such as affirming the link between smoking and increased risk of lung cancer, or alcoholism and liver disease.

Most medical scientists specialize in some area of biology such as microbiology or biochemistry.

Here are definitions for many of the areas of specialization:

Anatomist

Anatomists study the form and structure of animal bodies and try to determine the ability of animal bodies to regenerate destroyed or injured parts. They also investigate the possibility of transplanting whole organs or tissue fragments, such as skin.

Biochemist

Biochemists study the chemical composition of living things. They try to understand the complex chemical combinations and reactions involved in metabolism, reproduction, growth, and heredity. Biochemists may investigate causes and cures of diseases, or study the effects of food, hormones, or other substances on various organisms.

Much of the work in biotechnology is done by biochemists and molecular biologists because this technology involves understanding the complex chemistry of life.

Biomedical Engineer

Biomedical engineers research and develop new ways to help people who are handicapped by the malfunction of a body organ. Biomedical engineers have created devices such as artificial hearts, kidneys, limbs, and joints.

Biophysicist

Biophysicists study the physical principles within living cells and organisms. These scientists specialize in issues such as how the eye converts light into a signal to the brain, or how radiation affects living matter.

Biotechnology

Advances in basic biological knowledge, especially at the genetic and molecular levels, continue to spur the field of biotechnology. Biological and medical scientists use this technology to manipulate the genetic material of animals or plants, attempting to make organisms more productive or disease resistant. The first application of this technology has been in the medical and pharmaceutical areas. Many substances not previously available in large quantities are starting to be produced by biotechnological means; some may be useful in treating cancer and other diseases.

Cellular Biologist

A typical cellular biologist looks at the organs and cells of the body by manipulating samples of cells with drugs or by physical means to see how they react under certain conditions.

Developmental Biologist

Developmental biologists, formerly known as embryologists, study the development of an animal from a fertilized egg through the hatching process or birth. They also study causes of healthy and abnormal development.

Epidemiologist

Epidemiologists study the patterns of disease within a population. They also investigate how diseases are caused and how they spread.

Geneticist

Geneticists study how different traits and disorders are inherited. They may also investigate methods for altering or producing new traits.

Immunologist

Immunologists study how the body protects itself against foreign invaders such as parasites, viruses, and transplanted organs. They research ways to develop vaccines to protect against disease and medicines to cure or prevent allergic reactions.

Microbiologist

Microbiologists investigate microscopic organisms such as bacteria, viruses, algae, yeasts, and molds. These scientists try to discover how such organisms affect animals, plants, and the environment. Some microbiologists specialize in medicine or agriculture, while others focus on particular organisms. Microbiology includes virology and bacteriology.

Molecular Biologist

Molecular biologists are interested in large molecules (usually DNA or protein) with the ultimate goal of discovering what they do in the animal. From advances in molecular biology there has been considerable industrial spin-off such as DNA fingerprinting and the manufacture of genetically engineered drugs and diagnostic tools.

Mycologist

Mycologists perform experiments on fungi to discover any that might be harmful to humans or could be useful to medicine, agriculture, and industry for the development of drugs, medicines, molds, and yeasts.

Pathologist

Pathologists study the nature, cause, and development of diseases and the changes to animals and plants caused by the diseases. They make diagnoses from body tissues, fluids, and other specimens. They also perform autopsies to determine the nature and extent of disease as well as the cause of death.

Pharmacologist

Pharmacologists develop new or improved drugs or medicines. They also conduct experiments to discover the effects of different drugs—the benefits and possible shortcomings or undesirable side effects.

DEFINITION OF THE CAREER PATH: CLINICAL TECHNICIANS AND TECHNOLOGISTS

Clinical laboratory testing plays a crucial role in the detection, diagnosis, and treatment of disease. Clinical laboratory technologists and technicians, also known as medical technologists and technicians, perform most of these tests.

Clinical laboratory personnel examine and analyze body fluids, tissues, and cells. They look for bacteria, parasites, or other microorganisms; analyze the chemical content of fluids; match blood for transfusions; and test for drug levels in the blood to show how a patient is responding to treatment. They also prepare specimens for examination, count cells, and look for abnormal cells.

They use automated equipment and instruments that perform a number of tests simultaneously, as well as microscopes, cell counters, and other kinds of sophisticated laboratory equipment to perform tests. Then they analyze the results and relay them to physicians.

Some medical and clinical laboratory technologists supervise medical and clinical laboratory technicians.

Technologists in small laboratories perform many types of tests, while those in large laboratories generally specialize.

Here are definitions for some of the specializations:

Blood bank technologists collect, type, and prepare blood and its components for transfusions.

Clinical chemistry technologists prepare specimens and analyze the chemical and hormonal contents of body fluids.

Cytotechnologists prepare slides of body cells and microscopically examine these cells for abnormalities that may signal the beginning of a cancerous growth.

Immunology technologists examine elements and responses of the human immune system to foreign bodies.

Microbiology technologists examine and identify bacteria and other microorganisms.

Medical and clinical laboratory technicians perform less complex tests and laboratory procedures than technologists. Technicians may prepare specimens and operate automatic analyzers, for example, or they may perform manual tests following detailed instructions.

Like technologists, they may work in several areas of the clinical laboratory or specialize in just one. For example, histology technicians cut and stain tissue specimens for microscopic examination by pathologists, and phlebotomists draw and test blood. They usually work under the supervision of medical and clinical laboratory technologists or laboratory managers.

POSSIBLE JOB TITLES

Also within this broad career path biology majors can use their undergraduate degrees as a stepping stone to advanced medical training as physicians, nurses, physical therapists, and the wide spectrum of other practitioners who work with patients.

In addition to the definitions of the professional job titles just examined, here is a list of possible job titles that biology majors with additional training can pursue in the health-care fields:

Audiologist	Nutritionist
Biomedical engineer	Occupational therapist
Chiropractor	Ophthalmologist
Dental assistant	Optician
Dentist	Optometrist
Dietitian	Pharmacist
Emergency medical technician	Phlebotomist
Genetic counselor	Physical therapist
Hospital administrator	Physician assistant
Industrial hygienist	Physician in specialty areas
Licensed practical nurse	Podiatrist
Medical illustrator	Radiologic technologist
Medical records librarian	Recreational therapist
Medical supply sales	Respiratory therapist
Mortician	Speech pathologist
Nurse	Veterinarian
Nurse practitioner	

POSSIBLE JOB SETTINGS

Many medical scientists are employed by county, state, and federal agencies or in the private sector such as an animal vaccine supply company, a clinical reference laboratory doing tests for physicians and health departments, or a pharmaceutical corporation, as well as by hospitals, blood banks, and colleges and universities.

Many industries require the expertise of scientists to ensure the safety of their products, such as the cosmetic industry, food processors, and the dairy industry. Environmental and pollution control companies and the biotechnology industry also are large employers of biological scientists.

Some medical scientists work in management or administration or as consultants to business firms or to government. They may plan and administer programs for testing foods and drugs, for example, or write for technical publications. Some work in sales and service jobs for companies manufacturing chemicals or other technical products.

Almost one in four nonfaculty biological scientists are employed by federal, state, and local governments. Federal biological scientists work mainly in the U.S. Departments of Agriculture, the Interior, and Defense, and in the National Institutes of Health. Most of the rest work in the drug industry, which includes pharmaceutical and biotechnology establishments; hospitals; or research and testing laboratories.

More than half the employed clinical technologists and technicians work in hospitals. Most others work in medical laboratories and offices and clinics of physicians. Some work in blood banks, research and testing laboratories, and in the federal government at the Department of Veterans Affairs hospitals and U.S. Public Health Service facilities.

WORKING CONDITIONS

Medical scientists generally work regular hours in offices or laboratories and usually are not exposed to unsafe or unhealthy conditions. But some do work with dangerous organisms or toxic substances in the laboratory, so strict safety procedures must be followed to avoid contamination.

Medical scientists also spend time working in clinics and hospitals, administering drugs and treatments to patients in clinical trials.

Hours and other working conditions vary according to the size and type of employment setting, especially for technologists and technicians. In large hospitals or in independent laboratories that operate continuously, personnel usually work the day, evening, or night shift, and may work weekends and holidays. Laboratory personnel in small facilities may work on rotating shifts rather than on a regular shift.

In some facilities, laboratory personnel are on call, available in case of an emergency, and work several nights a week or on weekends.

Clinical laboratory personnel are trained to work with infectious specimens. When proper methods of infection control and sterilization are followed, few hazards exist.

Laboratories generally are well-lighted and clean; however, specimens, solutions, and reagents used in the laboratory sometimes produce odors. Laboratory workers may spend a great deal of time on their feet.

TRAINING REQUIREMENTS

The complexity of tests performed, the level of judgment needed, and the amount of responsibility workers assume depend largely on the amount of education and experience they have.

Many students planning to enter medical schools, or dentistry or veterinary colleges will fulfill part of their entrance requirements by taking courses or even completing bachelor's degrees in biology and zoology.

There is an increasing trend for medical researchers to have both Ph.D. and M.D. degrees. Many universities have integrated these programs.

In addition to these routes into health care, there are numerous positions available as technicians and technologists both in clinical and research laboratories. In many cases, it is possible to find employment as a biomedical technician with a bachelor's degree but it should be noted, however, that the operation of diagnostic equipment often requires training beyond a degree.

People with a bachelor's degree in biological science are usually not called biological scientists, but find jobs as science or engineering technicians or health technologists and technicians.

For biological scientists, the Ph.D. degree generally is required for college teaching, for independent research, and for advancement to administrative positions.

A master's degree is sufficient for some jobs in applied research and for jobs in management, inspection, sales, and service. The bachelor's degree is adequate for some nonresearch jobs.

Some graduates with a bachelor's degree start as biological scientists in testing and inspection, or get jobs related to biological science such as technical sales or service representatives. In some cases, graduates with a bachelor's degree are able to work in a laboratory environment on their own projects, but this is unusual. Some may work as research assistants.

Biological scientists should be able to work independently or as part of a team and be able to communicate clearly and concisely, both orally and in writing.

Those in private industry who aspire to management or administrative positions should possess good business skills and be familiar with regulatory issues and marketing and management techniques. Those doing field research in remote areas must have physical stamina.

Medical scientists who administer drug or gene therapy to human patients or who otherwise interact medically with patients (such as excising tissue or performing other invasive procedures) must have a medical degree. It is particularly helpful for medical scientists to earn both Ph.D. and medical degrees.

In addition to their formal education, medical scientists are usually expected to spend several years in a postdoctoral position before they are offered permanent jobs. Postdoctoral work provides valuable laboratory experience, including experience in specific processes and techniques (such as gene splicing), which are transferable to other research projects later on. In some institutions, the postdoctoral position can lead to a permanent position.

The usual requirement for an entry-level position as a medical or clinical laboratory technologist is a bachelor's degree with a major in medical technology or in one of the life sciences. Universities and hospitals offer medical technology programs.

It is also possible to qualify through a combination of on-the-job and specialized training. Bachelor's degree programs in medical technology include courses in chemistry, biological sciences, microbiology, and mathematics, and specialized courses devoted to knowledge and skills used in the clinical laboratory.

Many programs also offer or require courses in management, business, and computer applications.

Master's degrees in medical technology and related clinical laboratory sciences provide training for specialized areas of laboratory work or teaching, administration, or research.

The Clinical Laboratory Improvement Act (CLIA) requires technologists who perform certain highly complex tests to have at least an associate's degree.

Medical and clinical laboratory technicians generally have either an associate's degree from a community or junior college; or a certificate from a hospital, vocational or technical school; or from one of the armed forces. A few technicians learn on the job.

Nationally recognized accrediting agencies in the clinical laboratory sciences include the National Accrediting Agency for Clinical Laboratory Sciences and the Accrediting Bureau of Health Education Schools (ABHES).

The National Accrediting Agency for Clinical Laboratory Sciences fully accredits 621 and approves 72 programs that provide education for medical and clinical laboratory technologists, cytotechnologists, histologic technicians, specialists in blood bank technology, and medical and clinical laboratory technicians.

ABHES accredits training programs for medical and clinical laboratory technicians.

Some states require laboratory personnel to be licensed or registered. Information on licensure is available from state departments of health or boards of occupational licensing.

Certification is a voluntary process by which a nongovernmental organization, such as a professional society or certifying agency, grants recognition to an individual whose professional competence meets prescribed standards. Widely accepted by employers in the health industry, certification is a prerequisite for most jobs and often is necessary for advancement. Agencies that certify medical and clinical laboratory technologists and technicians include the Board of Registry of the American Society of Clinical Pathologists, the American Medical Technologists, the American Society for Clinical Laboratory Science, and the Credentialing Commission of the International Society for Clinical Laboratory Technology. These agencies have different requirements for certification and different organizational sponsors.

Clinical laboratory personnel need analytical judgment and the ability to work under pressure. Close attention to detail is essential because small differences or changes in test substances or numerical readouts can be crucial for patient care. Manual dexterity and normal color vision are highly desirable.

With the widespread use of automated laboratory equipment, computer skills are important. In addition, technologists in particular are expected to be good at problem solving.

Technologists may advance to supervisory positions in laboratory work or become chief medical or clinical laboratory technologists or laboratory managers in hospitals.

Manufacturers of home diagnostic testing kits and laboratory equipment and supplies seek experienced technologists to work in product development, marketing, and sales. Graduate education in medical technology, one of the biological sciences, chemistry, management, or education usually speeds advancement.

A doctorate is sometimes needed to become a laboratory director. However, federal regulation allows directors of moderately complex laboratories to have either a master's degree or a bachelor's degree combined with the appropriate amount of training and experience. Technicians can become technologists through additional education and experience.

CAREER OUTLOOK

Demand will remain strong for biological and medical scientists to research health problems and discover new treatments. Employment of biological and medical scientists is expected to increase faster than the average for all occupations through the year 2005. Nevertheless, job seekers can expect to face considerable competition for highly sought-after basic research positions. Biological and medical scientists will continue to conduct genetic and biotechnological research and help develop and produce products through new biological methods. In addition, efforts to clean up and preserve the environment will continue to add to growth. More biological scientists will be needed to determine the environmental impact of industry and government actions and to correct past environmental problems.

Expected expansion in research related to health issues, such as AIDS, cancer, and the Human Genome project, should also result in growth.

Biological and medical scientists are less likely to lose their jobs during recessions than those in many other occupations because most are employed on long-term research projects or in agricultural research. However, a recession could influence the amount of money allocated to new research and development efforts, particularly in areas of risky or innovative research. A recession could also limit the possibility of extension or renewal of existing projects.

Employment of clinical laboratory workers is expected to grow about as fast as the average for all occupations through the year 2006 as the volume of laboratory tests increases with population growth and the development of new types of tests.

Hospitals and independent laboratories have recently undergone considerable consolidation and restructuring that have boosted productivity and allowed the same number of personnel to perform more tests than previously possible. As a result, competition for jobs has increased and individuals may now have to look longer to find employment than in the past.

Technological advances will continue to have two opposing effects on employment through 2006. New, more powerful diagnostic tests will encourage more testing and spur employment. However, advances in laboratory automation and simpler tests, which make it possible for each worker to perform more tests, should slow growth.

Research and development efforts are targeted at simplifying routine testing procedures so that nonlaboratory personnel, physicians, and patients in particular can perform tests now done in laboratories. Also, robots may prepare specimens, a job done now by technologists and technicians.

Although significant, growth will not be the only source of opportunities. As in most occupations, many openings will result from the need to replace workers who transfer to other occupations, retire, or stop working for some other reason.

EARNINGS

According to the National Association of Colleges and Employers, beginning salary offers in private industry in 1997 averaged $25,400 a year for bachelor's degree recipients in biological science; about $26,900 for master's degree recipients; and about $52,400 for doctoral degree recipients.

Median annual earnings for biological and life scientists were about $36,300 in 1996; the middle 50 percent earned between $28,400 and $50,900. Ten percent earned less than $22,000, and 10 percent earned more than $66,000.

For medical scientists, median annual earnings were about $34,300; the middle 50 percent earned between $25,200 and $52,200. Ten percent earned less than $18,700, and 10 percent earned more than $74,000.

In the federal government in 1997, general biological scientists in non-supervisory, supervisory, and managerial positions earned an average salary of $52,100; microbiologists averaged $58,700; physiologists, $65,900; and geneticists, $62,700.

Median weekly earnings of full-time, salaried clinical laboratory technologists and technicians were $520 in 1996. Half earned between $403 and $706. The lowest 10 percent earned less than $298, and the top 10 percent more than $852.

According to a Hay Group survey of acute care hospitals, the median annual base salary of full-time laboratory technicians was $26,500 in January 1997. The middle 50 percent earned between $23,700 and $29,500. Full-time salaried staff medical laboratory technologists earned about $35,100; the middle 50 percent earned between $32,500 and $37,900.

The average annual salary for medical technologists employed by the federal government was $40,680 in early 1997. Medical technicians earned an average of $26,130.

CLOSE-UPS

CARLA LEE SUSON, MICRO/MOLECULAR BIOLOGIST

Carla Lee Suson has worked as a research assistant and chemical technician for a medical school and a chemical company, both in Texas. She has been in the field since 1985 and started her first lab job in her last year of college.

She has a B.A. in molecular biology from the University of Texas, Dallas, at Richardson, Texas, and graduated in 1986. She has also taken some master's level classes at Texas A&M University in Kingsville.

Getting Started

"I always wanted to be in the medical field for as long as I could remember. I discovered in high school that I did not have the stomach to be a doctor or nurse but loved working in the lab. I was very good at science. I decided to become a research scientist. In college, I became even more attracted to working with microscopes, centrifuges, and lab equipment. The work was fun and fascinating.

"I was trained at the University of Texas at Dallas as a micro/molecular biologist (B.A.). While there, I worked with mouse mitochondria DNA, separating it by gel electrophoresis and then putting it on special paper using western blots. I did not kill the mice but they were killed, the livers ground up into cellular mush, and the mitochondria taken out. We were investigating what the DNA sequence was in mitochondria. This was a mix of cellular and molecular work.

"My first lab job was as a tissue culture technologist at the Southwestern Medical School in Dallas. We studied the cellular causes of arthritis and rheumatism. Here we separated out vein cells from human placentas and white blood cells (t-cells) from blood samples and looked at how t-cells migrated across a vein cell barrier under the influence of a given drug. This is strictly cellular work.

"My second job involved more use of radiation labels to trace the amount of proteins in a cell. We isolated certain growth proteins from blood, labeled them with radioactive isotopes, and then added them to the media on top of foreskin fibroblasts (sort of muscle cells). Eventually we harvested the cells and isolated the DNA to see if the protein caused the cells to grow. The more DNA you have, the more cells you grew. This work involved a lot of column chromatography, radio-immuno assays, and cell work.

"My husband moved down to a small university town for his job (physics) and unfortunately, their biology department was animal-oriented. They studied snakes mostly. I wasn't really employable there so I got a job as a test technician at the local chemical factory. The factory was trying to make ibuprophen and acetomediphen (main ingredients in Advil and Tylenol) but was having trouble with their quality control.

continued

continued

"Under their chemist, I tested samples for purity and the waste waters for trace compounds. This involved a lot of wet chemistry techniques, HPLC (high pressure liquid chromatography), gas chromatography, and spectrometry."

The Day to Day

"The actual laboratory work is very repetitive from day to day. When you are trying to prove some drug works against some disease, you have to repeat the experiment many different times and with many different small changes. An average research project can easily lead to six months or a year of doing very similar experiments over and over again. Most experiments will last for several days doing different procedures (working on different equipment) at different steps. After you get your raw data back, you then have to analyze it to see if it has any meaning.

"Frequently the whole week's experiments are wasted because for one reason or another, the experiment didn't work. A person has to have clean habits and very good record keeping ability to be a success at this. Being even slightly dirty, or unaware of what you are doing, not only can ruin the experiments but can also create a health hazard. A technician I knew had a habit of eating donuts in the lab. She ruined all her experiments with sticky fingers and almost ate a mold-infested donut one day. It was horrible. If you don't keep good records, by the time you get your data back, you don't have any idea what effect you are looking for. An average experiment may mean working with 100 or more tubes of solutions. If you don't know what exactly is in every tube (and what amount), then your experiment is ruined. It helps to be highly organized, too. The more organized you are about your time, the less overtime you have to work.

"The work is very independent. I was often given my instructions at the beginning of the week and then left to do it at whatever pace was needed. I liked not having to be monitored all the time, but you have to have discipline to do the work in a timely manner. Labs can be quite small (one to three people who don't interact much) or very large (five or more people with lots of shared responsibility), but everyone I've ever met in labs or working at labs grouped together have always been very friendly and very intelligent.

"In the larger groups, the supervising doctor (usually a Ph.D.) encourages the technicians to have group meetings to discuss papers they have read that may impact the work. The opportunity for furthering your informal education in different techniques never stops. I've been in large lab groups that had frequent parties (birthdays, baby showers) and lunch get-togethers, all to create a strong social group.

"The work week cannot be compared to a normal 9 to 5 position. When you are working with animals or cells, you have to be prepared to do the experiment when they are ready. In many situations, this can be timed so that all the work happens during the week with only an occasional Saturday afternoon. Frequently I did all my data analysis work at home on my computer so that the time in the lab was actually spent working with test tubes. There are times when the workload increases because the supervisor wants to give a paper or a talk or needs the information for a grant. During those times, the work hours can be long. You have to be willing to be flexible with your time.

"During the average week, there are periods of time that you are simply waiting for something to finish 'cooking.' Those periods are filled with ordering supplies, making media, cleaning the lab (a never-ending task), doing work on machines, doing your hazard test checks (such as radiation checks), and generally doing the paperwork that is found in most work situations.

"Unless you have a master's degree or a Ph.D., you will not travel to conferences (it's very rare) or have your name published as a co-author on any paper. The bosses rarely have money to allow their workers to travel and usually the graduate students must take preference because they need to present papers in order to graduate.

"The lower tech jobs are also more at risk because of lab closures, loss of grant money, or downsizing. However, with the techniques you know, it is usually easy to get hired into another lab (usually at the same place) doing similar work. There is always a need for qualified technicians and assistants at any medical school."

continued

continued

The Upsides and Downsides

"I love the experimenting because it is like figuring out a puzzle. Once you know the truth behind what you are doing, it is wonderful. I love the chance to 'play' with all the high-tech equipment. I'm not actually playing, of course, but it is a lot like being a big kid in a gadget shop.

"I also love the idea that I am making some small effort to change mankind or help it through knowledge. When a professor or doctor receives an award or publishes a paper, even though you don't get public acclaim for it, the whole lab celebrates. Without your little contribution, the experiment would not have happened.

"The downsides are that grant money is fickle and your job can disappear even after years of service. You must live near bio-industrial companies or medical schools for employment. This is not the kind of job that you can find anywhere. Most universities, especially the small ones, do not hire outside help. It is cheaper for them to hire work-study students to work in the labs. It's better for the students, too, in that they gain experience, but it is rotten for the career-minded technician.

"When you tell nonscience people you work in a lab, they usually have this odd reaction, like you are the cruelest person on earth. My physicist husband frequently gets comments like 'you must be so smart to do that,' whereas the reaction to my work is 'oh gosh, I couldn't hurt small animals like that.' There is the assumption that biologists are not as smart as other scientists and have a proclivity and great desire to torture mice. It is actually very rare for the molecular/microbiologist to even work with animals.

"But in some labs you may have to work with animals, including killing them for certain organs (it is called sacrificing). This is done in a very pain-free manner, but most people can't do it. Alternately you may have to work with human tissue from cadavers, or discarded tissue such as foreskins from babies or placentas. This easily grosses out most people but also it carries a hazard of disease. Technicians have little chance of catching any illness if they are careful, but their chances are higher than other professions. If you are scared of catching any disease, this is not the job for you."

Salaries

"The technician salary is more or less equivalent to a school-teacher's salary at the beginning of your career. Of course, the more you know, the more experience you have, the better pay you will get.

"Industrial jobs pay about one and a half times more than medical schools. My starting salary in 1986 was about $15,000 a year. Today I would expect to get a salary of about $22,000 a year at a university or medical school. Of course that includes a good benefits package of insurance, retirement, and child care help. Most schools have good benefits for their staff."

Advice from Carla Lee Suson

"Take classes in computers, chemistry, and statistics, as well as your normal biology classes. The knowledge can only help you. There are growing new fields in biophysics, radiation physics, and computer theoretical biology (a very new field) that will need new people and are paying top salaries.

"Work in labs while in school as much as you can and get experience in many different lab techniques. When you get out of school, your experience will give you the edge over other applicants.

"Make great grades. Most college kids think that C is good enough. When you apply for any science-oriented job, they will take a close look at your school transcripts (even when you have 10 years' experience in the field). Science work is one of the few professions that look at your academic record almost as much (if not more so) than your work experience. If they don't like the grades you made, they won't hire you. Bad grades will haunt you the rest of your life. The A student gets hired more quickly."

MELISSA TIPPENS, CLINICAL MICROBIOLOGIST

Melissa Tippens worked in two hospital labs and an industrial lab, all in Georgia, for a total of three years, before she left the field to raise her children. In 1984 she earned her B.S. in biology from Western Kentucky University in Bowling Green and in 1986 her Master's of Medical Science (MMSc) from Emory University in Atlanta, Georgia, in clinical microbiology.

"I had a high school biology teacher who taught a unit on bacteriology and I absolutely loved it. From there I took a college course in microbiology and my mind was made up.

"In college I majored in biology but had to get a graduate degree to get in my field of interest.

"My first job was at the Emory University Hospital Clinical Microbiology Laboratory where I had done my training as well as holding a part-time job. They had a full-time opening shortly after I graduated.

"My second job was a fluke. I had recently moved, was tiring of the commute, and happened to meet the microbiology supervisor of the local hospital. They were planning to fill a position at that time and I applied. My next job was a brief foray into industrial microbiology. I was looking for Monday through Friday positions, saw the job in the newspaper, and applied. Then in 1989 I decided to leave the field to become a homemaker."

The Day to Day

"Duties vary depending on the size and type of lab. At a larger hospital microbiology lab, I was assigned a certain area and bench each day/week. The different areas were bacteriology, parasitology, mycology, virology/serology, and AFB (Acid-Fast Bacilli).

"In bacteriology, the different benches included primary plating, respiratory cultures, miscellaneous cultures (such as body fluids, wounds, tissues), urine and stool cultures, blood cultures, anaerobic cultures, and identification and sensitivities.

"A typical day in primary plating would involve receiving specimens, logging them in, setting them up on the appropriate nutritive media, and placing them in the proper incubation temperature and atmosphere. If Gram's stains were made, they would be examined under the microscope and recorded

"A typical day at most of the other benches would include examining the cultures for growth, differentiating between normal flora and pathogens, and isolating the pathogens for further identification. Once a pure culture of the pathogen was obtained, it was sent to the I.D. and Sensitivity bench. Here an automated system identified the organism and tested different antibiotics to see which ones would inhibit growth. This information would help doctors decide which treatment would be most effective.

"The blood cultures bench was different in that an automated system was used to detect the growth of bacteria in the bottles of blood. If any were detected, a Gram's stain was made. If we found bacteria on the stain the doctor was notified immediately. Then the media was inoculated to grow the bacteria for I.D. and sensitivity.

"General responsibilities of a technologist included entering preliminary or final results in the computer so doctors and other health-care providers can keep abreast of the progress of the cultures. Techs might also be responsible for running quality control checks before performing certain tests. In addition, they are responsible for cleaning and sanitizing their work area.

"Smaller labs may have one tech working in more than one area because of the lower volume of specimens. A smaller lab may also send certain types of cultures and organisms out to reference labs if they don't have the capability to deal with them.

"Working in an industrial lab calls for a very different type of microbiology. I was in production and my duties included making antiserum and fluorescent antibody stains.

"Hospital work was fast-paced most of the time. I had to learn to be very efficient. Some days the workload was very high so I had to move through the cultures as rapidly as possible without sacrificing accuracy. Mistakes could be costly for a patient.

continued

continued

"The atmosphere was relaxed, but professional. In my experience the workers became friends and even socialized outside work. The supervisors were very available and helpful, while maintaining high standards and expecting our best.

"For the most part, the work was very interesting, especially when unusual organisms were isolated. And knowing that you may have given the doctor information that could help save a patient's life was very rewarding.

The Upsides and Downsides

"My favorite part of the job was doing just that—taking an unknown organism, using all that I had learned along with all the tests available, and identifying it. It was like solving a mystery. Other upsides included having set hours with very little overtime, good health insurance coverage, and some room for advancement.

"The part of working in a hospital that I liked the least was having to work weekends and holidays. In addition to missing out on normal weekend/holiday activities, these times were extremely busy since we worked with a reduced staff.

"Other downsides included the level of pay as well as risk associated with working with infectious agents (although any reputable workplace should have adequate precautions and safety equipment).

"At the time I was working we were paid an hourly rate based on education, experience, and periodic evaluations. I started at around $8 per hour and progressed to around $10 to $11 per hour. I made slightly more, however, when I held an interim supervisory position."

Advice from Melissa Tippens

"My advice to anyone who enjoys biology, specifically microbiology, is to investigate different universities to check out their undergraduate and graduate programs (my master's program at Emory University is no longer available). If someone is more interested in research, a Ph.D. may be necessary. And another option for those interested in other areas of the clinical lab would be to consider a medical technology program. All in all, I think a person interested in the subject matter who is patient and who doesn't mind detail work would be happy in the field of clinical microbiology."

SHARON GRATA, MEDICAL LABORATORY TECHNICIAN

Sharon Grata works for Conemaugh Health Systems at Memorial Medical Center, western Pennsylvania's major trauma center and teaching hospital.

She earned an associate's degree in education from Mount Aloysious College in Cresson, Pennsylvania, and is working toward her B.S. in medical technology at St. Francis College in Loretto, Pennsylvania. She also had one year of clinical medical technician training through Lee Hospital School in Johnstown, Pennsylvania, where she started her career in 1976. She is certified by the American Society of Clinical Pathology.

"As long as I can remember I wanted to do something in the medical profession. In high school after a friend died from leukemia I decided then to do something with the analysis of blood and body fluids.

"After college I had a year of study as well as clinical training in all the departments of a hospital laboratory. After training at the hospital they hired me.

"At the hospital I am what they call a 'generalist' or a rotator. I worked in all the laboratory departments . . . phlebotomy (blood drawing), hematology, chemistry, blood bank, urinalysis, and microbiology. In other words, a jack of all trades.

"In hematology I ran blood counts. This is the test that gives the physician a lot of information in very little time. A machine actually counts how many red cells and white cells are in a cubic milliliter in the blood sample and then calculates how many are in the body. A high white count indicates a bacterial infection where a low one means a possible viral infection.

continued

continued

"This is where the manual differential is performed. A thin smear of blood is taken through a staining process and the lab technician (now machines do this) looks in a microscope to see what types of white blood cells and what percentage of these cells are present. This is the procedure in which leukemia can be detected among other infections such as mononucleosis.

"In the chemistry lab, serum is run through machines to measure the glucose, blood urea nitrogen, sodium, potassium, chloride, cholesterol, cardiac enzymes, and liver enzymes to give a chemical profile of each patient.

"The blood bank is where a person's blood typing and Rh factor are determined. After this, it is crossmatched with a 'donor' unit for transfusion purposes.

"Urinalysis checks for filtration function of the kidneys, glucose, ph, bilirubin, protein, blood, and for bacteria. A dipstick is dipped into the specimen and the strip is placed in the machine and checked for the above tests. Then a portion of the urine is centrifuged and looked at under the microscope for different cells and bacteria and other sediments that may indicate kidney problems or a bladder infection.

"Microbiology is the department that checks for bacterial infections throughout the body. A swab of the throat, eye, or ear, for example, is sent and the lab tech 'plants' the inoculated swab on various media that are poured and set in petri dishes. After incubation, bacteria form colonies and these colonies are identified and run through an antibiotic sensitivity to see which one will kill the bacteria present.

"Laboratory work has changed considerably from the time I first entered the field. Whether it's for the better depends on whom you talk with. It has gone from manual analysis and sometimes tedious work to automation and computerization.

"In 1976 when I started, doctors wanted all the lab tests they could get on a patient as fast as they could get them. Now with HMOs and the insurance companies having so much control over what is paid and what is not paid, they get less for their money and want it faster.

"Back in 1976 lab technician was ranked as one of the ten most stressful jobs and I am positive today it would rank even higher. A normal day starts at four A.M. That is when most of the blood is collected on the patients because we must get our specimens before the patients get their breakfast or are transported to another area of the hospital for other tests or surgery. Yes, we are the ones who wake you up early in the morning and get called everything from vampire to blood sucker to even nastier phrases. Most patients accuse us of doing this just to torture them.

"Sometimes you leave work with the face of a person who was just killed in an automobile accident or a gunshot wound etched in your mind. You don't remember the names because when you get called they are just a color code. Names come the next day if they survive, or if they don't, you see it in the obituary, but you never forget the face.

"Is it worth it? Yes. There isn't a day that goes by that I wonder how I can handle another day of stress, but then I look into the eyes of the patients and realize they are why I come back. The gratitude in their eyes is worth it.

"What I like most is the interaction with patients. If I can make someone who is in pain smile, laugh, and maybe forget their pain for a few seconds, it makes my day.

"The downside is the danger involved, working with body fluids. One wrong move, just a blink of an eye, and at anytime the technician could become infected with a dangerous disease such as hepatitis or HIV. And the pay does not compensate for the risks involved. I make only $22,000 a year."

Advice from Sharon Grata

"My advice for anyone interested in this field is to continue your education and go into a research lab. Hospital laboratories are gearing up for more automation over a human workforce. But the research part of the field is opening up more. Become a hematologist or a Ph.D. chemist or obtain a master's degree in microbiology.

"If you choose not to go for the higher level of education, then look into design and repair of robotic equipment that is making its way into the labs. And know computers inside and out."

PROFESSIONAL ASSOCIATIONS

Accrediting Bureau of Health Education Schools (ABHES)
Secretary
2700 S. Quincy Street
Suite 210
Arlington, VA 22206

For a list of training programs for medical and clinical laboratory technicians accredited by ABHES.

American Association of Anatomists
9650 Rockville Pike
Bethesda, MD 20814

American Association of Blood Banks
8101 Glenbrook Road
Bethesda, MD 20814-2749

American Association of Immunologists
9650 Rockville Pike
Bethesda, MD 20814

American Dietetic Association
216 W. Jackson Boulevard
Chicago, IL 60606-6995

American Medical Technologists
710 Higgins Road
Park Ridge, IL 60068

American Physiological Society
Membership Services Department
9650 Rockville Pike
Bethesda, MD 20814

American Society for Biochemistry and Molecular Biology
9650 Rockville Pike
Bethesda, MD 20814

American Society for Clinical Laboratory Science
7910 Woodmont Avenue
Suite 1301
Bethesda, MD 20814

American Society for Microbiology
Office of Education and Training-Career Information
1325 Massachusetts Avenue NW
Washington, DC 20005

American Society for Pharmacology and Experimental Therapeutics
9650 Rockville Pike
Bethesda, MD 20814

American Society of Clinical Pathologists
Board of Registry
P.O. Box 12277
Chicago, IL 60612

American Society of Cytopathology
400 W. 9th Street
Suite 201
Wilmington, DE 19801

Association for Professionals in Infection Control and Epidemiology
1016 Sixteenth Street NW
Sixth Floor
Washington, DC 20036

Association of Medical Illustrators
1819 Peachtree Street, N.E.
Suite 620
Atlanta, GA 30309

Biomedical Engineering Society
P.O. Box 2399
Culver City, CA 90230

Biophysical Society
9650 Rockville Pike
Bethesda, MD 20814

Biotechnology Industry Organization
1625 K Street NW
Suite 1100
Washington, DC 20006

Genetics Society of America
9650 Rockville Pike
Bethesda, MD 20814

International Society for Clinical Laboratory Technology
917 Locust Street
Suite 1100
St. Louis, MO 63101-1413

National Accrediting Agency for Clinical Laboratory Sciences
8410 W. Bryn Mawr Avenue
Suite 670
Chicago, IL 60631
For a list of accredited and approved educational programs for clinical laboratory personnel.

National Association of Health Career Schools
750 First Street NW
Suite 940
Washington, DC 20002
For information about a career as a medical and clinical laboratory technician and schools offering training.

Society for Developmental Biology
9650 Rockville Pike
Bethesda, MD 20814
Information on federal job opportunities is available from local offices of state employment services or offices of the U.S. Office of Personnel Management, located in major metropolitan areas.

CHAPTER FOURTEEN

PATH 5: BIOLOGY EDUCATORS

*T*eaching is the career path of choice for many people who feel that their love of and a depth of knowledge in the subject area are best expressed by sharing it and encouraging it in others.

No matter the area of specialization—botany or zoology, microbiology or the medical sciences—there are qualities and skills that all teachers must possess. In addition to being knowledgeable in their subjects, the ability to communicate, inspire trust and confidence, and motivate students, as well as understand their educational and emotional needs, are essential for teachers. They also should be organized, dependable, and patient, as well as creative.

DEFINITION OF THE CAREER PATH

There are many career paths an educator can take, many different age groups to work with, and many different settings to work in. For the purposes of this chapter we will look at the two most traditional teaching paths for biology majors: secondary school and college and university teaching. Alternative suggestions are given later in this chapter under "Possible Job Settings."

To understand fully the career path, though, we first must look at the role of a teacher. It is changing from that of a lecturer or presenter to one of a facilitator or coach. Interactive discussions and hands-on learning are replacing rote memorization, especially in the earlier grades. For example, rather than merely telling students about biology or mathematics, a teacher might ask students to help perform a laboratory experiment or solve a mathematical problem and then discuss how these apply to the real world.

As teachers move away from the traditional repetitive drill approaches, they are using more props or manipulatives to help students understand abstract concepts, solve problems, and develop critical thought processes. For example, young children may be taught the concept of numbers or adding and subtracting by playing board games. As students get older, they may use more sophisticated materials such as tape recorders, science apparatus, or cameras.

Classes are becoming less structured, and students are working in groups to discuss and solve problems together. Preparing students for the future work force is the major stimulus generating the changes in education. To be prepared, students must be able to interact with others, adapt to new technology, and logically think through problems. Teachers provide the tools and environment for their students to develop these skills.

Secondary Education

Secondary school teachers help students delve more deeply into subjects introduced in elementary school and learn more about the world and about themselves. They specialize in a specific subject, such as biology, Spanish, mathematics, history, or art. They may teach a variety of related courses, for example, botany and zoology.

Teachers may use films, slides, overhead projectors, and the latest technology in teaching, such as computers, telecommunication systems, and video discs. Telecommunication technology can bring the real world into the classroom. Through telecommunications, American students can communicate with students in other countries to share personal experiences or research projects of interest to both groups. Computers are used in many classroom activities, from helping students solve math problems to learning English as a second language. Teachers must continually update their skills to use the latest technology in the classroom.

Teachers design their classroom presentations to meet student needs and abilities. They also may work with students individually. Teachers assign lessons, give tests, hear oral presentations, and maintain classroom discipline. Teachers observe and evaluate a student's performance and potential. Teachers increasingly are using new assessment methods, such as examining a notebook of a student's research progress to measure student achievement. Teachers assess the results at the end of a learning period to judge a student's overall progress. They may then provide additional assistance in areas where a student may need help.

In addition to classroom activities, teachers plan and evaluate lessons, sometimes in collaboration with teachers of related subjects. They also prepare tests, grade papers, prepare report cards, oversee study halls and homerooms, supervise extracurricular activities, and meet with parents and school staff to discuss a student's academic progress or personal problems.

College and University Teaching

College and university faculty teach and advise over 14 million full-time and part-time college students and play a significant role in our nation's research. They also study and meet with colleagues to keep up with developments in their field and consult with government, business, nonprofit, and community organizations.

Faculty generally are organized into departments or divisions, based on subject or field. They usually teach several different courses in their department: introduction to biology, zoology, oceanography, marine science, and animal behavior, for example. They may instruct undergraduate or graduate students, or both.

College and university faculty may give lectures to several hundred students in large halls, lead small seminars, and supervise students in laboratories. They also prepare lectures, exercises, and laboratory experiments, grade exams and papers, and advise and work with students individually.

In universities, they also counsel, advise, teach, and supervise graduate student research. They may use closed-circuit and cable television, computers, videotapes, and other teaching aids.

Faculty keep abreast of developments in their fields by reading current literature, talking with colleagues, and participating in professional conferences. They also do their own research to expand knowledge in their fields and write about their findings in scholarly journals and books.

Most faculty members serve on academic or administrative committees that deal with the policies of their institution, departmental matters, academic issues, curricula, budgets, equipment purchases, and hiring. Some work with student organizations. Department heads generally have heavier administrative responsibilities.

The amount of time spent on each of these activities varies by individual circumstance and type of institution. Faculty members at universities generally spend a significant part of their time doing research; those in four-year colleges, somewhat less; and those in two-year colleges, relatively little. However, the teaching load usually is heavier in two-year colleges.

POSSIBLE JOB SETTINGS

Here we will look at all the settings in which a biology teacher can be employed. Some settings will expect teachers to follow a traditional, basic biology curriculum; others will want the work to focus on a specialty area. For example, a botanist or horticulturist, while not certified to teach in a public school system, could happily find work for the Cooperative Extension Service, a garden center, or botanical garden. The qualifications you'll need will vary depending on the work setting. Each setting has its own requirements of and expectations for its teachers, but each provides an environment where biology majors dedicated to teaching can practice their art.

Adult education centers	Garden centers/Nurseries
Alternative schools	Overseas schools
Aquariums	Overseas universities
Botanical gardens	Peace Corps
Community centers	Prisons
Community colleges	Private schools
Computer online services	Public schools
Cooperative Extension Service	Recreational centers
Department of Defense schools	Rehabilitation centers
Four-year colleges and universities	Zoos

WORKING CONDITIONS

Secondary Education

Secondary school teachers teach from five to seven periods in a day and have extracurricular responsibilities as noted earlier, such as coaching sports or chaperoning school outings.

In some secondary schools—and the problem is not limited to just inner-city schools—maintaining discipline has become a weighty part of the teacher's role.

On the positive side, secondary school teachers may help shape a student's future and assist in choosing courses, colleges, and careers. Special education teachers may help students with their transition into special vocational training programs, colleges, or jobs.

Teachers also participate in education conferences and workshops. Many enjoy several weeks' vacation during the school year and two months off in the summer. Others, though, to supplement their incomes, will teach summer school or find other part-time, summer work.

College and University Teaching

College faculty generally have flexible schedules. They must be present for classes, which usually adds up to 12 to 16 hours a week, and for faculty and committee meetings. Most establish regular office hours for student consultations and assistance, usually three to six hours per week. Otherwise, they are relatively free to decide when and where they will work and how much time to devote to course preparation, grading papers and exams, study, research, and other activities.

They may work staggered hours and teach classes at night and on weekends, particularly those faculty who teach older students who may have full-time jobs or family responsibilities during the weekdays. They have even greater flexibility during the summer break and school holidays, when they may teach or do research, travel, or pursue nonacademic interests. Most colleges and universities have funds used to support faculty research or other professional development needs, including travel to conferences and research sites.

Part-time faculty generally spend less time on campus than full-time faculty since they usually don't have an office. In addition, they may teach at more than one college, requiring travel between their various places of employment.

Faculty may experience a conflict between their responsibilities to teach students and the pressure to do research. This may be a particular problem for young faculty seeking advancement. Increasing emphasis on undergraduate teaching performance in tenure decisions may alleviate some of this pressure, however.

POSSIBLE JOB TITLES

There is not a wide latitude in job title for the professional biology teacher. We often apply the term *teacher* to indicate professionals in elementary school as well as the professionals filling the top posts at colleges and universities. Despite the subject area, rank, or setting, the teaching role essentially remains the same. They are all, to some extent, teachers.

TRAINING AND QUALIFICATIONS

To work in most public school systems, the bachelor's degree with a teaching certification is required. In other settings, such as some community colleges and most four-year universities, postgraduate degrees are required.

Secondary

Aspiring secondary school teachers either major in biology as the subject they plan to teach while also taking education courses, or major in education and take biology courses as their subject.

Alternative Teacher Certification

Many states offer alternative teacher certification programs for people who have college training in the subject they will teach but do not have the necessary education courses required for a regular certificate. Alternative certification programs were originally designed to ease teacher shortages in certain subjects, such as mathematics and science. The programs have expanded to attract other people into teaching, including recent college graduates and mid-career changers. In some programs, individuals begin teaching immediately under provisional certification. After working under the close supervision of experienced educators for one or two years while taking education courses outside school hours, they receive regular certification if they have progressed satisfactorily.

Under other programs, college graduates who do not meet certification requirements take only those courses that they lack and then become certified. This may take one or two semesters of full-time study.

Aspiring teachers who need certification may also enter programs that grant a master's degree in education, as well as certification. States also issue emergency certificates to individuals who do not meet all requirements for a regular certificate when schools cannot find enough teachers with regular certificates.

Competency Testing

Almost all states require applicants for teacher certification to be tested for competency in basic skills such as reading and writing, teaching skills, or subject matter proficiency. Almost all require continuing education for renewal of the teacher's certificate. Some require a master's degree.

Reciprocity

Many states have reciprocity agreements that make it easier for teachers certified in one state to become certified in another. Teachers may become board certified by successfully completing the National Board for Professional Teaching Standards certification process. This certification is voluntary, but may result in a higher salary.

Information on certification requirements and approved teacher training institutions is available from local school systems and state departments of education.

Colleges and Universities

Most college and university faculty are in four academic ranks: professor, associate professor, assistant professor, and instructor. A small number are lecturers.

Most faculty members are hired as instructors or assistant professors. Four-year colleges and universities generally hire doctoral degree holders for full-time, tenure-track positions, but may hire master's degree holders or doctoral candidates for certain disciplines or for part-time and temporary jobs.

Doctoral programs usually take four to seven years of full-time study beyond the bachelor's degree. Candidates usually specialize in a subfield of a discipline, for example, microbiology, entomology, or plant physiology, but also take courses covering the whole discipline. Programs include 20 or more increasingly specialized courses and seminars plus comprehensive examinations on all major areas of the field. They also include a dissertation, a report on original research to address some significant question in the field.

Students studying the sciences usually do laboratory work; in the humanities, they study original documents and other published material. The dissertation, done under the guidance of one or more faculty advisors, usually takes one or two years of full-time work.

Advancement

With additional preparation and certification, teachers may become administrators or supervisors, although the number of positions is limited. In some systems, highly qualified, experienced teachers can become senior or mentor teachers, with higher pay and additional responsibilities. They guide and assist less experienced teachers while keeping most of their teaching responsibilities.

Some faculty, based on teaching experience, research, publication, and service on campus committees and task forces, move into administrative and managerial positions, such as departmental chairperson, dean, and president. At four-year institutions, such advancement requires a doctoral degree.

STRATEGIES FOR FINDING JOBS

College Career Placement Centers

Check with your college career office. Career offices regularly receive mailings of job openings. You can also leave your resume on file there. Prospective employers regularly contact college career offices looking for likely candidates.

Help Wanted Ads

Seek out all newspapers in your area or in the geographic location in which you'd prefer to work. A trip to the library will reveal periodicals you might not have been aware of and will be less of a burden on your budget.

The Internet

This is an incredible source for job hunting. Use any of the search engines available to you and type in key words such as "employment," "biology," "teaching," and "jobs." You will discover a wealth of information online—organizations, educational institutions, publications, and a wide variety of potential employers and job search services—most of which are available to you at no charge above the online time your Internet provider charges you.

Internships and Volunteering

Biology educators, especially those hoping to land a job with a zoo or botanical garden, will find internships and volunteering stints to be the most important keys in that particular setting. These settings cry out for volunteer help and internships can be arranged through your university. Once in the door, make yourself indispensable. When a job opening occurs, you'll be there on the spot, ready to step in.

Direct Contact

Walk right in, set your portfolio or resume down on the appropriate desk, and you might find you have just landed yourself a job. This approach works best in adult education centers, community centers, and other related settings, as listed under "Possible Employers" earlier in this chapter.

The Chronicle of Higher Education

This is the old standby for those seeking positions within two- and four-year colleges and universities. The *Chronicle of Higher Education* is a weekly publication available by subscription or in any library or your college placement office.

Placement Agencies

For private schools particularly, both at home and abroad, placement agencies can provide a valuable source for finding employment. Some charge both the employer and the prospective employee a fee; others charge just one or the other.

CAREER OUTLOOK

School Systems

Overall employment of school teachers is expected to increase faster than the average for all occupations through the year 2005, fueled by dramatic growth among special education teachers. However, projected employment growth varies among individual teaching occupations. Job openings for all teachers are expected to increase substantially by the end of the decade as the large number of teachers now in their forties and fifties reach retirement age.

Assuming relatively little change in average class size, employment growth of teachers depends on the rates of population growth and corresponding student enrollments. The population of 14- to 17-year-olds is expected to experience relatively strong growth through the year 2005, spurring demand for secondary school teachers.

The supply of teachers also is expected to increase in response to reports of improved job prospects, more teacher involvement in school policy, greater public interest in education, and higher salaries. In fact, enrollments in teacher training programs already have increased in recent years. In addition, more teachers should be available from alternative certification programs.

Some central cities and rural areas have difficulty attracting enough teachers, so job prospects should continue to be better in these areas than in suburban districts. Mathematics, science, and special education teachers remain in short supply. Concerns over a future work force that may not meet employers' needs could spur demand for teachers who specialize in basic skills instruction, reading, writing, and mathematics. With enrollments of minorities increasing, efforts to recruit minority teachers may intensify.

The number of teachers employed depends on state and local expenditures for education. Pressures from taxpayers to limit spending could result in fewer teachers than projected; pressures to spend more to improve the quality of education could mean more.

Higher Education

Employment of college and university faculty is expected to increase about as fast as the average for all occupations through the year 2005 as enrollments in higher education increase. Many additional openings will arise as faculty members retire. Faculty retirements should increase significantly from the late 1990s through 2005 as a large number of faculty who entered the profession during the 1950s and 1960s reach retirement age at this time.

Enrollments increased in the early and mid-1980s despite a decline in the traditional college-age (18–24) population. This resulted from a higher proportion of 18- to 24-year-olds attending college, along with a growing number of part-time, female, and older students. Enrollments are expected to continue to grow through the year 2005, particularly as the traditional college-age population begins increasing after 1998, when the leading edge of the baby-boom echo generation (children of the baby boomers) reaches college age.

In the past two decades, keen competition for faculty jobs forced some applicants to accept part-time or short-term academic appointments that offered little hope of tenure, and others to seek nonacademic positions. This trend of hiring adjunct or part-time faculty should continue through the mid- to late-1990s due to financial difficulties universities and colleges are facing.

Many states have reduced funding for higher education. As a result, colleges increased the hiring of part-time faculty to save money on pay and benefits.

Once enrollments and retirements increase in the late 1990s, opportunities should improve for college faculty positions and for tenure, and fewer faculty should have to take part-time or short-term appointments.

Job prospects will continue to be better in fields such as the physical sciences, health science, business, engineering, computer science, and mathematics, largely because very attractive nonacademic jobs will be available for many potential faculty.

Employment of college faculty also is related to the nonacademic job market through an echo effect. Excellent job prospects in a field, for example, computer science from the late 1970s to the mid-1980s, caused more students to enroll, increasing faculty needs in that field. On the other hand, poor job prospects in a field, such as history in recent years, discourages students and reduces demand for faculty.

EARNINGS

School Systems

According to the National Education Association, the estimated average salary of all public elementary and secondary school teachers in the 1995–96 school year was $37,900. Public secondary school teachers averaged about $38,600 a year, while public elementary school teachers averaged $37,300. Private school teachers generally earn less than public school teachers.

In 1996, over half of all public school teachers belonged to unions—mainly the American Federation of Teachers and the National Education Association—that bargain with school systems over wages, hours, and the terms and conditions of employment.

In some schools, teachers receive extra pay for coaching sports and working with students in extracurricular activities. Some teachers earn extra income during the summer working in the school system or in other jobs.

Higher Education

Earnings vary according to faculty rank and type of institution, geographic area, and field. According to a 1995–96 survey by the American Association of University Professors, salaries for full-time faculty averaged $51,000. By rank, the average for professors was $65,400; associate professors, $48,300; assistant professors, $40,100; lecturers, $33,700; and instructors, $30,800.

Faculty in four-year institutions earn higher salaries, on the average, than those in two-year schools. Average salaries for faculty in public institutions—$50,400—were lower in 1995-96 than those for private independent institutions—$57,500—but higher than those for religious-affiliated or private institutions—$45,200.

In fields with high-paying, nonacademic alternatives—notably medicine and law but also engineering and business, among others—earnings exceed these averages. In others—such as the humanities and education—they are lower.

Most faculty members have significant earnings in addition to their base salary, from consulting, teaching additional courses, research, writing for publication, or other employment, both during the academic year and the summer.

Most college and university faculty enjoy some unique benefits, including access to campus facilities, tuition waivers for dependents, housing and travel allowances, and paid sabbatical leaves.

Part-time faculty have fewer benefits than full-time faculty, and usually do not receive health insurance, retirement benefits, or sabbatical leave.

RELATED OCCUPATIONS

Teaching requires a wide variety of skills and aptitudes, including a talent for working with people; organizational, administrative, and record keeping abilities; research and communication skills; the power to influence, motivate, and train others; patience; and creativity.

Workers in other occupations requiring some of these aptitudes include counselors, librarians, education administrators, writers, consultants, lobbyists, policy analysts, employment interviewers, preschool workers, public relations specialists, sales representatives, social workers, and trainers and employee development specialists.

CLOSE-UPS

Below, two biology teachers working in different settings discuss their jobs.

BOBBIE PFEIFER, HIGH SCHOOL BIOLOGY TEACHER

Bobbie Pfeifer taught biology and physical sciences in the Auburn/Washburn Unified School District #437 at Washburn Rural High School in Topeka, Kansas, from 1984 to 1990.

In 1985 she earned her B.S. in biology with a minor in chemistry and physics and a degree in secondary education at Washburn University of Topeka, Kansas. Her master's degree in secondary education in curriculum and instruction and special education is in progress.

The Attraction to the Field

"At the early age of 8, I can remember wanting to be a teacher. However, it wasn't until high school that my interest in science became apparent. It was during these years that I set my goals on becoming a science instructor. There were no other teachers in my family to emulate. Looking back, it was that one 'special' science instructor I had in high school that sparked my aspirations, coupled with great instructors at the university. It was their greatness I aimed to achieve."

Getting Started

"Just prior to graduation, while completing my student teaching assignment, I signed my first full-time teaching contract. That contract was offered by the very district in which I had been assigned to student teach. Keep in mind that there was a shortage, nationwide, for teachers of mathematics and science. When I graduated in 1985, a very low percentage of graduates nationally had chosen to major in these fields. This created vast opportunities for those of us who did. Those shortages were apparent in the corporate world, and more so in the teaching profession. To my knowledge, these shortages still exist today and may have even become more critical. Therefore, aspiring teachers who choose these areas of concentration will probably have no problems with job placement, and may even be hired, as I was, before actually graduating."

The Realities of the Job

"The nice thing about secondary education, for most people, is that you have your own room, your own rules, guidelines, expectations for student achievement, and your own methods of teaching and grading student performance. In many ways, teaching is a very independent environment. As a teacher of science, you're likely to have your own lab and equipment.

"My teaching assignments were Advanced Placement (college level) Biology; Honor Physical Science (combined Chemistry and Physics); and Regular Physical Science.

"My duties involve planning lessons that match the district's or department's overall teaching philosophy, goals, scope and sequence, or course syllabus. In nearly all cases you, as the teacher, have the freedom to plan and create these lessons and lab experiences to match your students' abilities, developing your own unique style.

"I also graded student performance and how well they mastered the material, then adjusted my teaching accordingly.

"Being in charge of a classroom has many great rewards. Contrary to the stories about how bad teaching is nowadays, I found one simple thing that seemed to work for me—set your expectations high for your students. For you see, there's a funny thing about kids—they'll rise to meet those expectations. Kids today are looking for direction. Start out the first day very firm, strict, and bordering on downright mean. Loosen up as time goes on.

"Establish right away who's in control, who's the boss, because if you lose that, it's impossible to regain. Just remember, if you expect them to be monsters, they'll fulfill that for you.

"And remember, respect is a two-way street. Give your students an incentive to perform to your expectations, and believe me, it doesn't take much."

A Typical Day

"My teaching day began at approximately 7:15 A.M. with prepping my lectures and labs for the day. Typically, around 7:35 A.M. teachers were expected to be present in the halls, as a method of crowd control. However, students often sought

continued

continued

out teachers to ask questions on something they didn't quite understand during this time.

"Warning bells for first class sound at 7:50 A.M. Classes begin at 8:00. Most schools in our area have a break for 20 minutes in the morning around 10:30. At this time students socialize in the halls, drink juice, and can purchase donuts, or they once again can seek the help of a teacher to ask questions. Naturally, since I taught science, I was flooded most days with students requiring help.

"Lunch times are divided into two or three groups and time slots. Teachers rotate between eating in the teachers' lounges and having hall duty. Afternoon classes end at 2:45. One hour each day is given to the teacher to do lesson planning and grading. After school, once again, students could come for extra help.

"In addition, all of my Advanced Placement Labs, which required 2–4 hours, were after school. Teaching is a hectic job, with bells ringing, classes changing, special duties, lessons to plan, labs to prepare, and students to educate.

"Everyone, including teachers, has something to learn. Sometimes I'd learn my most valuable lessons from the very students I was hired to teach. Boring is not a term I'd associate with teaching. Every day is different and unique, challenging and rewarding, and something memorable to be experienced.

"As former students, each of us knows what the work atmosphere is like. However, what most students don't know is that teachers within a school become a family, forming friendships that endure a lifetime."

The Upsides and Downsides

"What I like most about teaching is the satisfaction, knowing I've made a difference in so many people's lives. I'm reminded of this each time I run across former students who go on about what they've accomplished in their lives and careers. The most memorable are the ones who admit I made a difference or inspired them.

"What I like least about teaching is that the pay isn't equal to comparable degreed jobs of importance. Think about it.

The job of a teacher is critical to our future, yet the pay makes it difficult for the profession to retain the best and brightest stars. This is a shame. Teaching is not an eight to five job. Teachers often work into the evening and weekends at home to complete lesson plans and grading. Yet, the salary remains the same."

Salaries

"Salaries in teaching vary from state to state, town to town, and district to district. But on the average, most beginning teachers make $20,000. The nice thing about teaching salaries, however, is that most districts have a salary schedule based on years of experience and education, allowing the beginning teacher's wage to increase from year to year. Again, even this increase varies from district to district. Teaching salaries are often based on nine or ten months, not twelve."

Some Advice from Bobbie Pfeifer

"When it comes to teaching, my advice is always follow your heart. Teaching's not for everyone. If you're looking for an area of concentration that will likely land you a job quickly upon graduation, consider mathematics or science. Either one of these fields also makes you marketable in the corporate world. In addition, check with your university about 'hardship' school districts. New teachers who sign commitment contracts for a certain number of years will have their education or student loans paid for, in much the same way doctors are encouraged to work in rural areas."

MICHELE GRAHAM, BIOLOGY LECTURER

Michele A. Graham is a biology lecturer at Cal-State Hayward University in Hayward, California.

She earned her B.A. in printmaking at the California College of Arts and Crafts in Oakland, California, in 1972. In 1984 she earned her M.S. in Biology at Cal-State Hayward

continued

continued

and in 1996 her Ph.D. at University of California, Berkeley, in evolutionary biology and entomology. She has been working in the field since 1984. She started out as a research assistant and graduate student instructor, then taught at various junior colleges before coming to work full-time at Cal-State Hayward.

The Attraction to the Field

"Because I love animals, I always wanted to be a zoologist. As a little girl I thought maybe I could convince people to care more about animals. As an adult I hope I can make a difference in our culture's perception about other life forms so that we and they might have a chance to survive our greed and misuse of the planet.

"I got my training through school, both master's and doctoral programs, and by observation of the manner in which people act toward the earth.

"It is very tough finding a university position, especially in California and especially in my field. Molecular biologists and biochemists are much more in demand than evolutionary ecologists. I did some undergrad work at Hayward so I knew the people there. Two years ago when I started looking for another job, I probably applied to 40+ colleges and universities all over the United States. Of those applications, maybe four or five were exactly in my field; the others were jobs I was stretching for."

The Realities of the Job

"As a college instructor your primary responsibility is to teach. Usually you teach one or two courses. This means that you develop and write your own lectures based on the information you feel your students need to have. You choose textbooks, write a syllabus, and in the case of biology, develop labs to go with the course.

"Your secondary responsibility is to conduct research. Research brings recognition to the department and money to the university or college and so is considered important. As someone interested in science, it would be expected that you enjoy doing research. Research is interesting because you can ask great questions and sometimes actually find answers, but it often requires tedious attention to detail. So, if detail isn't your bag, research may not be much fun.

"Sometimes, a way around doing research in some institutions is to write books, articles, and textbooks. In junior colleges, where I taught before I received my Ph.D., research is not expected and the primary responsibility is teaching.

"Additionally, as a college instructor you are required to participate in faculty meetings, larger campus committees, and in the general business of the institution. In California it's called 'shared governance' and it takes up a large amount of your time.

"In a typical day you might give a lecture, meet with a lab or two, monitor your research projects, meet with graduate or undergraduate students who work with you, meet with a departmental or college committee, take time to read newly published research in your areas of interest, and work on lecture notes.

"Things are always busy and never dull. Although you are expected to perform well and publish research papers, the atmosphere is relaxed and friendly. At least in California, folks generally wear jeans and shirts and look like biologists. You are, however, usually on your own in your teaching and research, working in isolation from your departmental colleagues.

"During your first years you should expect to work 60 to 70 hours per week. During this time you are trying to do a lot of research in order to publish as many papers as possible by the time of your review for tenure. Once you have tenure, things calm down and relax a bit. But this is a demanding way to make a living so you need to really love it to make it worthwhile."

The Upsides and Downsides

"What I really love about my work is (1) working with students and (2) playing with ideas. Working with students, especially students who want to know about biology, is wonderful, exciting, never boring, and always challenging. When a student's mind first begins to wrap itself around a wholly

continued

new idea and then the idea begins to take hold and the student breaks through to see the many implications of this idea in his or her own life and the world, it is awe inspiring. To be part of this process as a teacher is a privilege and it is the part of my job that gives it real meaning.

"The part of my job that I hate is trying to work with administrators who are no longer academics but M.B.A.'s and who fundamentally think that education is a service-oriented business. Their ideas include refusing to offer any class that has a registration below a certain level (often 20 students or less.) This kind of thinking will eventually eliminate many important academic disciplines (Latin and Greek, or electron microscopy, etc.), as well as many esoteric disciplines (Sanskrit) that, nevertheless, have a place in the academic environment and may have important significance to other disciplines."

Salaries

"As a full-time instructor, given my experience, I make between $45,000 and $50,000 per year. This varies because I sometimes teach an additional class. Just starting out, new Ph.D.'s make between $30,000 and $40,000. Note, this is not a field to enter if money is a consideration. No one who does the actual teaching makes much money, considering the amount of education needed."

Advice from Michele Graham

"My advice to all is to do something you love, regardless of how much money you will earn or how feasible it seems, or how difficult to accomplish. Work takes up a lot of time and a lot of years, and if you don't get up every day to something you love doing, your life is going to be miserable. So, the greatest quality to possess is being in love with your job.

"Being a biologist will require that you get at least a master's degree. To teach in college, you have to get a Ph.D. This will require at least five additional years of college, but be forewarned, it is getting more difficult to get a Ph.D. because the requirements of the research are stiffer. So it may, and often does, take considerably longer than five years. Once you get into graduate school everything will flow from there."

PROFESSIONAL ASSOCIATIONS

Information on careers in teaching science can be obtained from:

National Science Teachers Association
1840 Wilson Boulevard
Arlington, VA 22201-3000

Association for Biology Laboratory Education
Nancy Rosenbaum
(ABLE Membership Chair)
Department of Biology, Yale University
P.O. Box 208104
New Haven, CT 06520-8104

Information on teachers' unions and education-related issues may be obtained from:

American Federation of Teachers
555 New Jersey Avenue NW
Washington, DC 20001

National Education Association
1201 16th Street NW
Washington, DC 20036

A list of institutions with teacher education programs accredited by the National Council for Accreditation of Teacher Education can be obtained from:

National Council for Accreditation of Teacher Education
2010 Massachusetts Avenue NW
2nd Floor
Washington, DC 20036

For information on voluntary teacher certification requirements, contact:

National Board for Professional Teaching Standards
300 River Place
Detroit, MI 48207

For additional information contact:

American Association for Higher Education
One Dupont Circle NW
Suite 360
Washington, DC 20036

American Association of Christian Schools
P.O. Box 2189
Independence, MO 64055

American Association of Colleges for Teacher Education
One Dupont Circle NW
Suite 610
Washington, DC 20036

American Association of State Colleges and Universities
One Dupont Circle NW
Suite 700
Washington, DC 20036

Association for Childhood Education International
11141 Georgia Avenue
Suite 200
Wheaton, MD 20902

Council for American Private Education
One Massachusetts Avenue NW
Suite 700
Washington, DC 20001-1431

National Association for the Education of Young Children
1834 Connecticut Avenue NW
Washington, DC 20009-5786

National Association of Independent Schools
75 Federal Street
Boston, MA 02110

Publications

The Journal of College Science Teaching (JCST) is a refereed journal published by the National Science Teachers Association (NSTA) for an audience of college and university teachers of introductory and advanced science courses. *JCST* communicates innovative, effective techniques to improve interdisciplinary teaching strategies for instructing both science majors and nonmajors.

JCST
National Science Teachers Association
1840 Wilson Boulevard
Arlington, VA 22201-3000

Chronicle of Higher Education
Subscription Department
P.O. Box 1955
Marion, OH 43305

APPENDIX

ADDITIONAL RESOURCES

To complement the resources provided at the end of each chapter, below you will find additional publications and associations and institutions to contact for more career or training information:

American Society of Agronomy
677 South Segoe Road
Madison, WI 53711

Institute of Food Technologies
221 N. LaSalle Street
Suite 2120
Chicago, IL 60601

National Association of Science Writers
P.O. Box 294
Greenlawn, NY 11740

PUBLICATIONS

The New Careers Directory: Internships and Professional Opportunities in Technology and Social Change. Lasky, Barry, ed. Student Pugwash USA. Washington, DC.

Prentice Hall Guide to Scholarships and Fellowships for Math and Science Students. Englewood Cliffs, NJ.

The Search for Solutions: How We Know What We Know About the Universe and How We Know It's True, by Horace Freeland Judson. Baltimore, MD: Johns Hopkins University Press.

Solving the Puzzle: Careers in Genetics. The Genetics Society of America and The American Society of Human Genetics. Bethesda, MD.

To Be a Scientist: The Spirit of Adventure in Science and Technology, by Donald Braben. New York, NY: Oxford University Press, 1994.

Women of Science: Righting the Record, by G. Kass-Simon and Patricia Farnes. Bloomington, IN: Indiana University Press.

Sea Grant Program Offices

The 31 Sea Grant institutions also are sources of information about oceanography, ocean research, and career opportunities. Inquiries should be directed to the publications office at the following addresses:

Alaska Sea Grant College Program
205 O'Neill Building
P.O. Box 755040
Fairbanks, AK 99775-5040

California Sea Grant College Program
University of California A-032
La Jolla, CA 92093

Connecticut Sea Grant Program
University of Connecticut
Building 24
Room 110
Avery Point
Groton, CT 06340

Delaware Sea Grant College Program
College of Marine Studies
University of Delaware
Newark, DE 19716

Florida Sea Grant College Program
G022 McCarty Hall
University of Florida
Gainesville, FL 32611-0103

Georgia Sea Grant College Program
Ecology Building
University of Georgia
Athens, GA 30602

Hawaii Sea Grant College Program
University of Hawaii
1000 Pope Road
Room 201
Honolulu, HI 96822

Illinois/Indiana Sea Grant Program
University of Illinois at Urbana/Champaign
1301 W. Gregory Drive
51 Mumford Hall
Urbana, IL 61801

Louisiana Sea Grant College Program
Center for Wetland Resources
Louisiana State University
Baton Rouge, LA 70803

Maine Sea Grant Program
Marine Advisory Program
30 Coburn Hall
University of Maine
Orono, ME 04469

Maryland Sea Grant College Program
H. J. Patterson Hall
University of Maryland
College Park, MD 20742

Michigan Sea Grant Program
University of Michigan
I.S.T. Building
2200 Bonisteel Boulevard
Ann Arbor, MI 48109-2099

Minnesota Sea Grant Program
University of Minnesota
116 Classroom Office Building
1994 Buford Avenue
St. Paul, MN 55108

Mississippi/Alabama Sea Grant Consortium
Caylor Building
Gulf Coast Research Laboratory
Ocean Springs, MS 39564

National Sea Grant College Program
NOAA, Sea Grant, R/OR1
SSMC-1, Fifth Floor
1335 East-West Highway
Silver Spring, MD 20910

National Sea Grant Depository
Pell Library
University of Rhode Island
Bay Campus
Narragansett, RI 02882

New Hampshire Sea Grant Program
Marine Program Building
University of New Hampshire
Durham, NH 03824

New Jersey Marine Science Consortium
Sea Grant Program
Building 22
Fort Hancock, NJ 07732

New York Sea Grant College Program
Duchess Hall
State University of New York at Stony Brook
Stony Brook, NY 11794-5001

North Carolina Sea Grant College Program
Box 8605
North Carolina State University
Raleigh, NC 27695-8605

Ohio Sea Grant Program
Ohio State University
1541 Research Center
1314 Kinnear Road
Columbus, OH 43212

Oregon Sea Grant College Program
ADS A418
Oregon State University
Corvallis, OR 97331

Puerto Rico Sea Grant Program
University of Puerto Rico
Department of Marine Sciences
Mayaguez, PR 00708

Rhode Island Sea Grant College Program
Marine Resources Building
University of Rhode Island
Narragansett, RI 02882

Sea Grant College Program
Massachusetts Institute of Technology
E38-302
Cambridge, MA 02139

South Carolina Sea Grant Consortium
287 Meeting Street
Charleston, SC 29401

Texas A&M University Sea Grant College Program
1716 Briarcrest
Suite 702
Bryant, TX 77802

USC Sea Grant Institutional Program
University of Southern California
University Park
Los Angeles, CA 90089-0341

Virginia Sea Grant College Program
Virginia Institute of Marine Sciences
Gloucester Point, VA 23062

Washington Sea Grant College Program
University of Washington
3716 Brooklyn Avenue N.E.
Seattle, WA 98105

Wisconsin Sea Grant Institute
University of Wisconsin
1800 University Avenue
Madison, WI 53705

Woods Hole Sea Grant Program
Woods Hole Oceanographic Institution
Woods Hole, MA 02543

ADDRESSES OF FEATURED INSTITUTIONS

Animal School, Inc.
Dr. Mary Nitschke
Koll Business Center
Building 9
7850 S.W. Nimbus Avenue
Beaverton, OR 97005

Detroit Zoological Institute
West Ten Mile Road and Woodward Avenue
P.O. Box 39
Royal Oak, MI 48068-0039

La Guardar Inc. Wildlife and Rehabilitation Center
4966 County Road 656
Webster, FL 33597

Lion Country Safari
2003 Lion Country Safari Road
Loxahatchee, FL 33470

Metro Washington Park Zoo
4001 S.W. Canyon Road
Portland, OR 97221

New England Aquarium
Central Wharf
Boston, MA 02110-3399

INDEX